Becoming a Secondary School Teacher

WITHDRAWN

Aimed at supporting those undertaking initial teacher training and the statutory Induction that follows, *Becoming a Secondary School Teacher* explores the skills, roles and knowledge needed to become a successful teacher in today's secondary schools. Providing detailed guidance on key areas of professional practice, the book helps the reader to link key theories and principles to the reality they will find in the classroom.

This edition has been fully updated to reflect the latest legislation and Teachers' Standards as well as changes in practice and expectations regarding learning, assessment and inclusion. Highly accessible and full of practical advice it includes:

- guidance on key skills for classroom success including lesson planning, classroom management and assessment;
- practical tips on handling areas of real concern such as discipline, workload, job interviews and relationships with colleagues;
- advice on teaching beyond your specialist subject and teaching in challenging circumstances;
- reference throughout to the Teachers' Standards that have to be met during training, what these mean in practice and how they might be evidenced.

With a strong reflective focus through case studies, action points and reflection points, this book is core reading for all students wanting to get the most out of their initial teacher training programme.

Peter Fleming is Lead Adviser for School Leadership and Workforce Development at North Yorkshire County Council. He has previously taught in both secondary schools and Higher Education and was Head of Teacher Training at York St John University.

Becoming a Secondary School Teacher

How to make a success of your initial teacher training and induction

2nd edition

Peter Fleming

Routledge
Taylor & Francis Group

LONDON AND NEW YORK

First edition published 2004
by Routledge

Second edition published 2013
by Routledge
2 Park Square, Milton Park, Abingdon, Oxon OX14 4RN

Simultaneously published in the USA and Canada
by Routledge
711 Third Avenue, New York, NY 10017

Routledge is an imprint of the Taylor & Francis Group, an informa business

British Library Cataloguing in Publication Data
A catalogue record for this book is available from the British Library

Library of Congress Cataloging in Publication Data
Fleming, Peter, 1957–
  Becoming a secondary school teacher: how to make a success of your
  initial teacher training/Peter Fleming. – 2nd ed.
  p. cm.
  Includes bibliographical references and index.
  1. High school teaching – Great Britain.   2. Education, Secondary –
  Great Britain.   I. Title.
  LB1737.G7F54 2013
  373.11020941 – dc23
  2012015704

ISBN: 978-0-415-52934-1 (hbk)
ISBN: 978-0-415-52935-8 (pbk)
ISBN: 978-0-203-11791-0 (ebk)

Typeset in Bembo and Helvetica Neue
by Florence Production Ltd, Stoodleigh, Devon

MIX
Paper from
responsible sources
FSC® C004839
www.fsc.org

Printed and bound in Great Britain by
TJ International Ltd, Padstow, Cornwall

Contents

1

Introduction

Becoming a secondary school teacher

Introduction

Congratulations on deciding to become a secondary school teacher. You have chosen an interesting and rewarding profession. You are embarking on a career that offers the opportunity to improve lives, but to be effective as a teacher you will first need to develop a wide range of skills and competencies. Successful secondary school teachers are able to convey a love of their subject to young people through a combination of enthusiasm, knowledge and effective classroom practice. With a genuine desire to do their best for pupils from all backgrounds, teachers can make a real difference to the lives of those they teach and in so doing contribute positively to our society.

A great deal is now known about what constitutes effective classroom practice and this 'science of teaching' helps to inform this book. However, the complexities of teaching and learning can never be reduced to a set of mechanically applied technical competencies. Teachers operate in real classrooms with real pupils and the schools in which they work are located in real communities. Teachers must take a whole range of factors into account when they plan and deliver their lessons, and the ability to adapt practice to meet the needs of very different classes and pupils in a particular context is very important. Analysis and reflection, therefore, inform the pedagogy used by effective teachers who understand that if they are to help all their students succeed they need to be flexible in the methods they use. All of the above is reflected in the Teachers' Standards (DfE 2011). These Standards underpin all Initial Teacher Training (ITT) and must be achieved consistently in order for you to be awarded Qualified Teacher Status (QTS). You will continue to be judged against the Standards during your Induction (which usually lasts one year for a teacher employed full-time) and beyond this the Standards will be used to inform your appraisal as a teacher.

There are many routes into teaching and information about these can be found on the Teaching Agency's website (http://www.education.gov.uk/get-into-teaching). At the time of writing this book the majority of secondary school teachers gain QTS by following a full-time Post Graduate Certificate in Education

(PGCE) programme, but some train part-time, some train 'on the job' through a Graduate Training Programme (GTP) or School Centred Initial Teacher Training (SCITT) and some follow a degree programme with QTS. In the future, specialist Teaching Schools will play a bigger role in organising and delivering ITT programmes, with the government planning to have 500 Teaching Schools designated by 2015. This book will be helpful to you, whichever route into teaching you have chosen and irrespective of the type of organization managing your training programme. It is written in a way that will introduce you to the essential knowledge and understanding that underpins the Standards and will encourage discussion and critical reflection.

In this chapter you will be asked to think about:

- Professional values;
- Roles and responsibilities during training;
- Looking after yourself during training;
- How to use this book.

Professional values

To guide teachers in their work the Standards document (DfE 2011) addresses Personal and Professional Conduct. Below are some statements that capture the flavour of how teachers should behave in order to uphold public trust in the profession:

- Treat pupils with dignity;
- Build relationships rooted in mutual respect;
- Observe proper boundaries appropriate to a teacher's professional position;
- Have regard to safeguarding pupils' well-being;
- Show tolerance and respect for the rights of others;
- Show respect for core values such as democracy, the rule of law and individual liberty;
- Show tolerance of those with different faiths and beliefs;
- Ensure personal beliefs are not expressed in ways which exploit pupils' vulnerability.

These statements immediately make clear that teachers operating in our diverse and complex multi-cultural society need to be mindful of the impact they can have on the thinking and behaviour of young people. Teachers can have influence beyond the teaching of their subject and as role models they need to ensure their behaviour and the ideas they express are appropriate. The implications for your practice of the statements above will become clearer as you work your way through this book and as you progress through your training programme.

Successful teachers are driven by a real desire to make a difference in pupils' lives. They want all their pupils to succeed and they take pride in seeing them do so. This moral purpose is what enables teachers to muster the energy needed to rise to the challenges that secondary school life can confront them with day after day. It is what gives them the determination and the heart never to give up on a pupil. It is worth thinking carefully about the values that drive you as you embark on your teaching career.

Your roles and responsibilities during training

The vast majority of new teachers gain QTS through conventional programmes in which trainees spend time in college or university as well as time in school (usually twenty four weeks in school for those on PGCE programmes). In this way the practical skills of classroom practice can be developed, informed by reference to underpinning theory and appropriately contextualised and analysed.

The success of school experience depends on a three-way partnership between the school, the trainee and the Higher Education Institution (HEI). The role of each partner is usually explained in school experience documentation provided by the HEI. It may also appear in your programme handbook. It is very important that you familiarise yourself with this, so that you are clear about who will have responsibility for making judgements about your progress towards the Standards.

It is during school experience that you are most likely to experience role confusion as a result of being seen as both a student (trainee) and a teacher. As a result you might sometimes feel unsure about what is acceptable behaviour in relation to both teachers and pupils. Towards the end of your final school experience you will be expected to take on most aspects of the role of teacher, but you will build up to this gradually. The stages you go through are typically as follows:

- Observation of experienced teachers, focusing on particular aspects of practice, for example effective questioning techniques;
- Small Group Teaching (micro teaching), where you work with a small group of pupils within a class or withdraw a group to teach away from the rest of the class;
- Team teaching, where you plan with an experienced teacher and share the delivery of the lesson;
- Whole class teaching, with the class teacher present;
- Whole class teaching, with the class teacher nearby but not in the same room.

You can see from this why role confusion can arise. For example, the way you work with pupils in a micro teaching situation will be different to the way you behave when teaching the whole class. Once you begin to teach whole classes, you are likely to develop through various stages of competence. Initially, you will be concerned with your presence in class (Do I look relaxed? Do I project my voice effectively?). This will be followed by concerns about class control and behaviour management (Will they do what I want? How do I stop them shouting out the answers to questions?). Then you will begin to focus on how successful you are at teaching the class (Are the pupils making progress? Are my lesson objectives being achieved?). Finally, you will begin to think about meeting the needs of particular pupils and groups of pupils within the class (Are *all* pupils learning? Does the work I set challenge *all* abilities of pupils in the class? Have I differentiated my approach for different groupings of pupils?). During your development the role of your school-based tutor (mentor) will be very important, as this will be the person who will support and guide you, offering advice on how you can improve your practice. It is important that you develop a good relationship with this key member of staff.

This is best done by ensuring you meet the school's likely expectations of trainees. You should work hard to come across as thoroughly professional and committed. You can do this by:

- Showing courtesy;
- Showing interest;
- Showing enthusiasm;
- Dressing in line with the school's dress code;
- Seeking advice and acting on it;
- Being flexible;
- Offering support where you can;
- Getting to know the school's policies on things such as uniform, homework and marking;
- Being tactful;
- Respecting confidentiality of information;
- Attending team meetings after school;
- Showing initiative (ask, don't wait to be told!);
- Trying hard to develop good relationships with all staff and pupils.

You should also show that you are very well organised and approach your work systematically. You should make sure you:

- Arrive at school with plenty of time to get organised before the day begins.
- Plan and prepare thoroughly – ask if you are unsure about what is expected of you.
- Prepare your own materials rather than always expecting to be able to use resources that already exist.
- Keep detailed records – as a minimum your teaching file should contain schemes of work, lesson plans, your lesson evaluations, records of pupils'

progress, examples of pupils' work, teaching aids you have produced and written feedback given to you following lesson observations.

- Discuss your lesson plans with your allocated mentor, especially important early on in your training.
- Seek advice on, and try out, different approaches in the classroom.
- Undertake any background reading needed to fill gaps in your own subject knowledge.

Looking after yourself during training

It is no exaggeration to say that becoming a secondary teacher will be one of the greatest challenges you will ever face. There is a massive learning curve for you to climb. You have a tremendous amount of new information to absorb, new skills to learn and new relationships to build. You will be working very hard and feeling very tired. It is important, therefore, that you give some thought to stress management and time management at the outset of your training. This should help you not only to survive the year, but to make a successful and enjoyable start to your chosen career.

Some thoughts on stress

According to the Education Service Advisory Committee (1992) stress is 'a process that can occur when there is a mismatch between the perceived pressures of a situation and the individual's ability to cope with it'. David Fontana (1989) defined stress as

> a demand made upon the adaptive capacities of the mind and body. If these capacities can handle the demand and enjoy the stimulation involved, then stress is welcome and helpful. If they can't and find the demand debilitating, then stress is unwelcome and unhelpful.

This definition is useful for several reasons. Firstly, it reminds us that stress can be both good and bad. Secondly, it isn't so much pressure that determines whether we're stressed or not, it is our reactions to it. Thirdly, if our body's capacities are good enough, we respond well to stress, if they aren't we give way. Typically, too little pressure results in boredom and frustration, a moderate level of pressure is stimulating and actually improves performance whereas too much pressure becomes debilitating and reduces performance (Figure 1.1).

Training to be a teacher is potentially very stressful, though each individual has a different capacity for dealing with pressure and so working for QTS may cause little anxiety for one person but considerable anxiety for another. Much depends on the individual's personality, experience and motivation, as well as factors such as support received from college and school-based tutors (mentors), school context

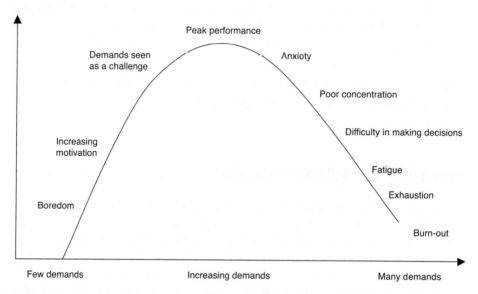

FIGURE 1.1 The effect of increasing pressure on performance

and domestic circumstances. Studies of stress in student teachers (Capel 1997; Hart 1987; Kyriacou and Stephens 1999) have shown a wide variety of causes of stress for trainees:

- Class control, discipline and disruptive pupils;
- Conflict with pupils;
- Meeting the needs of pupils with a wide range of abilities within a class;
- Practical teaching skills;
- Planning lessons;
- Being observed and receiving feedback;
- Disagreements with tutors and mentors;
- Excessive workload.

Most trainees feel under the greatest pressure during final school experience. High standards are expected of trainees who must demonstrate a competent level of planning, teaching and assessing over time, as well as maintaining order in the classroom and forging productive relationships with staff and pupils. Trying to take on board and demonstrate a complex array of skills in the classroom is no easy matter. You may spend a long time travelling to and from your placement school and you will have to spend time in the evenings and at weekends planning your lessons and marking work. All of this can feel manageable if your classroom experience is positive and you are succeeding. However, if you encounter difficult pupils, receive large amounts of negative feedback on your classroom performance and feel you are not making progress, it is very likely that you will begin to feel overwhelmed and stressed. According to Williams (1999) teaching is so personal that when Ofsted inspectors visit a school many teachers feel *they* are being assessed, not their teaching. If their teaching is criticised they can begin to feel worthless as *individuals*. Likewise, if their teaching is praised their self-esteem is boosted and they feel good about *themselves*, not just their teaching. It is easy to see the parallels here with the scrutiny of the classroom performance of trainees by tutors and mentors.

Coping with stress

Psychologists identify some individuals as being more stress prone than others. They are usually people who have high expectations of themselves, are very task and result orientated, tend to work very quickly and find inefficiency in others very frustrating. It is, of course, much harder for such people to control stress than other personality types, but not impossible. Recognising your potential for stress and being proactive in controlling stress are both very important. Recognising that training to teach is potentially stressful will help you to develop strategies that will prevent you becoming stressed rather than waiting until you feel stressed and then considering what you ought to do about it. Here are a few pointers on reducing stress:

- Get your time management right (see below). This will make you much more effective in all aspects of your life.

- Maintain a sense of humour. Take what you do seriously but be able to laugh at yourself and see the funny side of mistakes you are sure to make. Sharing stories of blunders you make with fellow trainees can be therapeutic.

- Remain optimistic. If you focus on the negative you will soon get yourself on a downward spiral. It is very important to think positive, and celebrate progress made rather than dwelling on the distance still to go. Clichéd as the phrase may be, it really is important to see your glass as half full rather than half empty.

- Have a life beyond your training course. It is essential that you engage in activities away from school and college. A successful family life and satisfying social life make you a more interesting and rounded person. Too many late nights at the computer or too many working weekends build tension and resentment. Build blocks of relaxation time into your week as this will help you work more efficiently by forcing you to do certain tasks in a limited time frame.

- Some teachers arrive at school an hour or more before the school day begins and work on until 5.00 or 5.30 p.m. and then take no work home. While this wouldn't suit everybody (flexibility over non-contact tasks can help greatly with child minding arrangements, for example) it is one way of clearly demarcating working life and home life, which really can help you to 'switch off' and relax once you leave the school buildings. As a trainee, you should use your non-contact time in school efficiently so as to limit the work you have to take home.

■ Accept that perfection is not possible. You must have high expectations of yourself, of course, but it is impossible for you to get everything right all the time. You will have to be able to cope with negativity and resistance from some students and classes. If a class gives you a hard time it usually isn't personal and other teachers will probably be finding the class a handful also. Expect to have some critical feedback on your teaching; you have a lot to learn and observation and feedback are a vital part of the learning process. Feedback is intended to help you focus on improving your practice and achieving the Standards. Accept it in this light and engage positively with the process. Always act on advice that is written on observation feedback sheets.

■ Exercise. It is important to engage in some form of regular exercise as a means of reducing stress through the release of endorphins.

Action and reflection point

Are you a stress-prone person?

Below are a series of questions to help you identify how stress prone you are. They are based on a questionnaire compiled by Cooper and Sutherland (1997). Give yourself a score on a 1–11 scale for the bi-polar statements provided. The first one has the scale included so you can see where low and high scores fall.

Casual about appointments	1 2 3 4 5 6 7 8 9 10 11	Never late
Not competitive	1–11	Very competitive
Good listener	1–11	Attempts to finish sentences for others
Never feels rushed, even when under pressure	1–11	Always rushed
Can wait patiently	1–11	Impatient while waiting
Does tasks one at a time	1–11	Tries to do many things at once
Slow, deliberate talker	1–11	Fast and forceful speaker
Slow doing things	1–11	Fast – eating, walking, etc.
Easy-going	1–11	Hard-driving, pushing yourself and others
Expresses feelings	1–11	Hides feelings
Many outside interests	1–11	Few interests outside work/ home
Unambitious	1–11	Ambitious
Casual	1–11	Eager to get things done

Reflection

The higher the score received on this questionnaire (143 being the maximum possible) the more firmly an individual can be classed as stress prone. The lower the score the more an individual can be classed as easy-going. Interestingly, people who are highly stress prone are often blind to their own behaviour. If you are scoring this questionnaire to assess yourself and suspect that you are stress prone, it is likely that you will find it hard to be completely honest in your self-assessment. To get a more accurate assessment it is useful to ask someone else who knows you well to complete the questionnaire based on their perceptions of your behaviour. Extreme scores at either end of the scale can actually be a problem for people wanting to be good teachers.

Psychologists who first did research in this area used the term 'Type A personality' for those who exhibit strong stress-prone tendencies and 'Type B personality' for those who are very easy-going. While these terms and the ideas behind them are now considered obsolete by many psychologists they nevertheless provide a helpful framework for trainee teachers to begin to consider their behaviour and its likely impact on those they work with.

Type A personalities tend to display the following characteristics:

- Devotion to work, working long hours, feeling guilty when not working;
- A chronic sense of time urgency;
- Attempting to schedule more and more into less and less time;
- Often attempting to do two or more things at the same time;
- Hate being kept waiting, especially in queues;
- Find it difficult to talk about anything other than work;
- A strong need to be in control;
- A very competitive outlook.

The reason why Type A people can be difficult to work with is because of their constant need to be productive. They tend not to be good listeners and like to keep strict control over what is going on. They often do jobs themselves rather than taking the time to show someone else what to do. They often expect everyone around them to work to their demanding pace and schedule, including long hours of working in order to meet unrealistic goals and deadlines. Imagine the effect on a class of pupils (diverse and with different aptitudes and abilities) that Type A behaviour might have. Interestingly, Type A people are often rewarded with early promotion because, in the short term, they accomplish tasks quickly. In the longer term, however, Type A behaviour can become dysfunctional for an organisation and Type A people can fail as team leaders, finding it difficult to manage those who are less driven.

Type B personalities are the opposite of Type A. They are generally patient, relaxed, easy-going and rarely display a sense of urgency. They tend to be good at listening to others but often fail to meet deadlines and don't fit in easily to an organisation where rapid change is needed or where targets have to be met. Their lack of urgency can sometimes be highly frustrating to their colleagues. Imagine the effect on a class of pupils (all needing challenge, provided through well-structured lessons and timely feedback, to achieve their exam targets) an extreme Type B personality might have.

It is important that trainees who recognise extreme Type A or Type B behaviour in themselves consider what effect they might have on fellow trainees (especially if they are placed in the same school for school experience) and on their pupils. Arguably, it is impossible to change personality but it is possible to modify some behaviour associated with personality. For example, trainees with Type A tendencies must understand the negative effect their desire to 'control' will have on pupils who need to develop as independent learners. They should consciously plan opportunities for pupils actively to lead learning in the classroom in response to this tendency to want control. Equally, trainees with a Type B personality need to realise that they may come across to their pupils as lacking in organisation and failing to set clear goals and boundaries. They would need to respond by incorporating clear expectations and deadlines into their planning and keeping to them. Both teachers would be failing their pupils, but in different ways, if they failed to moderate their extreme tendencies. Reflect on your behaviour. Through knowledge comes strength and with greater self-awareness you can begin to adapt your behaviour so that your personality doesn't become a barrier to you developing into an effective teacher.

Some thoughts on time management

You are joining a demanding profession and so effective time management is vital for survival. Far too many teachers find themselves *living to work* rather than *working to live*; a situation not entirely down to personality type and one that is simply not sustainable in the long run and which can cause burn-out and serious health problems. Many teachers devote very long hours to their work out of genuine commitment and a desire to do the best for the children they teach. While this is admirable in some ways (and is related to the sense of moral purpose mentioned earlier) *expecting* teachers to devote every evening and weekend to their jobs in order to maintain the nation's education system is simply not acceptable and is actually a recipe for stress-related illnesses and marriage breakdowns amongst teachers.

Effective teachers learn to use time efficiently. It is very revealing to discover that those complaining the most in staff rooms about lack of time are often very inefficient in their use of time. Likewise, teachers who are actively involved in extra-curricular activities and award bearing continuing professional development (CPD) are often also the very members of staff who can be relied upon to get a job done efficiently. Indeed, it is very likely that they also have fulfilling family lives and an active social life. Some people seem to be *naturally* good time managers and this is reflected in all areas of their lives. Even so, there are strategies that everybody can learn to become better time managers.

How is effective time management achieved?

Working smarter not harder is the way to survive in a highly demanding job such as teaching and this requires a systematic approach to work and to life in general. According to Wood (1991) there are three characteristics of effective time management, which he calls the 'three Ts'.

- *Thought:* Achieve your goals by thinking about what you have to do, questioning its value and prioritising.
- *Technique:* Plan when and how you will undertake each task so as to optimise your use of time.
- *Temperament:* Try not to panic when new tasks come along because you should realise that worrying wastes time and solves nothing. Likewise, when things go wrong do not spend hours thinking 'if only I had . . .'. Instead, you should conduct a review of why things went wrong and then plan to ensure that the same mistakes are not made in the future.

Planning, priorities and deadlines

There is a cliché that suggests that if we fail to plan then we plan to fail. All effective teachers need to plan so that they can spread their workload and prioritise. Making effective use of a planner/diary (paper or electronic) is essential.

Covey (1994) suggests a variation on planning through the use of a Time Management Matrix (Table 1.1). All tasks should fit into one of the quadrants. Obviously, the urgent and important matters require your immediate attention. Items in the other boxes must be dealt with in order of priority; your aim is to work as much as possible in the important but not urgent box. Non-urgent and unimportant tasks should probably be crossed off your list altogether. It is useful to try and predict the amount of time needed for each activity beforehand. Bear

TABLE 1.1 Covey's Time Management Matrix

	URGENT	*NOT URGENT*
IMPORTANT	Crises Pressing problems Deadline driven projects, meetings	Preparation Prevention Planning Values clarification Relationship building Empowerment
NOT IMPORTANT	Interruptions, some phone calls Some mail, some reports Some meetings Many pressing matters Many popular activities	Trivia Junk mail Some phone calls Time wasters 'Escape' activities

in mind, though, that as a trainee it is likely that you will underestimate the time required for many tasks undertaken routinely by experienced teachers. With practice you will become more accurate, and the knowledge gained will prove invaluable for future planning.

Setting deadlines for the activities on your list is a good way of focusing the mind and avoiding 'drift' (which results in important but not urgent tasks never being tackled in a planned fashion). Deadlines for all tasks must be realistic and you should avoid setting deadlines that result in you putting off tasks until the day before they have to be completed. 'Working to the wire' is a bad habit and one that you should avoid. It allows no further time to reschedule the work should a crisis arise. Set your own target date for completing each task some time in advance of the school or college deadline. This provides a safety net should a crisis arise.

Delegation

Most teachers spend time doing things which should or could be done by someone else. Under the Labour administration, during the first decade of this century, *workforce remodelling* was encouraged in schools with one of its aims being to remove routine administrative jobs from teachers to enable them to focus their time and energy on teaching and learning. Teachers now have access to administrative support and in some secondary schools this is provided by an administrator being attached to a faculty for a number of hours each week. Discuss with your school-based tutor how you can make use of this person (if they exist in the structure) and how you access administrative support more generally for routine tasks such as photocopying. In lessons, save time by using pupils to give out books, collecting books in open at the page you need to start marking, and marking some pupils' books as you circulate (this is good practice as it allows you to discuss work with individual pupils and monitor progress and misunderstandings).

Avoiding delays

Procrastination can be a great time waster. While it is a mistake to make snap decisions, you must be able to weigh up the options fairly quickly and then act. For example, spending hours trying to decide on the most appropriate picture or PowerPoint image to illustrate one small point to a class doesn't represent a good use of time, given all the other jobs you are likely to have to do. Another form of procrastination is continually putting off jobs you don't like doing. Competent time managers identify the tasks they least like doing and use strategies to help them overcome their natural reticence to do them. Strategies include:

- Setting deadlines for completion of unpopular tasks;
- Breaking tasks down into manageable stages;
- Tackling difficult jobs early in the day when they are fresh;
- Rewarding themselves for finishing a task.

During your training period, you will have a number of assignments to complete, as well as planning and marking related to school experiences. Towards the end of your training, you might also be applying for jobs. You must plan carefully, spreading the timing of tasks if you are to cope successfully with these competing demands on your time.

There are several strategies that can be used to improve time management. Consider the following advice and then do the *opposite*:

- Don't use a planner and never have your diary or e-planner to hand – you have a good memory and that should be enough.

- Don't bother with setting yourself targets – you might feel too pressured.

- Never prioritise the tasks you have to do – you work more efficiently when you suddenly realise an assignment is due in the next day.

- Don't make a daily list of things to do; if a task is really necessary someone will remind you it needs doing.

- Never delegate; you need to prove that you can do everything.

- Never reply to memos from your tutors immediately; decisions are always better for being given plenty of thought.

- Allow people to interrupt you at all times of the week; it shows you care about your friends.

- Each day and at weekends take as much work home as you can; the more you have with you the more you are likely to do.

- Don't store class lists, lesson plans, schemes of work, worksheets, test papers, etc. on a computer; you will need to rewrite them anyway so what's the point?

How to use this book

While this book has been designed to act as a useful core text to support initial teacher training programmes and the Induction, no single book can do justice to all the areas and issues you will encounter during training, and you are encouraged to read beyond this book in order to further enhance your knowledge and understanding. Throughout the book the term 'trainee' has been used and reference is made to 'Initial Teacher Training (ITT)'. This ensures consistency with the terms you are likely to encounter in official documentation. However, the term 'training' is unlikely to do justice to the programme you will follow for the award of QTS. Initial Teacher Education (ITE) is a more appropriate description of the process you will go through to gain QTS.

Reflection point

What is the difference between training and education? Why is this distinction important?

Training is associated with teaching a precise set of skills; we can train dogs to perform tricks to order, for example. Education suggests something more worthy; it is associated with developing people intellectually. Training is certainly one element of ITE programmes (there are pedagogical methods and behaviour management techniques to be learnt) but it is too simplistic to reduce effective teaching to a set of competencies that simply have to be learnt in order for the trainee to become a successful practitioner. The successful application of learnt techniques *in context* requires reflection leading to modification of learnt procedures to maximise their impact.

At the core of teacher education are a number of key attitudes:

- *Reflective practice.* During your programme you should be encouraged to analyse, reflect on and evaluate your own performance and to strive for continuous improvement. This attitude is vital and lies at the heart of self-improvement as well as being a key to raising pupils' attainment.

- *Collaboration and teamwork.* The importance of collaborative learning has long been understood by educationalists and it is important that you learn the craft of the classroom through collaborative practice as well as encouraging collaborative learning in your pupils. Many highly successful schools see themselves as 'learning organisations' in which teachers continue to develop through collaboration both within and beyond the school. It is highly likely that your training will bring you into contact with teachers from schools designated as 'Teaching Schools'. Be open about taking on board the messages such experienced and successful teachers give you.

- *Critical engagement.* Teachers need to have the intellectual capacity to make judgements about a range of professional issues, such as approaches to teaching and learning, school policy and national policies on education. It is important that you learn to think rationally and become capable of evaluating a range of evidence to reach sound judgements. Try and understand your 'teacher training' by reference to a wider critical framework in order to assist you in developing as an autonomous thinker.

- *Clear values based on fairness, equality and inclusion.* It is important that you are able to make a valuable contribution to educating children for an increasingly pluralistic and multi-cultural society. Understanding barriers to achievement and how to remove them is essential in a society that values equality of opportunity. This requires understanding leading to commitment and is not something that can be achieved by mechanistic behaviours. As already stated, these values are embedded in the national Teachers' Standards (DfE 2011).

Throughout this book you will be given the opportunity to reflect critically on particular issues and you will be encouraged to work collaboratively on some tasks with fellow trainees. However, this might not always be easy. As much of your time will be spent in school you will not always have access to other trainees or even a library. This book will still be useful in these circumstances, as it provides basic information and guidance on most issues you are likely to encounter.

There are several ways in which this book can be used:

- You could read the whole book from cover to cover – this will provide you with basic information you will need to succeed in your training as well as helping you to focus your thinking. Doing this at the outset of your training will help you prepare for lectures and seminars that you will receive.

- You could dip into it at times when you feel you need help in a particular area. The chapter headings should give you a very clear idea of the issues being covered. It is likely that each chapter will support a theme covered in your university programme or a concern you encounter on school experience. Using it this way will help you to analyse a problem you are facing or indeed avoid problems arising in the first place.

- You can use it with fellow trainees and your university/school tutors to focus your discussion on particular issues. The tasks and opportunities for reflection are especially useful for this purpose.

- If you are following a GTP or SCITT programme, opportunities to reflect on your practice away from school may be fewer than those enjoyed by students following a PGCE or BA/BSc with QTS programme. The reflection opportunities and tasks provided in the book should help you to think carefully about your work in the classroom.

At various points opportunities to enhance your learning are provided:

Reflection point

This is an opportunity to think through your own ideas and beliefs on an issue. It should help you clarify your thinking and also realise that you already have views on this aspect or issue that are likely to influence you during training. By sharing your reflections with others you will begin to realise that attitudes and practice in education are influenced by wider society, politics and the culture in which we live. Consequently, policies, decisions and practice in schools are often contested and specific decisions teachers make are very often not black or white, right or wrong.

Action point

This asks you to do an activity. Activities range from compiling a list to focus your thinking to engaging in some practical research in a school context. The intention of directing you to undertake activities in school is to bring alive an issue and help you to see how things play out in the real world of schools and young people.

Case studies

These are intended to develop your thinking on a particular issue by helping you to see what a real situation might look like. Case studies are followed by opportunities for reflection or action.

The standards for teachers

Please bear in mind that the chapters in this book are, to some extent, artificial divisions. The different topics connected with becoming a teacher cannot be so easily separated in real life; the separations here provide a convenient way of thinking about a particular aspect but you always need to make connections in your thinking and practice. For example, planning, teaching, learning and behaviour are all connected and it is impossible to work on one aspect divorced from the other three. The index will help you to locate references to things that are mentioned in several chapters.

The same logic can be applied to the Standards. They are not a tick list and shouldn't be used as such. Although breaking down the various aspects of what effective teachers do that makes them effective is helpful as a means of understanding their complex work, successful teaching isn't done 'by numbers'. Your tutors know this very well and will help you understand the connections between the various Standards. You will find in this book that each chapter relates to several Standards, driving home this point (Table 1.2).

TABLE 1.2 Standards for teachers and relevant chapters

STANDARDS FOR TEACHERS	RELEVANT CHAPTERS
TEACHING	
1. *Set high expectations which inspire, motivate and challenge pupils*	
– establish a safe and stimulating environment for pupils, rooted in mutual respect;	2, 3, 5, 6, 8, 10
– set goals that stretch and challenge pupils of all backgrounds, abilities and dispositions;	2, 3, 4, 6, 7
– demonstrate consistently the positive attitudes, values and behaviour which are expected for pupils.	2, 5, 6, 8, 10
2. *Promote good progress and outcomes by pupils*	
– be accountable for pupils' attainment, progress and outcomes;	2, 3, 4, 5, 6, 7, 8, 10
– plan teaching to build on pupils' capabilities and prior knowledge;	2, 3, 7
– guide pupils to reflect on the progress they have made and their emerging needs;	7, 8

continued . . .

TABLE 1.2 Standards for teachers and relevant chapters . . . *continued*

STANDARDS FOR TEACHERS	RELEVANT CHAPTERS
TEACHING	
– demonstrate knowledge and understanding of how pupils learn and how this impacts on teaching;	2, 3
– encourage pupils to take a responsible and conscientious attitude to their own work and study.	3, 5, 7, 8
3. *Demonstrate good subject and curriculum knowledge*	
– have a secure knowledge of the relevant subject(s) and curriculum areas, foster and maintain pupils' interest in the subject, and address misunderstandings;	2, 3, 4
– demonstrate a critical understanding of developments in the subject and curriculum areas, and promote the value of scholarship;	2, 3
– demonstrate an understanding of and take responsibility for promoting high standards of literacy, articulacy and the correct use of standard English, whatever the teacher's specialist subject;	4, 8
– if teaching early reading, demonstrate a clear understanding of systemic synthetic phonics;	
– if teaching early mathematics, demonstrate a clear understanding of appropriate teaching strategies.	
4. *Plan and teach well-structured lessons*	
– impart knowledge and develop understanding through effective use of lesson time;	2, 4
– promote a love of learning and children's intellectual curiosity;	2, 3, 4, 8
– set homework and plan other out-of-class activities to consolidate and extend knowledge and understanding pupils have acquired;	4, 9
– reflect systematically on the effectiveness of lessons and approaches to teaching;	1, 4, 7, 12
– contribute to the design and provision of an engaging curriculum within the relevant subject area(s).	4, 12
5. *Adapt teaching to respond to the strengths and needs of all pupils*	
– know when and how to differentiate appropriately, using approaches which enable pupils to be taught effectively;	2, 3, 4
– have a secure understanding of how a range of factors can inhibit pupils' ability to learn, and how best to overcome these;	5, 6, 8, 10
– demonstrate an awareness of the physical, social and intellectual development of children, and know how to adapt teaching to support pupils' education at different stages of development;	2, 3, 4

continued . . .

TABLE 1.2 Standards for teachers and relevant chapters . . . *continued*

STANDARDS FOR TEACHERS	RELEVANT CHAPTERS
TEACHING	

– have a clear understanding of the needs of all pupils, including those with special educational needs; those of high ability; those with English as an additional language; those with disabilities; and be able to use and evaluate distinctive teaching approaches to engage and support them.	3, 6, 7

6. *Make accurate and productive use of assessment*

– know and understand how to assess the relevant subject and curriculum areas, including statutory requirements;	7
– make use of formative and summative assessment to secure pupils' progress;	2, 4, 7
– use relevant data to monitor progress, set targets, and plan subsequent lessons;	4, 7
– give pupils regular feedback, both orally and through accurate marking and encourage pupils to respond to feedback.	2, 4, 7

7. *Manage behaviour effectively to ensure a good and safe learning environment*

– have clear rules and routines for behaviour in classrooms, and take responsibility for promoting good and courteous behaviour both in classrooms and around the school, in accordance with the school's behaviour policy;	5, 8
– have high expectations of behaviour, and establish a framework for discipline with a range of strategies, using praise, sanctions and rewards consistently and fairly;	5, 8
– manage classes effectively, using approaches which are appropriate to pupils' needs in order to involve and motivate them;	2, 3, 4, 5, 6
– maintain good relationships with pupils, exercise appropriate authority, and act decisively when necessary.	5, 6, 8, 10

8. *Fulfil wider professional responsibilities*

– make a positive contribution to the wider life and ethos of the school;	9, 12
– develop effective professional relationships with colleagues, knowing how and when to draw on advice and specialist support;	12
– deploy support staff effectively;	4, 5, 6, 12
– take responsibility for improving teaching through appropriate professional development, responding to advice and feedback from colleagues;	12
– communicate effectively with parents with regard to pupils' achievements and well being.	8, 12

continued . . .

TABLE 1.2 Standards for teachers and relevant chapters . . . *continued*

STANDARDS FOR TEACHERS	*RELEVANT CHAPTERS*
PERSONAL AND PROFESSIONAL CONDUCT	
• *Teachers uphold public trust in the profession and maintain high standards of ethics and behaviour, within and outside school, by:*	2, 5, 6, 8, 9, 12
– treating pupils with dignity, building relationships rooted in mutual respect, and at all times observing proper boundaries appropriate to a teacher's professional position;	
– having regard for the need to safeguard pupils' well-being, in accordance with statutory provisions;	
– showing tolerance of and respect for the rights of others;	
– not undermining fundamental British values, including democracy, the rule of law, individual liberty and mutual respect, and tolerance of those with different faiths and beliefs;	
– ensuring that personal beliefs are not expressed in ways which exploit pupils' vulnerability or might lead them to break the law.	
• *Teachers must have proper and professional regard for ethos, policies and practices of the school in which they teach, and maintain high standards in their own attendance and punctuality.*	5, 8, 12
• *Teachers must have an understanding of, and always act within, the statutory frameworks which set out their professional duties and responsibilities.*	1, 6, 8, 9, 12

Summary

Becoming a secondary school teacher requires commitment, determination and resilience. The Teachers' Standards (DfE 2011) used to inform the award of QTS are, quite rightly, very demanding. You will need to demonstrate a good understanding of your subject and how it should be taught, high standards of professionalism and effective classroom practice in order to succeed. Committing yourself to critical reflection and realising the power of collaborative learning from the outset will help you succeed. You will also need to understand how to manage your time effectively and how to minimise the impact of the potentially stressful situations you will face during training. This book will provide basic information you need on all the key elements of your training programme, regardless of your subject specialism. To get the most from each chapter you are advised to undertake the recommended reflection and action activities. If you haven't already done so, it is a good idea to familiarise yourself with the Standards (Table 1.2). As you embark on your training think about the implications of Part Two of the Standards: Personal and Professional Conduct and consider what the implications are for your outlook and behaviour as a trainee.

References

Capel, S. (1997) 'Changes in Students' Anxieties After Their First and Second Teaching Practices' in *Educational Research*, 39(2) 211–228.

Cooper, C. and Sutherland, V. (1997) *Thirty Minutes to Deal with Difficult People*, London: Kogan Page.

Covey, S. (1994) *First Things First: Coping with the Ever Increasing Demands of the Workplace*, London: Simon and Schuster.

DfE (2011) *Teachers' Standards*, Crown copyright.

Education Service Advisory Committee (1992) *Managing Occupational Stress: A Guide for Managers and Teachers in the School Sector*, London: HMSO.

Fontana, D. (1989) *Managing Stress*, London: Routledge.

Hart, N.I. (1987) 'Student Teachers' Anxieties: Four Measured Factors and Their Relationship to Pupil Disruption in Class' in *Educational Research*, 29(1) 12–18.

Kyriacou, C. and Stephens, P. (1999) 'Student Teachers' Concerns during Teaching Practice' in *Evaluation and Research in Education*, 13(1) 18–31.

Williams, E. (1999) 'Sleeplessness? Irritability? Low self-esteem? You must have Ofsteditis', in *Times Educational Supplement: Mind and Body Supplement*, TES (26th March 1999).

Wood, I. (1991) *Time Management in Teaching*, London: Network Educational Press.

2

Teaching

Introduction

Before you begin your training programme it is important you spend some time thinking about teaching. Your response to this suggestion is probably that you have already spent a great deal of time thinking about teaching; you thought long and hard about the profession before you applied for a place on a training programme. While this is no doubt true, you now need to think carefully about exactly what a teacher does in order to be effective.

Good teachers make teaching look easy! A casual observer in a secondary school classroom would know nothing of the preparation that has led up to the lesson delivery and would probably fail to see the subtleties of organisation and interaction being performed smoothly by the teacher. In this chapter you will be introduced to research findings on effective teaching and you will be invited to reflect on and analyse the work of the teacher in a systematic way that will take you beyond casual observation. Doing this at the start of your training programme will help you make more sense of classroom life when you observe teachers at work. It should also help you to begin to reflect on your own attitudes to teaching, and the competencies you will need to develop, which experienced teachers often employ with such skill they no longer consciously think about them.

Thinking about effective teaching

You will have experienced many teachers during your time at school. Did you respond to some teachers better than others? If your answer is 'yes', did all pupils respond well to these teachers or only certain groups of pupils (the most able, the least able, boys, girls, confident pupils, shy pupils, gregarious pupils, studious pupils, those keen on the subject, those with little interest in the subject)?

You may conclude from your reflections that personality has something to do with a teacher's level of success and that people with certain personality types are therefore more likely than others to make successful teachers. Alternatively, you may have reached the conclusion that a range of people with different personality types can be successful as teachers, but that certain types of pupils respond differently to people with different personalities. Either way, you are probably associating certain attitudes and behaviours or 'styles' of teaching with effectiveness.

Reflection point

Spend a few minutes thinking about teachers you were taught by. Can you identify different teaching styles (think about approaches to classroom management to help focus your ideas)? Do you think there is a link between personality and teaching style? Are there any personality types that are unsuited to teaching? How does a teacher's style impact on learners and learning?

There are three 'styles' described below to get you thinking. It is unlikely that you will find extreme versions of any of these styles except 'authoritative' in today's secondary schools. Nevertheless, it is probable that you will come across teachers who veer towards, or show elements of, the other two styles.

Authoritarian

Extreme authoritarian teaching is consistent with teaching styles from the early twentieth century. Classrooms are quiet, ordered and strictly patrolled by the teacher. Pupils know their place within the classroom and if they deviate from the task in hand they 'face the consequences'. Hawley (1997) suggests that 'this type of teacher gives no indication that s/he cares for the students, and little praise or encouragement is given if at all'. Pupils fear teachers of this type, who hold on to power by controlling all aspects of learning. Students are discouraged from initiating self-motivated learning, and skills associated with verbal communication and discussion are inhibited. Students dislike this style of teaching. Teachers who favour it tend to find it difficult to relate to pupils and vice-versa. Pupils find such teachers 'strict and scary' (Cowley 2001).

Consider why this approach might be ill suited to a democratic society in which individuality is valued and/or to an education system required to turn out autonomous thinkers.

Authoritative

Authoritative teachers are able to adapt their teaching style to fit the situation they find themselves in. They place limits and controls on their pupils, but also encourage them to think independently by asking appropriate questions and challenging them to investigate for themselves. Unlike authoritarian teachers, these teachers *earn* the respect of their pupils by being fair, kind and nurturing in their attitude. The authoritative teacher can manage the classroom by involving children within the lesson and praising good work and effort, but using reprimands when the need arises. Children know that although such teachers are approachable and 'human' there are consequences if unacceptable behaviour is displayed.

Why do you think the most effective teachers in today's schools are likely to be using the authoritative approach? Does it have any downsides? Will all pupils respond to this approach?

The nurturer

The extreme nurturer places few demands on pupils, believing that they should be free to explore learning in their own time. Such teachers have a rather idealistic view of their pupils, believing that they are all basically motivated to learn and that if they are provided with the necessary emotional support then they will take control of their own learning. Priority is given to emotional and social development as these teachers believe pupils only learn well in an environment where they feel safe and secure and if they have a positive sense of self.

Why would teachers who use a solely nurturing approach be unable to survive in today's secondary schools? Are there any stages of education or contexts in which this approach would be acceptable?

It is clear from the above typologies that the authoritative style is the one you should try to cultivate. Do bear in mind, though, that there will be occasions when teachers who favour the authoritative style 'turn on' the authoritarian because a particular set of circumstances make it necessary. Likewise, the authoritative teacher may need to become the nurturer with certain pupils. An ability to adapt style according to circumstances is very important. Though personality might be important in explaining why some teachers find it easier than others to develop the authoritative approach, it is possible for all teachers to learn many of the basic techniques associated with this style.

A consideration of overall style is just a starting point. You now need to think beyond these general descriptions to get at what makes teachers effective. You need to unpack exactly what the effective teachers you have experienced did that made them more successful than other teachers. You need to identify the behaviours that were common to all effective teachers you can remember.

Action point

Spend a few minutes listing the things your most effective teachers did. What characteristics did they display? How did they manage pupils? If you run out of ideas think about the things your less effective teachers did (or didn't do) and suggest the opposite!

You have probably managed to produce a reasonable list of things that you believe make teachers effective. How does it compare with the list below? This was produced by pupils I taught some years ago, as part of a whole school initiative to improve the quality of teaching in my school. I think you will agree that the list is full of common sense points and shows that secondary school pupils are more than capable of reflecting with maturity on the teaching and learning process. The pupils were asked to brainstorm the points, and this is a summary of things that were mentioned by every group the activity was conducted with. They are not listed in order of importance (though you might like to consider whether or not all the points are equally important).

A 'good' teacher . . .

- Is welcoming and friendly;
- Has a sense of humour;
- Treats pupils with respect;
- Is enthusiastic;
- Explains things clearly;
- Makes the subject interesting and easy to understand;
- Praises pupils;
- Gets to lessons on time;
- Expects good behaviour;
- Is fair;
- Doesn't rush homework instructions;
- Marks books regularly;
- Is well organised;
- Doesn't shout and scream;
- Shows interest in pupils;
- Helps pupils who don't understand;
- Has a tidy classroom;
- Lets pupils have a say in how things are organised.

Many of these points have also been identified by writers and researchers interested in teacher effectiveness. Barber and Brighouse (1992), for example, associated the following qualities and characteristics with 'good' teachers:

- Good understanding of self and of interpersonal relationships;
- Generosity of spirit;
- Sense of humour;
- Sharp observational powers;
- Interest in and concern for others;
- Infectious enthusiasm for what is taught;
- Imagination;
- Energy;
- Intellectual curiosity;
- Professional growth and understanding of how children learn;
- Ability to plan appropriate learning programmes for classes/groups/individuals;
- Understanding of their curriculum in the context of the school as a whole.

This list goes further than the one produced by pupils in my school and begins to include points that might not be so evident to teenagers thinking about why they learn better with some teachers than others. For example, the ability to plan appropriately might not be obvious to pupils; they would identify interesting lessons or making a subject easy to understand as characteristics of effective teaching, without realising that a great deal of planning had gone into making lessons interesting and teaching complex concepts by breaking them down into understandable stages.

From this list we begin to see that effective teaching occurs as a result of thorough planning and good understanding of the curriculum and how children learn, though there is still much importance made of teachers displaying a set of appropriate attitudes and behaviours that will make their success in the classroom more likely. In recent years much greater emphasis has been placed on identifying the precise behaviours and skills that characterise effective teaching. Teaching has been deconstructed in an effort to identify a precise set of competencies that result in effectiveness in the classroom. These are reflected in the Standards that you will have to demonstrate by the end of your training period, in order to be awarded qualified teacher status (QTS).

Action point

List things effective teachers might do before, during and after a lesson to ensure that they are effective. If the lesson is the tip of the iceberg (the bit we see), what lies hidden from view?

The list you produced is likely to contain such things as:

- Learning pupils' names;
- Reading up on the concepts to be taught;
- Planning for the particular abilities of the pupils to be taught;
- Evaluating what pupils learnt in the previous lesson and using this to assist planning;
- Organising the classroom in a way that is suited to the nature of the lesson;
- Greeting the pupils and ensuring an orderly start to the lesson;
- Giving clear instructions;
- Using the whiteboard to note key ideas;
- Ensuring that the lesson has pace and variety;
- Asking questions during the lesson to aid learning and assess level of understanding;
- Responding quickly and fairly to any misbehaviour;
- Ensuring that the lesson has an orderly conclusion and that homework instructions are understood;

- Using work produced during the lesson to assess learning;
- Using other adult support effectively.

This is not an exhaustive list, of course, but it does help to demonstrate that once you begin to analyse exactly what teachers are doing, it becomes clear that there is much more to teaching than standing in front of a class and talking. David Reynolds (1999) summarised research on effective teaching from a number of different countries. He noted great consistency in the research findings, with the following traits common to all successful teaching:

- Intellectual challenge through high expectations, exciting interest and appropriate questioning;
- Strong classroom structures with a limited range of goals;
- Efficient use of time with well handled lesson transitions and good use of homework.

In 2000 Hay McBer published a model of teacher effectiveness. They had conducted extensive research into what exactly effective teachers do, by talking to a number of 'star teachers', their pupils and their colleagues. They also observed these teachers at work in an effort to identify practices and characteristics common to all of them, even though they came from a variety of types of school and a range of geographical areas. The research confirmed much of what was already known about teacher effectiveness and concluded that a combination of interconnected factors contributed to overall effectiveness. These factors were classified as teaching skills, professional characteristics and classroom climate.

The full report can be found in various places on line (e.g. http://dera.ioe.ac.uk/4566/1/RR216.pdf) and a consideration of some of the findings now will help your reflections on effective teachers.

Teaching skills

Teaching skills are 'micro-behaviours' that the effective teacher exhibits when teaching a class. The behaviours looked for in the Hay Mcber research were clustered under the headings used by Ofsted inspectors when making judgements about quality of teaching. The following summarises what the research concluded about the teaching skills of the very best teachers.

Effective teachers communicate *high expectations* directly to pupils. They encourage effort, accuracy and good presentation. They have differentiated objectives for pupils of different ability but are consistent in expecting all pupils to do their best. They use a variety of techniques to motivate pupils, they draw on pupils' own experience in lessons and give pupils opportunities to take responsibility for their own learning.

Effective teachers' *planning* is thorough and systematic. Each lesson is considered in the context of the longer-term scheme of work and takes into account what pupils learnt in the previous lesson and for homework. Account is taken of the needs of different ability groups within the class. Lesson intentions (expected learning outcomes) are shared with pupils and instructions given are clear. Lesson objectives are reviewed with the class.

Effective teachers employ a variety of teaching strategies. Many activities are led by the teacher. Information is presented with enthusiasm and clarity and the lessons move at a brisk pace. Individual work and small group activities are common. The learning is often 'active'. The teacher uses questioning regularly and in a sophisticated way to help move pupils' understanding on.

Effective teachers have a clear strategy for pupil behaviour management. Their classrooms are places where a sense of order exists. They set clear expectations and boundaries for behaviour. They nip inappropriate behaviour in the bud. They make sure they know what is going on everywhere in their classroom (360° vision). In schools where there are significant numbers of children with more challenging behaviour effective teachers have a very structured approach to each lesson, with regard to behaviour. For example, they stand at the classroom door to greet pupils. These approaches are used alongside the longer-term approach of getting to know the pupils well and making them feel valued as individuals.

Effective teachers make good use of time and resources (including other adults in class). Lessons are started briskly, activities are well paced with effective transitions between activities, and there is time for review built in at the end of a lesson. The teacher's time is allocated fairly among pupils. Resources are organised efficiently in the classroom so that the lesson runs smoothly. For example, books and materials needed by pupils are set out in advance of a lesson to ensure time is not wasted and pace is maintained.

Effective teachers use a range of assessment methods to monitor pupils' progress. Tests, competitions, questions in class and regular written work are all used. Pupils are encouraged and helped to assess their own work and set targets for improvement. Critical and supportive comments are provided on pupils' written work. Effective teachers use the information gathered from assessment to inform planning, for example, to plug learning gaps.

Effective teachers make good use of homework. This is set and marked regularly and is integrated into the work being covered in the lesson.

The professional characteristics identified in the report are defined as 'deep-seated patterns of behaviour which outstanding teachers display more often, in more circumstances and in greater degree of intensity than their colleagues' (Hay McBer 2000). These characteristics include:

- Professional behaviour characterised by respect for others, self-confidence, creating trust and a willingness to challenge and support pupils.
- Clear thinking, enabling cause and effect to be recognised (analysis) and patterns and links to be made (conceptualisation).
- Channelling energy into planning and setting expectations. These teachers are committed to improvement and are willing to seek out information that will help them to get the best out of their pupils.

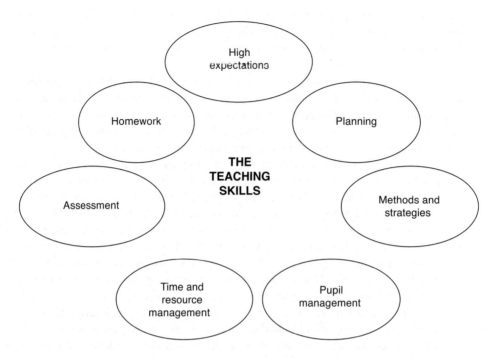

FIGURE 2.1 The teaching skills

■ Leadership abilities demonstrated through motivating pupils, adaptability and flexibility and a willingness to hold their pupils to account for their achievement and behaviour.

■ Good inter-personal skills leading to the formation of productive relationships with colleagues, effective teamwork and the capacity to influence other people.

Finally, the report makes reference to 'classroom climate'. Essentially, the researchers tried to uncover what it feels like for a pupil to be in a good teacher's classroom and identify exactly what features that make up the ethos of the classroom help to motivate pupils. The following points were identified as being important:

■ Clarity about the purpose of the lesson;

■ A feeling of order in the classroom;

■ Clear standards relating to behaviour;

■ Fairness (no favouritism);

■ The opportunity to participate;

■ Support;

- A safe classroom (free from bullying and fear);
- A stimulating classroom (where pupils' interest is developed);
- A clean and comfortable environment.

You now have a much clearer picture of the characteristic behaviours associated with effective teachers. You have a model of excellence, which will help you to find your bearings when you are undertaking school experience as part of your training programme. It is likely that your training provider will expect you to undertake some fairly structured observations of experienced teachers during the early stages of your time in school. The observation schedule (Table 2.1) provided at the end of this chapter should help you to relate what you have read about effective teaching to what you see going on in school. By observing teachers systematically, you will begin to see how many of the characteristics identified above are used 'in action'.

At this stage, you may be feeling quite daunted by what you will have to be able to do in order to become an effective teacher. Don't panic! Literally thousands of other trainees have had similar feelings but have gone on to become very accomplished practitioners. If you are passionate about your subject and are determined to do the best you can to help every child you teach to 'grow', then you are starting your training with the right attitude to become a successful professional. As far as the practical skills teachers exhibit go, accept that it will take a while for you to develop these. Concentrate on the basics: starting a lesson, presenting information, asking questions, and learn from how you see good teachers handling these aspects of teaching. As your confidence grows, you will begin to handle classes more naturally.

Of course, even the basics mentioned above are more complex than at first appears and there is not always an absolutely right way to do things (though there are certainly wrong ways to do things). Making judgements about how to handle particular classes and children in order to maximise their learning is partly what makes teaching so highly skilled. This is why you will be encouraged to develop as a 'reflective practitioner' during your time in training.

Effectiveness – a health warning

Throughout this chapter regular use has been made of the word 'effective' but what this means exactly has not been defined. An assumption has been made that all readers will have a similar understanding of what effective means. It is likely that you regard an effective teacher as one who is successful in generating interest and enthusiasm for their subject, and one who gets the best possible academic results for the ability of children taught. This is an acceptable definition, but a bit more discussion is called for.

Some people would prefer a more precise definition of effective. There are those who believe that in education, as in many other walks of life, effectiveness should be measurable. Such people would put great faith in school league tables and in Ofsted judgements about the effectiveness of schools. Relating this to individual teachers, they would argue pupils' results in national tests and exams provide a reliable measure of how effective a teacher has been. This is problematic for a number of reasons. Raw results from national tests take no account of the social or ethnic background of the pupils. This makes it very difficult to make judgements about how effective individual teachers have been, as few would argue that a pupil's background has no impact on their interest in education and the level of support they receive away from school. In order to get round this problem, value-added data is used. This takes into account the level of achievement of pupils when they enter a school or commence an examination course. This means that some schools in which pupils receive lower GCSE grades than other schools might be considered more effective, despite lower raw results, because they have added greater value to pupils' learning during their time at the school. Some value-added techniques, for example the Year 11 Information System (YELLIS) and the 'A' Level Information System (ALIS), even take into account the 'cultural capital' of the pupils (assessed by the use of a questionnaire) so that schools know how they are doing compared with schools catering for very similar children (for full details go to www.cemcentre.org.uk). While these approaches are clearly of more value than raw scores, they are not without their critics. Some would argue that no two schools or even two pupils are the same, and that measures of social class, such as parental occupation or eligibility for free school meals, rarely provide an accurate and valid picture of particular schools and children. Bearing this in mind, any attempt to measure teacher effectiveness based on test and examination results *alone* must be treated with caution. Effectiveness is multidimensional. Teachers differ in their effectiveness with different types and ages of pupils and with different aspects of pupils' development.

Helping pupils to gain academic qualifications is not the only thing that teachers should be doing. However, in these days of accountability, there is a danger that teachers might focus on this aspect of their work at the expense of all else. This could have unintended consequences. For example, teachers might 'teach to the test' rather than exploring with their pupils potentially more interesting aspects of a subject. The experience gained by pupils could, therefore, be diminished even though their exam results improve. Teachers might focus on pupils likely to gain better exam results, at the expense of the less able. For example, pupils who are borderline D/C in a GCSE class may be given considerable help in order to boost a school's position in the league tables, where the percentage of pupils gaining grades A★–C is an important measure of success. More worrying still, teachers might neglect the human side of teaching because of the pressure to generate results. They might be less inclined to devote time to troubled youngsters who need a shoulder to cry on or less likely to participate in extra-curricular activities, instead focusing on getting as many pupils as possible 'through the test'. As a new entrant to the profession, you need to be aware that effective teaching cannot be measured by test results alone.

Reflection point

Can you think of any criteria other than exam results that might be used when making judgements about a teacher's effectiveness? Try and discuss your findings with other trainees.

This is a difficult area, as so much of what a teacher does isn't measurable. Indeed, a teacher might never know the impact s/he has had on particular pupils. It is certainly the case that some young people are inspired to study particular academic disciplines by their teachers, but there are other ways in which teachers might be influential. There are many adults I have met who admit to having wanted to be like their teachers. Many strong women teachers have been an inspiration to the girls they have taught, and the current drive to increase the number of teachers from minority ethnic groups is an indication of the importance being placed on teachers as role models. Many testimonials from adults who found their adolescent years to be a time of turbulence offer thanks to teachers who devoted time and energy to helping them through a difficult time in their lives and providing emotional support. Their teachers were effective, but they might not have thought so at the time, and what they achieved never featured in a league table of academic results.

Ofsted and teacher effectiveness

Ofsted (The Office for Standards in Education, Children's Services and Skills) make judgements about the quality of teaching when they inspect schools. Over the years the schedule they use when judging a lesson has evolved, with much more emphasis now being placed on the impact on learning of what teachers do in class. The Ofsted schedule published in December 2011 makes clear that 'the judgement on quality of teaching must take account of evidence of pupils' learning and progress' (www.ofsted.gov.uk/resources/090098). Inspectors observing lessons are asked to consider a number of things including: the extent to which teaching strategies engage *all* pupils; how well pupils understand how to improve their learning as a result of feedback from teachers; the extent to which teachers enable their pupils to develop the skills to learn for themselves. This helps to clarify for you, at the start of your teaching career, that teachers who are merely performers at the front of the class (however entertaining they may be) will not be using a sufficient range of pedagogical skills to be effective. Similarly, teachers who enable some pupils – but not all pupils – to learn will be falling short of what is required of a satisfactory teacher. The case study below helps to further explain this point.

Case study

As a young head of department, I was keen to become involved in training teachers. I agreed to have two trainees in my department. I was to be their mentor and was determined to make a success of my role. I observed both trainees regularly. I was initially very happy with one of the trainees. She was a very good communicator and held the attention of the children by the way she performed at the front of the class. Her self-confidence helped her class control. I felt at an early stage that she would develop into a very good teacher. The other trainee I was less sure about. She was more quietly spoken and not a natural extrovert. Her lesson introductions were less polished. However, as time went on the second trainee grew in confidence. Her planning was detailed (and showed differentiated activities for different groups of pupils according to prior attainment) and she spent most of each lesson speaking to pupils individually about their work and helping them with misunderstandings. She knew all the children's names and showed a quiet interest in each one of them. Meanwhile, the first trainee had reached a plateau in terms of her development. Her personality meant that she was a natural performer, but she showed interest in only the most able and extrovert pupils in her classes. Her planning wasn't differentiated to meet the needs of all abilities. The quality of work the pupils in her classes produced was not as good as the quality of work produced by pupils in the classes of the quieter trainee. This was not what I expected from the judgements I made when I first observed them. I worked with both trainees to try and support their development; the quieter trainee flourished, responding to advice and working hard; the more self-confident trainee was simply not prepared to put in the effort and time needed to improve, despite being a natural performer.

The important thing to learn from this is that there is more to teaching than 'performance'. Teaching must result in pupils learning and for this to happen for all pupils a whole range of skills is needed as well as dedication and hard work.

Action point

If you are at the start of your training programme

- Think carefully about your own personality, attitudes and skills. Write down the things you feel you already have in place that will enable you to make a success of your training. Then list the things you know you will need to work on, with an action plan of how you intend to do this.
- When you get the opportunity to observe an experienced teacher at work, use the observation schedule (Table 2.1) to help you focus on effective behaviour. Once you are clear that the elements on the list are usually present in successful lessons you can begin to consider how each one supports pupils' learning.

If you are well into your training programme and have already had some experience of whole class teaching or you are commencing your Induction

- Try and get a fellow trainee or NQT (someone you feel at ease with) to observe one of your lessons and to complete an observation schedule (Table 2.1) for you. List the areas you need to work on (behaviours that are absent) and write an action plan of what you intend to do. Don't forget that judgements made will be likely to be 'gut reactions' rather than a scientific measure of how you performed.

TABLE 2.1 Lesson observation schedule

LESSON OBSERVATION SCHEDULE	YES	NO

PLANNING

Are the lesson objectives communicated clearly to the class?
Is the lesson structured into a number of clear 'chunks'?
Is the lesson reviewed with the class at the end?
Has the teacher planned differentiated activities for pupils at different
   stages/levels of understanding?

TEACHING

Is the lesson linked to previous learning?
Are the pupils' ideas and experiences drawn upon?
Is a variety of questioning used (open and closed questions)?
Are explanations clear?
Does the lesson move at a good pace?
Is interaction between teacher and pupils relaxed but purposeful?
Does the teacher modify his/her language for different learners?
Does the teacher clarify misunderstandings that emerge?

LEARNING ETHOS AND BEHAVIOUR MANAGEMENT

Do pupils show self-control throughout?
Do pupils work effectively together (e.g. on paired or group tasks)?
Is misbehaviour dealt with promptly?
Are all pupils treated fairly?

ASSESSMENT

Are questions used to assess understanding?
Does the teacher address pupils' misunderstandings?
Does the teacher circulate and read pupils' written work in class?
Do comments in pupils' books help them know what is needed to improve?

USE OF TIME AND RESOURCES

Are all required resources easily to hand?
Are teaching assistants clear about what is expected of them?
Are transitions between parts of the lesson handled with little loss of pace?

HOMEWORK

Is homework set?
Are instructions about homework clear?

ACHIEVEMENT

Were all pupils 'on task' for most of the lesson?
Did the learning outcomes (objectives) seem to be achieved?
Did pupils of *all* levels of ability seem to make progress?

Summary

This chapter introduced you to some of the research that exists on teacher effectiveness and prompted you to reflect on the approach to teaching taken by good teachers you have encountered during your own school days. This should have helped you to be clearer about what the qualities, aptitudes and behaviours of effective teachers are. When you go into classrooms as part of your training year and begin to observe teachers at work, see if they are displaying the approach and behaviours outlined in this chapter. You should also be beginning to prepare yourself mentally for using techniques that have been identified. Honing effective questioning skills and developing successful lesson transition points will take some time, of course, but by visualising yourself handling these aspects of a lesson you will begin to build your confidence and be more likely to make a success of them when you are at last let loose on a class!

While it is true that effective teachers use an identified set of techniques, it is also the case that there is an important element of individuality involved in teaching. There is no such thing as the identikit teacher. Teachers with quite different personalities can achieve equal success with pupils. Terry Haydn (2003), commenting on the findings of his research into pupil disaffection, said, 'Teacher characteristics are more important to kids than anything else. What their teacher is like really does make a difference'. (More information on this can be found at www.uea.ac.uk/~m242/nasc)

It is likely that all successful teachers will exhibit most of the behaviours we have discussed, but in ways that appear unique to children. High expectations can be transmitted to pupils in different ways by different teachers, for example. The techniques teachers use to keep children 'on task' or the ways in which they praise children can be tremendously varied. This variety is partly what makes school life interesting for pupils. Likewise, the way in which identified behaviours are modified to meet the needs of particular ages and abilities of children is very important. The way good teachers praise eleven-year-olds is different from the way they praise fifteen-year-olds. Try and identify these differences in approach before you begin practising your skills in the classroom.

The following words from a Year 8 pupil provide an appropriate way to end this chapter devoted to a consideration of what makes a good teacher.

A good teacher . . .

Is kind
Is generous
Listens to you
Encourages you
Has faith in you
Likes teaching children
Likes teaching their subject
Takes time to explain things

Helps you when you're stuck
Tells you how you are doing
Allows you to have your say
Doesn't give up on you
Cares for your opinion
Makes you feel clever
Treats people equally
Stands up for you
Makes allowances
Tells the truth
Is forgiving.
　　　　(Hay McBer 2000)

References

Barber, M. and Brighouse, T. (1992) *Enhancing the Teaching Profession*, London: IPPR.

Cowley, S. (2001) *Getting the Buggers to Behave*, London: Continuum.

Hawley, C. (1997) *Teacher Talk – What is Your Classroom Management Profile?* http://education.Indiana.edu/cas/tt/v/1i2/what.html.

Hay McBer (2000) *Research into Teacher Effectiveness*, London: DfES.

Haydn, T. (2003) quoted in Thornton. K. 'Friendly, Fun but Fair – the Ideal Mix' in *Times Educational Supplement*, TES (25th May 2003).

Ofsted (2012) *The Evaluation Schedule for the Inspection of Maintained Schools and Academies*, Crown copyright.

Reynolds, D. (1999) 'Can Good Teaching be Measured?' in *Times Educational Supplement*, TES (1st August 1999).

3

Learning

Introduction

For those who are new to teaching it can seem strange that a key part of their training programme will focus on pupils' learning. Surely, the novice will reason, if teachers use their classroom skills effectively then pupils will learn. The assumption here is that pupils learn when teachers teach. This seems logical, but you will know from your own experience and observations that teachers are differentially effective. As we discussed in Chapter 2, some have more success with certain classes and certain pupils than others. One of the key ingredients of success in the classroom is to be able to match teaching methods to the learning needs of pupils. This can only be achieved through some understanding of how children learn. It is quite possible for a teacher to give a lively performance at the front of the classroom, displaying a detailed knowledge of their subject, but for pupils to learn very little, because the teaching method chosen (in this case a didactic approach) doesn't suit the learners.

During your training programme for the award of QTS, you will be going through a period of rapid learning. Much of your learning will take place in the classroom (on the job) as you grapple with developing the skills required of a teacher. Throughout your training try and think about how *you* learn. By doing this you will begin to see that pupils, just like you, learn in a wide variety of ways. You will realise that at times they may feel daunted by what they are expected to learn, they may be anxious about the possibility of failure and different pupils will require different levels of support with their learning. Thinking about how *you* learn will get you started on thinking about the possible learning needs of your pupils.

In this chapter different ideas about learning will be explored. You will be introduced to some of the major theories and writers that have influenced the way in which teachers approach their work. This will help you to see the link between ideas about learning and pedagogic strategies, which in turn should help you reflect on the implications for teaching and learning in your subject area. Learning theories will not tell you how to teach; this is a matter of professional judgement.

However, they will help you to decide on the strategies you might use with particular pupils or classes. The important starting point is to remember that teaching is a means to an end (pupils' learning) not an end in itself. If you teach but your pupils don't learn, or only some of them learn, you are not being effective.

Thinking about learning

Before we consider major learning theories it is worth thinking about some fundamental factors that might influence pupils' learning.

Reflection point

Spend a few minutes thinking about why some pupils in schools appear to learn more easily than others.

You are likely to have produced a list that includes the following points:

- Ability
- Self-esteem
- Motivation
- Personality
- Aptitude
- Learning style
- Support from home
- Peer influence
- Previous experience.

You may have considered the point that some pupils do learn easily but are not as successful as they could be because they lack motivation or parental support or because they belong to friendship groups where success is not seen as 'cool'. Equally, other students may not learn quite so easily, but achieve through sheer determination and hard work. Explaining pupils' success in learning involves the consideration of a range of factors. In the past, many have argued that ability, and more specifically, intelligence, together with motivation explains why some pupils learn more easily than others. While these factors are significant, it is now accepted that intelligence is far from easy to define (and is certainly not fixed) and that such things as learning styles and self-esteem are also important. A better understanding of the links between all these factors has helped to raise achievement in schools in recent years.

Intelligence

Intelligence as an explanation of success in learning is contentious. A commonly accepted definition of intelligence is difficult to find and there is no consensus on approaches to measuring intelligence and establishing the intelligence quotient (IQ) of an individual. Clearly, social circumstances have a major influence on the development of 'intelligence', whatever potential an individual may have in terms of their genetic make up. The 'nature–nurture' debate has been a subject of research and argument among scientists and educationalists for many decades. Intelligence testing is an attempt to identify the innate ability of an individual. Cyril Burt's theories formed the basis of accepted wisdom on the nature of intelligence for generations of school children from the 1950s onwards. His theories influenced the 11+ exam, used to determine which children would be given a place in a grammar school during the years of selective education. Burt was much criticised for his deterministic approach, and the discrediting of the 11+ exam was a key factor in the move away from selection to comprehensive schools in the 1970s.

> Possibly the worst educational innovation of the twentieth century was the so called intelligence test . . . let us put the record straight . . . we all have the ability to improve and expand our own intelligence; it is not fixed.
>
> (Dryden and Vos 1994)

In the 1960s and 1970s socio–cultural factors began to be seen as more important determinants of intelligence than heredity. While individual differences in intelligence were acknowledged, educators argued that social inequalities had a greater influence on children's capacity for learning. This was why, they argued, middle class children generally did much better than working class children in the 11+ exam. By the 1990s, politicians were accusing teachers working in schools in inner-city areas of having low expectations of their pupils and of using children's social and cultural backgrounds as an excuse for under-achievement. Clearly, the nature–nurture debate and arguments about the link between intelligence and pupils' ability to learn go on. As a teacher, it is important that you don't jump to conclusions about a child's level of intelligence. Indeed, we will see later in this chapter that it is helpful to think in terms of multiple-intelligences when considering children's abilities. Also, don't make assumptions about a child's capacity for learning based on their social background; avoid 'labelling' and have high expectations of all the children you teach.

Motivation

Motivation is a key factor in learning and is linked very closely to attitude. Motivation in a school context can be seen as 'a person's aroused desire for participation in a learning process' (Curzon 1990). Many teachers would argue that by the time pupils reach Year 8 of secondary school some of them are losing motivation and developing negative attitudes towards schooling. Indeed, over the years HMI have commented on pupils' attitudes in some schools as being a cause for concern. 'In too many lessons the bad behaviour and poor attitude of a minority of pupils adversely affect the learning of others' (HMI 2000).

There can be no simple explanation for this falling off in attitude and lack of motivation. However, one important factor is worthy of discussion as, arguably, it is something teachers can have some influence over. According to the Elton Report (DES 1989), 'Many children who behave badly in school are those whose self-esteem is threatened by failure. They see academic work as "unwinnable". They soon realise that the best way to avoid losing in such a competition is not to enter it'. In school, pupils who enjoy success will see themselves as being good at learning. They will be motivated to continue working hard. Their self-esteem will be high and they will be developing a healthy self-image. Often, those who do not enjoy success have, by the age of 13, decided that they are 'failures' and that school learning is not for them. Their self-esteem will be low and their self-image is likely to be negative. Like adults, all teenagers want to feel good about themselves. Those unable to succeed academically may seek kudos from elsewhere. This may be from sport or music, but is more likely to come from gaining the approval of peers through larking about or, depending on circumstances, more serious anti-social behaviour and crime.

Teenagers have a mental image of the type of person they are compared with others. They also have a mental image of their ideal-self – the kind of person they want to be. In lower secondary school, pupils are beginning to get a sense of what their futures might hold, based on their successes and failures to date. Pupils with high self-esteem will be those whose self-image is very close to their ideal-self. Low self-esteem can result when there is a wide gap between self-image and ideal-self. If pupils develop a self-image of academic failure, this can bring about a self-fulfilling prophecy. Pupils who are consistently disruptive in class may be closing the gap between their self-image and ideal-self as pupils who are not 'swots' and do not get on in school.

As the teacher in charge of the learning of your pupils you must never forget just how important it is to set up opportunities for your pupils to experience success. Don't allow yourself to take the view that some pupils aren't worth bothering about because of their attitude. Hart's research (1987) identified the importance of teacher–pupil relationships for pupils' feelings of self-worth in relation to learning competence. All pupils are motivated in the sense that they have needs and drives. If these needs and drives are at odds with your expectations this is probably because these pupils have experienced failure for much of their school life. Always believe that it is never too late to make a difference. Never allow pupils' past failures to shape your expectations of what they might potentially achieve. As HMI note 'In the most effective schools teachers had high expectations of what all pupils could do and achieve' (HMI 2011). We will return to the theme of self-esteem in Chapter 5 (Climate for Learning and Behaviour Management) and Chapter 9 (Teaching Beyond your Subject Specialism).

Learning theories

It is not the intention in this chapter to provide an in-depth study of learning theories, but to present an overview of the main theoretical perspectives and consider their implications for teachers. No one theory can supply a blueprint for how we learn or how you should teach, but each offers insights which can be helpful to teachers in thinking about how best to approach the delivery of particular subjects to particular pupils.

Cognitive Development Theory

Jean Piaget saw intellectual and moral development as sequential, with the child moving through stages of thinking driven by the need to understand the world. According to Piaget, the stages through which the child's thinking moves is linked closely to age. The stages identified by Piaget are summarised in Table 3.1. 'Operations' is the term he used to describe the skills and mental activities used by the child in interacting with new experiences. In short, we can see that the operations associated with each stage marks the development from practical thought to abstract thought. Children need to explore and manipulate materials as well as being taught, when dealing with new concepts. They are unable to learn in formal and theoretical ways until they have reached the right stage of maturity.

Piaget has been criticised for lack of rigour in his methodology and it is easy to challenge some of the conclusions he reached. For example, is the process of cognitive development necessarily age-related or is it more to do with the range and depth of learning experiences that children are exposed to? Is it only mature adults who can think abstractly? Are there some adults who don't operate at the formal operational stage of thinking?

Piaget's work has been especially influential in primary education, particularly in the use of 'concrete' objects with young children. The idea that pupils need to

TABLE 3.1 Piaget's stages of cognitive development

AGE	STAGE	CHARACTERISTICS
0–2	Sensory-motor	This stage comes before the development of language skills. The child makes reflex responses and explores the world through feeling, seeing and tasting.
2–6 years	Pre-operational	The child begins to realise others have a viewpoint. She can handle objects with confidence, classifying them into groups, and recognise and use symbols.
7–11	Concrete-operational	The child develops the ability to do complex mental operations and logical thinking develops.
12+	Formal-operational	The child develops abstract thinking skills; the ability to think about events that have never happened or things s/he has never seen. Deductive thinking becomes possible and the child develops the ability to empathise and appreciate different perspectives.

be at a particular developmental level in order to cope with certain learning tasks is a powerful one. However, research studies have substantially challenged this belief. Flavell (1982) has argued that, while stages of development linked to age are too rigid, Piaget's ideas about the sequences learners go through are valid and of some use to teachers in planning learning for pupils. Put simply, teachers need to examine the level of difficulty of topics and curriculum materials and tasks in deciding how appropriate they are for particular age groups and ability levels. They must also monitor the progress of individuals in order to decide when to increase the intellectual demands placed on them. It is now believed that through appropriate interventions children can be helped towards more sophisticated levels of understanding, so as a teacher you shouldn't limit your expectations of pupils based rigidly on theoretical stages of development.

Social Constructivist Theory

Whereas Piaget considered language to be a tool of thought in the child's developing mind, *Lev Vygotsky* held that language was generated from the need to communicate and was central to the development of thinking. He emphasised the importance of socio-cultural factors in the development of language and reasoning. Vygotsky's work highlighted the importance of talk as a learning tool and the significance of social learning. He introduced the concept of the zone of proximal development: internal developmental processes associated with learning that are triggered through interaction with people. 'What a child can do today in co-operation, tomorrow he will be able to do on his own' (Vygotsky 1962). The teacher, taking a facilitating role, has to present the child with problems that are at the very edge of their current understanding. The importance of learning through play is well understood by Early Years professionals. The talk involved in play is a mechanism by which young children work through challenges and problems, thus making sense of the world. Most secondary school teachers now accept the significance of talk in learning and in recent times collaborative learning has been encouraged in classrooms, for example, peer tutoring and group work and talk-partners are now commonplace. However, the teacher remains critical to the success of such approaches by setting up appropriate tasks and providing effective guidance and intervention.

Reflection point

Can you think of examples of how 'talk' and other active learning strategies might be used to aid learning in your subject lessons?

One very successful approach that works well is to divide the class into groups and then provide suitable materials or references to enable each group to research a particular area of a topic. Each group must make sense of what they have researched by discussing it, and they must then report back to the whole class. In addition to the benefits of co-operative learning suggested by Vgotsky, there are other advantages too:

- The pupils are provided with some insight into all areas of a topic, even though they have only had to cover one area, so time is saved;

- Having to report back to the whole class provides an extra incentive to get it right;

- Groups can be created by carefully mixing abilities and allocating areas and resources accordingly.

Jerome Bruner, one of the most distinguished cognitive psychologists of the post-war years, argued that pupils learn effectively through structured interventions. He advocated a spiral curriculum in which children revisit topics and concepts as they mature, adding new layers to their understanding each time. For example, very concrete examples and hands on experience will be provided for young children, whereas older pupils will be able to discuss topics in a more abstract way. Teaching addition to young children will involve the use of actual objects, such as counters, that can be manipulated to demonstrate what adding numbers together actually means. With older children, more complex addition may be done as a mental exercise. Learning involves the active restructuring of knowledge through experience; it takes place in a cultural context, according to Bruner. The skilled teacher will ensure that pupils are supported appropriately and encouraged to discover principles for themselves. For example, the way a teacher uses questions to focus a child's thinking or designs materials to develop pupils' understanding one step at a time will help to ensure that they develop the next layer of understanding. Bruner called this process 'scaffolding' (Bruner 1983). Learners are encouraged to carry out parts of tasks that are within their ability, and the adult 'fills in' or 'scaffolds' the rest. The scaffolding involves gaining the learners' interest, reducing their choices, maintaining their interest, highlighting critical aspects of the task, controlling their frustration, and demonstrating possibilities to them. It is clear that different pupils will need different scaffolding strategies, depending on the level of their understanding. Wood (1988) has developed Bruner's ideas and suggests five levels of support that can be given:

- General verbal encouragement;
- Specific verbal encouragement;
- Assistance with pupil's choice of materials or strategies;
- Preparation of material to be assembled by pupils;
- Demonstration of task.

It easy to see how these forms of assistance could also be applied to the production of academic work, such as an essay.

Constructivism

This theory of learning draws on the work of Bruner and Vygotsky, but places more importance on learners' individual conceptions. It is founded on the idea that people make their own sense of things in unique ways. They assess new ideas and knowledge against their existing ideas and experiences and by so doing come to modify their views of the world. Teachers using constructivist approaches will therefore create situations that facilitate pupils constructing their own knowledge. If pupils hold misconceptions, the teacher must make it possible for these misconceptions to be unpacked and reassessed. Science is one clear area in which misunderstandings held by pupils have to be challenged.

Multiple intelligences

According to the psychologist Howard Gardner (1983), learners all have the capacity to develop at least seven types of intelligence:

- Linguistic: the intelligence of words;
- Mathematical: the intelligence of numbers;
- Spatial: the intelligence of pictures and images;
- Musical: the intelligence of tone, rhythm and timbre;
- Kinaesthetic: the intelligence of the whole body and hands;
- Interpersonal: the intelligence of social understanding;
- Intrapersonal: the intelligence of self-knowledge.

Handy (1997) argues that intelligence comes in many forms. He cites eleven intelligences, which need not and often do not correlate with each other:

- Factual intelligence: the ability to remember information;
- Analytical intelligence: the ability to reason and conceptualise;
- Numerate intelligence: the ability to use numbers easily;
- Linguistic intelligence: a facility with language and languages;
- Spatial intelligence: an ability to see patterns in things;
- Athletic intelligence: the skill exemplified by athletes;
- Intuitive intelligence: an aptitude for sensing what is not automatically obvious;
- Emotional intelligence: self-awareness and self-control;
- Practical intelligence: the ability to be realistic and get things done;
- Interpersonal intelligence: the ability to achieve goals with and through others;
- Musical intelligence: the intelligence of tone, rhythm and timbre.

Critics of mass education would argue that only a very small number of these intelligences are recognised and encouraged in our schools. Indeed, pupils are likely to be regarded as intelligent, and do very well in examinations, if they display capability in just the first four areas on Handy's list (whereas success in life may depend on practical and interpersonal intelligence). While teachers cannot change a system that rewards a narrow range of intelligences, they can show awareness of the full range displayed by their pupils, and try and praise and encourage pupils who show capability in any area. This will help to build pupils' self-esteem, which in turn will help their performance in all areas.

Learning style

It is now understood that just as we receive information about the world around us through our five senses, we also have individual sensory preferences as to how we make sense of that information. Some people have a visual preference, some auditory and some kinaesthetic. This preference doesn't mean that the individual cannot use other styles, but it does mean that being able to use their preferred style will greatly aid learning and understanding. According to Smith (2001) 29% of us prefer to learn by seeing, 34% of us have an auditory preference and 37% of learners prefer to engage with the experience physically.

Visual

A visual preference means a person can easily construct imagined scenes. They can visualise themselves operating in different contexts. They will often associate words and feelings with images. When spelling, they may see the word before writing it out. Visual learners will look upwards when accessing remembered information and many speak rapidly and make use of pointing gestures with hands outlining or describing the information presented. They are likely to use phrases like 'I see what you mean', 'it looks good to me', 'just imagine' and 'I can't picture that'.

Auditory

A preference for auditory learning means a person enjoys language generally and is good at internal dialogue and self-talk. When remembering spellings, such a person may sound out a word in their heads before writing it. When thinking about new situations they are likely to think about what will be said to them and what they will say. Auditory learners usually speak clearly and at an even, rhythmic tempo, with skilled use of modulation to clarify meaning. Auditory learners often use accompanying hand gestures such as counting out points on their fingers.

Kinesthetic

A kinaesthetic learner will find feelings, emotions and tactile sensations very important. Such a person may spell a word by 'feeling' it being written letter by letter before they actually begin. Before entering a new situation, a kinaesthetic learner will imagine what it is going to feel like. Such learners often fidget and find it difficult to concentrate without regular breaks. They may use phrases like 'can you handle this?', 'it feels good to me', 'I've changed my stance on the issue' and 'I feel backed into a corner'.

Reflection point

What are the implications of this for teachers? How can a teacher cater for pupils with different preferred learning styles?

The most obvious thing for a teacher in a secondary school to do is to ensure that in their approach to teaching and learning they use a variety of techniques to ensure that there is 'something for everyone'. That is to say, the needs of visual, auditory and kinaesthetic (VAK) learners are taken into account. This is likely to mean that the teacher incorporates elements in his repertoire that he himself would not naturally favour. Table 3.2 provides a summary of the most common approaches to suit the VAK styles of learning. In some schools, all children are assessed for their preferred VAK style, and this information is then used by teachers when considering how best to meet pupils' needs.

Accelerated learning

In recent years a body of literature has appeared on the subject of accelerated learning. Advances in brain science mean that we now know a lot more about the learning process, yet many teachers are ignorant of these findings and continue to organise lessons in ways which will not promote learning for all. Paying attention to the different needs of visual, auditory and kinaesthetic learners is one way in which learning can be improved, but there are many others.

Here are some things that we now understand about the brain and learning:

■ The brain uses in excess of 20% of the body's oxygen and it requires water, rest and protein to function effectively. When children sit down, their heart rates slow and the amount of oxygen that gets to the brain decreases.

■ When people feel threatened or are placed under negative stress they are unable to learn effectively. People learn best in a state of *relaxed alertness*.

■ The average concentration span of children is limited to approximately chronological age in minutes plus two minutes, with the average concentration span of an adult being around twenty minutes.

■ The two hemispheres of the brain operate in different ways. The left-brain processes information logically and deals with reading, writing and listening whereas the right-brain is more intuitive and responds to images and music. However, we now know that both sides of the brain are involved in virtually all activities and if one side is emphasised at the expense of the other, learning will be restricted. There is some evidence that children suffering from attention deficit hyperactivity disorder (ADHD) are strongly right-brain dominant, while those with Asperger's Syndrome are strongly left-brain dominant. All children need help in developing the use of both sides of the brain.

■ The brain is not designed for remembering large amounts of information but it remembers context and unusual and dramatic events naturally.

■ Most information stored in the brain is forgotten unless regular review occurs.

Reflection point

What are the implications of this for learning in school? How might teachers use this information when planning their lessons?

There are many practical ways in which learning might be improved, based on what we know about the brain.

Many children leave home each morning not having eaten breakfast. Many go through the day without drinking adequately. Some schools run breakfast clubs to ensure that children have the opportunity to eat at the start of the day and many schools now allow children to have bottles of water in class. Some movement during lessons will ensure children's brains have the oxygen they need for learning. Having a pile of books or some materials that pupils need to leave their desks to get is a simple way of ensuring movement without disorder!

Many children feel threatened in class. They might feel worried by bullies in class, they might be frightened of the teacher. If they are 'put on the spot' and unable to answer a question, this will reduce their ability to think clearly. Teachers can do a lot to create an atmosphere in which children can learn. Following the suggestions made in Chapter 2 should ensure that you get things right. Greeting pupils with a smile and being positive and upbeat at the start of a lesson are obvious ways in which you create the right atmosphere. Also, giving pupils a sense of control can help to reduce anxiety. For example, many pupils feel worried at the mention of a 'test'. By giving them the impression that they have some control over this

TABLE 3.2 Taking account of pupils' preferred learning styles

VISUAL	AUDITORY	KINESTHETIC
• Use body movements and gestures	• Use paired and group discussion	• Use mime
• Use display opportunities in your classroom	• Invite in guest speakers	• Demonstrate concepts through movement and gestures
• Use video, slides, Power-Point presentations, OHP, flip chart and coloured marker pens	• Have class debates	• Have design and build activities
• Use lively and colourful posters and textbooks	• Use chants and verse	• Arrange field-trips and visits
• Display key words around the room	• Use dramatic readings	• Use physical movement, for example use children in the playground to reconstruct troop positions on a battle ground
• Use spider diagrams, flow charts etc.	• Use tapes of broadcasts	
	• Use mnemonics	• Demonstrate abstract concepts practically, e.g. trade or wealth can be explained by getting the children to use substitutes for money and goods to simulate real world events
	• Have music to accompany parts of the lesson	

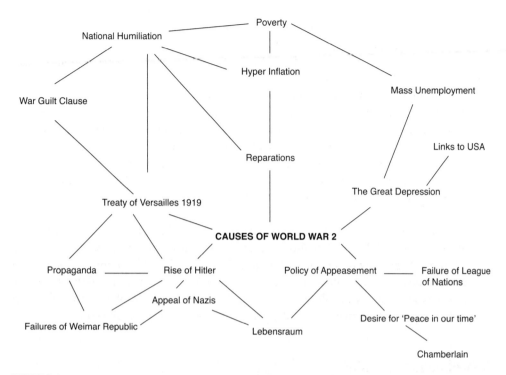

FIGURE 3.1 A memory map on the causes of World War 2 created by pupils in Year 9

(when it will be, choice of areas to be tested, short responses or essays) anxiety can be greatly reduced. The teacher is, of course, really in control, but the pupils *feel* that they have some control and this is what is important.

Many teachers spend too long telling pupils about the new theme or topic they are introducing. Even with the use of questions, most children will have 'switched off' if this goes much beyond fifteen minutes. Learning is more effective if the teacher's initial input is limited to 10–15 minutes and a series of short learning activities are built into a lesson. We also know that children will learn more effectively if the first fifteen minutes and last ten minutes of a lesson are used well. This means, a very sharp start to a lesson is required, with the new learning points being introduced as soon as possible. A plenary session should be provided at the end of the lesson, where learning can be reinforced. This part of the lesson can be fun, with *relaxed alertness* achieved by sometimes allowing versions of 'Mastermind' or 'The Weakest Link' to be used as a means of assessing learning. The middle bit of the lesson can be broken up by collecting in homework, thus allowing some movement at the very time when children are beginning to 'wilt'.

Effective learning based on an understanding of the brain will be whole-brain learning. Children spend a lot of time in lessons reading, writing and listening. This is left-brain activity. Right-brain activity can be encouraged through using music, displays, imagination and graphs. Try and plan activities that encourage crossover between the two hemispheres of the brain. For example, by asking pupils to describe information they read from a graph or by putting information from a text into a memory-map format (Figure 3.1). This crossover activity can often be fun. For example, asking pupils to think of a character they have read about as a car or animal, and to justify their choice, can be very effective.

The more children are encouraged to be active in a lesson the more they will remember. Creating a context in which children learn actively (group work, role play, model making) will increase the chances of children remembering the content of the lesson. Also, if you are able to add a dramatic episode or a surprise to a lesson it is more likely to be remembered. If you dress up as a vagrant from Elizabethan England and tell your story, the children are more likely to remember more about your appearance and plight than if they read about Elizabethan poverty in a book!

Try and provide opportunities for regular review of learning. This should happen at the end of each lesson, but also at various points during the year. When reviewing, ask pupils to put key points into diagrammatic form, tell the key points to a neighbour or turn the key words into a mnemonic (SUNWAD helps me to recall the Yorkshire rivers Swale, Ure, Nidd, Wharfe, Aire and Derwent, for example). Such techniques will increase the chance of key ideas and concepts being remembered.

Learning and teaching

This brief consideration of learning should have enabled you to reach some tentative conclusions about approaches to teaching. It was suggested in Chapter 2 that the authoritative style of teaching is most effective. Weight has been added to this view by what we now know about learning. Authoritative teachers tend to work in a more student-centred way, facilitate learning opportunities, give some control over learning to their pupils and focus on the process of learning as well as the outcomes (Figure 3.2). From what we know about the brain, motivation and learning styles we can conclude that the authoritative teaching style will be the most effective. When you are on school experience, you should find most of the key ideas outlined in this chapter being used.

Action point

When you are on school experience, get a few pupils to complete one of the questionnaires designed to enable pupils to assess their preferred learning styles (Figure 3.3). Try and observe these pupils in lessons. Does their behaviour bear out what we know about their preferred learning style? Do you think they are effectively catered for by the teaching approach adopted by their teacher? What could teachers do to help to maximise their learning? What could these pupils do themselves to increase their learning?

Authoritarian	Authoritative
Teacher centred	Student centred
Student passive	Student active
Didactic	Facilitative
Negative stress	Relaxed alertness
Focus on outcomes	Focus on outcomes and process
Measurable outcomes only	Not all learning is measurable

FIGURE 3.2 Teaching style and learning

Look at each statement below in turn. Think about whether it is true of you. If it is really true, score 5. If it is completely untrue, score 0. Use the numbers in between if the statements are not completely true or untrue for you. Circle your scores and then add them to the key at the bottom. Discuss your results with your teacher.

1.	I like to listen to music when I work	0	1	2	3	4	5
2.	I enjoy making things in class	0	1	2	3	4	5
3.	To spell correctly, I write the word first	0	1	2	3	4	5
4.	I can picture in my head lots of places I have visited	0	1	2	3	4	5
5.	I can remember the titles to my favourite TV programmes	0	1	2	3	4	5
6.	I really enjoy Art lessons	0	1	2	3	4	5
7.	At break I like to play outdoor ball games or running	0	1	2	3	4	5
8.	I like looking at pictures in books	0	1	2	3	4	5
9.	I easily remember the words to songs	0	1	2	3	4	5
10.	When I spell, I see the word as I spell it	0	1	2	3	4	5
11.	I can remember the theme tunes to my favourite TV programmes	0	1	2	3	4	5
12.	I love to sing	0	1	2	3	4	5
13.	I'd rather play sport than watch it	0	1	2	3	4	5
14.	PE is my favourite lesson	0	1	2	3	4	5
15.	When I spell I say the word in my head	0	1	2	3	4	5
16.	I can remember a lot from when I was younger	0	1	2	3	4	5
17.	I enjoy it when we discuss things in groups	0	1	2	3	4	5
18.	I find it difficult to sit still for more than a few minutes	0	1	2	3	4	5

Marking Your Questions

Visual	Score	**Kinesthetic**	Score
Question 4	____	Question 2	____
Question 5	____	Question 3	____
Question 6	____	Question 7	____
Question 8	____	Question 13	____
Question 10	____	Question 14	____
Question 16	____	Question 18	____
Total	____	**Total**	____

Auditory	Score
Question 1	____
Question 9	____
Question 11	____
Question 12	____
Question 15	____
Question 17	____
Total	____

FIGURE 3.3 VAK learning preference questionnaire

Summary

This chapter has briefly outlined some major learning theories as well as introducing you to some of the implications of recent developments in our understanding of how people learn and how the brain functions. From this it is possible to list a number of things that teachers should try and do in order to maximise the learning of their pupils. These things include:

- Having high expectations of all pupils;
- Trying to give all pupils the opportunity to experience success;
- Creating an atmosphere of relaxed alertness in your classroom;
- Using a variety of teaching techniques and props so that all styles of learners (VAK) are included in your lessons;
- Trying to build concrete experiences into your lessons;
- Using scaffolding techniques to aid differentiation;
- Using strategies to develop whole-brain activity;
- Not talking to a class for more than 15–20 minutes without a change of activity;
- Making maximum use of the first and last 10–15 minutes of every lesson;
- Allowing some movement in the middle of a lesson;
- Having regular reviews of learning;
- Giving pupils some control of what happens during lessons.

Of course, exactly how you apply the above suggestions will vary from class to class, pupil to pupil and subject to subject. Experienced teachers make such judgements every day of their lives. As a teacher in training, you should try to build variety into your lessons and ensure that you make good use of the beginning and end of each lesson. Getting these things right will put you in a good position to work on some of the other aspects of learning support, such as effective interventions at the very edge of a pupil's understanding. Getting everything right will not happen straight away and you may find that it is not always possible to do what you know should maximise learning. For example, you know the importance of making good use of the first ten minutes of a lesson. Even if you have decided to save taking the register until later in the lesson so that you get on to the key learning points straight away, you may be thwarted by pupils arriving late, possibly due to no fault of their own. Likewise, you know it makes sense to allow pupils to learn collaboratively through discussion, but some classes may take advantage of this and not concentrate on the task in hand. You may be forced to have them working individually until you feel they understand and respond to your high expectations. Don't become disheartened; continue to strive to use methods that you know will maximise learning, but vary them according to each situation you are in and don't try and walk before you can run. Remember, you are learning too, and will continue to do so throughout your career.

References

Bruner, J. (1983) *Child's Talk: Learning to Use Language*, Oxford: Oxford University Press.

Curzon, L.B. (ed.) (1990) *Teaching in Further Education*, London: Cassell.

DES (1989) *Discipline in Schools* (The Elton Report), London: HMSO.

Dryden, G. and Vos, J. (1994) *The Learning Revolution*, Stafford: Network Educational Press.

Flavell J.H. (1982) 'Structures, Stages and Sequences in Cognitive Development' in W.A. Collins (ed.) *The Concept of Development: The Minnesota Symposia on Child Psychology*, Vol. 15, 1–28.

Gardner, H. (1983) *Frames of Mind: The Theory of Multiple Intelligence*, New York: Basic Books.

Handy, C. (1997) 'Schools for Life and Work' in P. Mortimore and Little V. M. (eds.) *Living Education: Essays in Honour of John Tomlinson*, London: Paul Chapman.

Hart, N.I. (1987) 'Student teachers' anxieties: four measured factors and their relationship to pupil disruption in class', *Educational Research*, 29 (1), 12–18.

HMI *Annual Report of Her Majesty's Chief Inspector 1999–2000*, London: The Stationery Office.

HMI *Annual Report of Her Majesty's Chief Inspector of Education, Children's Services and Skills 2010–2011*, London: The Stationery Office.

Smith, A. (2001) *Accelerated Learning in Practice*, Stafford: Network Educational Press.

Vygotsky, L.S. (1962) *Thought and Language*, Cambridge, Mass.: MIT Press.

Wood, D. (1988) *How Children Learn and Think*, Oxford: Blackwell.

4

Planning

Introduction

As a trainee teacher the old adage, '*If you fail to plan, you plan to fail*' has never been truer. It is ironic, therefore, that when you observe experienced teachers in their classrooms, you will rarely see them following highly detailed lesson plans.

The reason why experienced teachers are rarely seen consulting lesson plans is probably two-fold. Firstly, they are likely to have planned schemes of work in some detail (probably in conjunction with other colleagues teaching the same subject) and so have a clear idea of what they expect the children to achieve and how they will ensure this happens over a sequence of lessons. Secondly, as experienced teachers they will have been teaching a particular syllabus or aspect of the curriculum for some years, and so will know from experience how best to ensure effective delivery. This doesn't mean they will have no plans but simply that the plans they use will be far less detailed than those expected of a trainee. Don't forget, after several years of teaching, many aspects of the job become almost instinctive, taking away the need for the detailed planning and rehearsing that provide essential support to trainees and recently qualified teachers. This is not unlike the car driver who, with increasing experience, no longer has to think through every gear change and manoeuvre. The experienced driver can also make a journey he knows well without the need for consulting detailed maps in advance.

As a trainee, you are unlikely to be given complete freedom in planning because many schools will have schemes of work in place for most year groups, possibly containing a breakdown of the key areas of the curriculum you will be expected to deliver week by week. You will have some freedom over *how* you teach particular lessons, but probably not over the content and sequence of lessons. However, it is important that as part of your training programme you are introduced to the principles of planning. To be effective in the classroom, you will need to be able to plan for the delivery of the curriculum for your subject and to translate this broad planning into well-structured lessons. When researching effective teaching Hay Mcber (2000) found that, 'In classes run by effective teachers, pupils are clear about what they are doing and why they are doing it.

They can see the links with their earlier learning and have some ideas about how it could be developed further'. As you embark on your work in the classroom, the only way you can achieve this clarity with your pupils will be through detailed and effective planning.

This chapter will introduce you to some curriculum development issues, as well as helping you to understand how to write schemes of work and lesson plans. It will encourage you to focus on the importance of clear objectives and to begin to think about how to plan for progression and coherence. Examples of planning sheets will be provided to help you get started on this complex area of a teacher's work.

The curriculum

Curriculum definitions

Explaining what is meant by 'curriculum' is not as obvious as might at first seem. Most people would take curriculum to mean the subjects followed by pupils during their time at school. However, the curriculum is far more than just a list of subject content. Pupils learn and develop as a result of how they access the curriculum (the process) as well as learning about the subjects on the curriculum. A simple example of this is that pupils asked to work in a group will hopefully be developing and using social skills (organisation, negotiation, delegation, listening) as well as learning the particular content associated with the subject. While most planning is concerned with the cognitive and skills domains, we mustn't forget to think about opportunities for developing the affective domain also.

This chapter will focus on planning for delivery of the formal curriculum, sometimes called the intended curriculum or the overt curriculum, but it is worth making a quick mention here of the *hidden* or *covert* curriculum. In the attitudes you display towards your pupils and the subject matter you teach you will, perhaps unintentionally, be conveying particular values and attitudes. Thus, you may be teaching your pupils things you are not aware of or not intending. For example, if you make little effort to include pupils with special needs in your lessons, this will send out signals about their value both to them and to the other pupils in your class. Likewise, if the textbooks you use in Science contain few images of women working in laboratories, the hidden curriculum message is obvious.

Curriculum control and content

Before 1988, when greater centralisation of education was introduced through the Education Reform Act, teachers had a great deal of freedom in deciding the content of the curriculum of their school. For some years now teachers in England have had to follow the National Curriculum, which lays down clear guidelines on what to teach to pupils at each stage of their journey through school. This means that most teachers have little choice in what they teach though they still have considerable autonomy over how best to teach it. At the time of writing, this situation is beginning to change as Government policy now allows Academies to decide their own curriculum.

What we need to remember is that no curriculum can remain unchanged. In every field of knowledge new developments are made which impact on what we teach in schools (ICT was not a curriculum subject even thirty years ago, for example). Views about the ultimate purpose of education change and these influence what we teach and how we teach it (think about why Latin now rarely features on the timetables of state schools). At different times, governments face different national priorities, and these will influence what we are expected to teach in schools. The idea that secondary school teachers 'just teach their subjects' is naïve, as the importance of their subject in the curriculum and even its content will reflect the views and priorities of the day, influenced by the government, wider society and world in which we live. The priority given to citizenship education in the first few years of the new millennium (see Chapter 8) is a good example of how a government priority can influence what teachers are teaching. Currently, the government focus on the so-called 'English Baccalaureate' (not a qualification but a league table measure recognising where pupils have secured a C grade or better across a core of academic subjects – English, mathematics, history or geography, the sciences and a language) is influencing what many state schools offer their pupils at Key Stage 4.

Although there is currently much discussion about the suitability and effectiveness of the National Curriculum, the existence and status of vocational courses in schools and the logic of Academies having greater curriculum freedom, the purpose of this book is not to enter into these debates. It is fair to say that the curriculum that all state secondary schools in England provide for their pupils is an attempt to introduce them to a range of forms of knowledge representing the ways people experience the world. At one level, then, it is an attempt to transmit wisdom (knowledge already developed) to future generations. There is also a strong focus on ensuring that future generations of pupils will be active and productive adults, able to make a contribution to maintaining our economic prosperity. The strong emphasis on ICT skills is a good example of this.

Reflection point

Before considering how to plan for the delivery of your particular subject, it is worth spending a little time considering why it features on the curriculum at all.

You were probably asked the above question at your interview for a place on a training course. Reminding yourself now will help you to clarify what you see as the overall aims and purposes of teaching your subject. It is important not to lose sight of these overall aims when you concentrate on the detail of a particular lesson or topic. Believing your subject has a legitimate place on the curriculum and is an essential part of children's education is important and will help you to feel more confident about planning for its delivery.

Schemes of work

Preparing an outline of work to be covered over a period of time involves writing schemes of work. Typically, schemes of work are written to cover a distinct unit of work, a bloc of teaching time, or both. Lesson plans are used to flesh out the skeleton provided by the scheme of work. The intention of both is to ensure that pupils learn the things you intend them to learn. Good schemes of work are not developed in isolation. They take account of what pupils have learnt already and what will be expected of them in future units of work. In this way continuity and progression is achieved. That is, developments in knowledge, skills and understanding are planned rather than accidental.

It is likely that during training you will be provided with schemes of work by teachers in the schools you are placed in for school experience. It is important to understand the thinking that has gone into writing these schemes of work. At the design stage, teachers will have answered the following questions:

- What are our aims (what are we trying to achieve with the pupils)?
- What key questions, concepts and words are involved?
- How does this unit link to earlier units (what are the pupils likely to know already)?
- How much time (how many lessons) have we got to deliver this unit?
- What resources do we need to support delivery?
- How will we structure the content to ensure there is progression?
- How will we ensure all abilities can access the content?
- How will we know we have achieved our aims (how will we assess pupils' learning)?
- How does this unit relate to later units in this subject and/or units in other subjects?

An example of part of a scheme of work for a Year 9 History unit is provided in Table 4.1. This is not the only format that can be used for schemes of work, and this format won't necessarily suit all subject areas. However, it gives you an idea of the kind of information included. A scheme of work should provide a clear overview of what you will be teaching; lesson plans allow you to translate this in a way that makes sense for particular classes you have to teach.

Action point

Get copies of relevant schemes of work from the first school in which you are placed for school experience. Do they provide you with as much information as you need for planning individual lessons? If not, discuss what you feel you need with your subject mentor. Look through children's books. Does the work they

TABLE 4.1 Extract from a scheme of work for Y9 history

YEAR 9 KEY STAGE 3 STUDY UNIT: THE TWENTIETH CENTURY WORLD

Aim: To provide pupils with an overview of some of the main events, personalities and developments of the twentieth century and enable them to understand how they have shaped the modern world.

KEY ISSUES	CONCEPTS/KEY TERMS	CONTENT	RESOURCES	POSSIBLE ACTIVITIES	ASSESSMENT	LINKS WITH OTHER AREAS
World War I Treaty of Versailles Life in the 1920s	Alliances World War Total War Allies Trench Warfare Treaty War Guilt League of Nations	Sides in the war Scale and nature of warfare War and social change Peace terms Attitudes to Germany in the 1920s	Department booklet: *Introduction to C20 World* Worksheets on trench warfare Textbook: *Era of Second World War* p.4–5 (basic and extension work) BBC Video: *The Lights Go Out in Europe*	Group activities listed in *Introduction* booklet Class discussion Creation of graphical displays on causes of war, trench warfare and results of war (differentiated) Text book exercises	Work in exercise books based on *Introduction* activities Group wall displays	Key Stage 3 Unit: *Britain 1750–1900*: Link between industrialisation, colonisation and World War I.
Hitler's Rise to Power Life in Nazi Germany (NB – link to Holocaust – see below)	Democracy Dictatorship Nationalism Communism Fascism Capitalism Police State Inflation Depression Propaganda Anti-Semitism Racism	The legacy of Versailles Problems facing the Weimar Republic Hitler's appeal Analysis of propaganda The Enabling Law Life under the Nazis: education, women,	Department booklets: *Hitler's Rise to Power* and *Life in Nazi Germany* A range of worksheets and homework sheets Textbook: *Era of Second World War* p.10–13 and 38–42	Teacher presentation and discussion, use of video clips for analysis and discussion group and paired responses to propaganda slides Guided web research and group	Exercise book work, presentations and homework sheets Test conditions: Assessment Sheet on *Hitler's Rise to Power*	Year 9 Citizenship unit on Prejudice GCSE RE unit on Current Social Issues GCSE History Unit on *The Road to War*

Topic	Key words	Content	Resources	Teaching activities	Assessment / activities	Links
		legislation, ideology, treatment of 'undesirables'	(basic and extension work) Various video extracts (see dept. list) Two sets of slides on Nazi Propaganda Appeal of Hitler resource box	presentations on how particular groups might have viewed Hitler, based on consideration of primary sources (differentiated – see Appeal of Hitler resource guide)		Year 9 Citizenship unit on Understanding Conflict GCSE History Unit on World War 2
World War 2 The Road to War Events The End of the War (NB – The Home Front presented as a depth study – see below)	Anschluss Lebensraum Appeasement Alliances Blitzkrieg Occupation Turning Points Atom bomb	A brief consideration of the key events leading to war and the reasons for appeasement. The key events and turning points of the war: Battle of Britain, Pearl Harbour, Russian Campaign, Hitler's death, Hiroshima and Nagasaki	Department booklet: World War 2 Textbook: Era of Second World War p.16–36 (basic and extension work) Various video extracts (see dept. list)	Text book exercises Presenting the events leading to war in flow-chart format Class debate on appeasement based on view-points expressed in the 1930s (differentiated sources) Pupils' taped radio broadcasts of key events from British and German points of view (based on consideration of bias and use of propaganda) Text book exercises	Posters on steps to war, letters in defence of or against appeasement, timeline with discussion of significance of key events, exercise book work. Formal assessment of level – essay: Who was to blame for World War 2?	

have done reflect the learning intentions set out in the scheme of work? Discuss with your subject mentor how far individual teachers are allowed to deviate from schemes of work. What are the advantages and disadvantages in allowing teachers freedom to deviate?

When teachers are given freedom to deviate from a scheme of work they are able to think creatively about what might be of greatest use or interest to their pupils. This can be especially important when planning for pupils who, for a variety of reasons, fail to respond to or have difficulty accessing the curriculum that most pupils are covering.

One of the opportunities for flexibility you may be given while on school experience is having some say in the order in which you teach topics within the syllabus or scheme of work you are asked to follow. Certain topics for certain subjects will have to be followed in the order that ensures pupils' skills and knowledge are being appropriately developed. Some topics will require pupils to have a level of knowledge and understanding on entry from the study of earlier topics. However, in some subjects a greater amount of flexibility may be possible. There are several ways in which you might establish your order of teaching. Here are some possibilities:

- An 'easy' topic first (one you think will be straightforward to teach);
- Your best topic first (the one you feel most confident about);
- Relevance of the topic (linking it to an issue in pupils' lives);
- Opportunistic (linking the topic to events in the news);
- The season (field-trip opportunities are greater in summer);
- Availability of resources (some schools rotate topics so that not all classes require the same resources at the same time);
- A controversial topic first (to stimulate interest);
- A non-threatening topic first (to build confidence);
- Safety considerations (avoiding a topic that requires the use of practical equipment until you feel fully in control of the class).

When experienced teachers select the order in which topics from a syllabus will be taught, they are also likely to consider how previous cohorts of pupils have responded to particular topics. They will know from experience what the examination will demand of pupils and this will also influence their thinking on the sequencing of topics. Some teachers involve pupils in deciding the order in which topics might be taught, thus giving them a sense of power and control.

Lesson plans

A lesson plan usually provides an outline of one lesson. It should be linked closely to the overall scheme of work. The lesson plan allows you to work out in detail how you will ensure that one part of the scheme of work is successfully delivered to a particular class. When planning a lesson you should think about the following key questions:

- Where are the students now? (What can they do already? What do they understand?)
- Where will they be by the end of the lesson?
- What are you going to do to check their progress and help them get there?
- How will you know they have?

Translating these questions into lesson plans means that plans normally include the following information:

- Prior learning of the group and/or individuals relevant to this lesson.
- Clear lesson objectives, sometimes expressed as learning outcomes (what you expect the children to know, understand and/or be able to do by the end of the lesson).

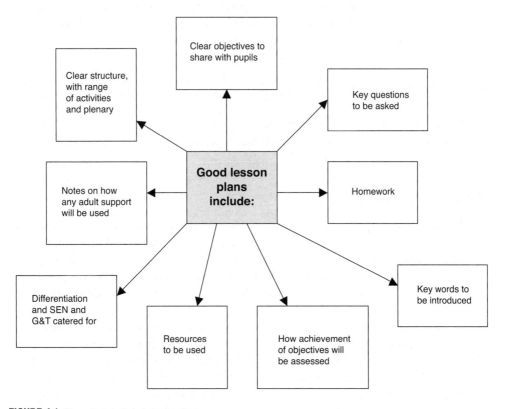

FIGURE 4.1 Elements to include in lesson plans

- Key questions you intend to ask/answer and key words you will introduce. This doesn't mean a detailed list of questions you will put to the pupils; it is a way of sharing with pupils what they will be learning (by the end of the lesson we will have answered the question 'Why do earthquakes occur?').

- Clear lesson structure with approximate times given to each part of the lesson (remember what was said in Chapter 3 about the need for pace, variety and distinct bursts of activity).

- The resources you intend to use at each stage of the lesson (including adult support), and how they will be used to achieve differentiation (bear in mind also what was said in Chapter 3 about preferred styles of learning).

- How children identified with Special Educational Needs (SEN) or those classed as Gifted and Talented (G&T) will be catered for (differentiation).

- Homework details (probably not needed for every lesson; refer to school policy on homework).

- An indication of how you will assess the progress made by the pupils (have the lesson objectives been achieved?).

An example of what a lesson plan might look like is given in Figure 4.2. This is not provided as an example of the perfect lesson-planning format (if, indeed, there is such a thing). It is intended to offer a possible way of summarising your lesson intentions on one side of A4 paper.

Action point

Discuss this format with an appropriate tutor and your subject mentor. Compare it with other formats you have seen and then devise a lesson-planning sheet that you think will meet your needs.

Thinking about objectives

Defining clearly what learning you want to take place in a lesson is very important. You need to be certain about what you expect the children to know, understand and be able to do as a result of the learning that takes place. It is helpful to phrase your lesson objectives as learning outcomes: by the end of the lesson pupils will be able to. . . . This should help you distinguish between aims (long term goals) and objectives (specific goals).

You need to avoid being vague when writing objectives. If you share them with the pupils (and this is something you should do) then they need to be able to tell from the objectives exactly what is expected of them by the end of the lesson. You need to get beyond thinking that your objective is to cover a particular chunk of a syllabus, to thinking about what precise knowledge and skills you expect the children to have mastered.

LESSON PLAN (expand lines and boxes as required)

Date............................... Class ....

Issues arising from last lesson (including any individual pupil needs)
....
....

New Objectives/Learning Outcomes
....
....

Key Words/Questions
....
....

Time	Teacher Activities	Pupil Activities (including differentiation, SEN, G&T)	Resources and Role of Adult Support

Evaluation/Development

Were objectives achieved (evidence)?
....
....

Any misunderstandings or points to develop next lesson
....
....

Individual pupil issues
....
....

FIGURE 4.2 Possible lesson plan format

The nature of objectives will vary from subject to subject, but it is always helpful to think in terms of the three domains of learning mentioned earlier in this chapter: cognitive, skills (or psychomotor) and affective.

The cognitive domain

This is the area that teachers of subjects classed as 'academic' focus on the most. Knowledge and understanding are central to this domain. Being able to explain 'how' and 'why', through the application of knowledge and the capability to assess and evaluate, fall into this area. The levels in the cognitive domain were identified by Bloom (1964). A simplified version of this is shown in Figure 4.3. Each category can be summarised as follows:

- Knowledge – recognition and recall of information;
- Comprehension – interpretation, translation and summarising of information;
- Application – using information in new contexts;
- Analysis – separating the whole into parts to make sense of relationships;
- Synthesis – combining ideas from different sources to create the whole picture;
- Evaluation – making judgements from evidence based on criteria or rationale.

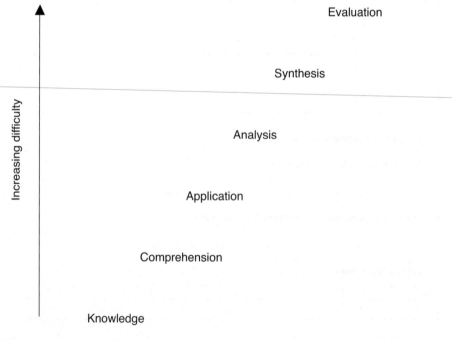

FIGURE 4.3 Major categories in the cognitive domain

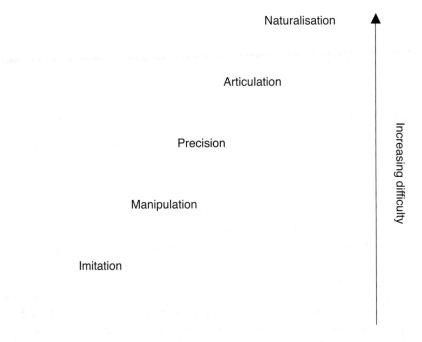

FIGURE 4.4 Major categories in the skills (psychomotor) domain

It is obvious that in order to achieve the more complicated thinking processes the lower level objectives must first have been achieved. For example, in order to achieve the application level, pupils must first possess knowledge and comprehension. Teachers bear this in mind when planning for progression and challenge. Being aware of pupils' prior level of knowledge and understanding is important. As a trainee teacher you will need to establish this through discussion with teachers, in order to get your planning right.

The skills domain

In some subject areas there is a greater focus on developing pupils' skills. A psychomotor skill consists of tasks that are integrated into a co-ordinated whole. Reece and Walker (2000) make reference to a taxonomy which is summarised in Figure 4.4. It is similar to the cognitive taxonomy in that the categories represent progression from simple to complex operations:

■ Imitation – observing a single skill and trying to copy it;

■ Manipulation – performing a single skill following instructions;

■ Precision – reproducing a single skill accurately and independently;

■ Articulation – successfully combining one or more skills in sequence;

■ Naturalisation – completing one or more skills automatically.

It is clear from this breakdown that each successive level within the domain requires more complicated forms of psychomotor skill. Teachers must plan to develop pupils' skills in stages from imitation to automatic performance. As with planning to develop the cognitive dimension, teachers planning to develop pupils' psychomotor skills must be clear about their skill level on entry.

The affective domain

This is the area that is most difficult to plan for and to assess. It is likely that you (and your department and school) will have some long-term aims that fall within the affective domain, but that these cannot easily be turned into specific lesson objectives. This is because the affective domain is concerned with pupils' attitudes and values. In some subjects the attitudes you are trying to develop are uncontroversial. Few, for example, would argue against trying to develop in pupils an automatic awareness of safety when working in a laboratory or workshop. Other values may seem unproblematic at first, but have the potential to become controversial. For example, all teachers would want their pupils to develop into caring and sympathetic adults. They would want their pupils to value diversity and not make judgements about others based on prejudice. However, in attempting to encourage these values some parents may misunderstand what is intended and feel (usually wrongly) that, for example, particular groups are being favoured at the expense of others, homosexuality is being encouraged or teachers are trying to inculcate their children with particular political views. How to handle the development of such values is discussed further in Chapter 8 and Chapter 9. For now, let us consider how Krathwohl et al (1964) categorised levels within this domain (see Figure 4.5):

- Receiving – passively listening to ideas;
- Responding – complying with expectations/ideas presented;
- Valuing – displaying behaviour consistent with expectation in situations where not forced to obey;
- Organising – behaving in a way that shows commitment to set of values;
- Characterising – behaviour totally consistent with internalised values.

In this domain, instead of developing from simple to complex ideas as with cognitive development, each successive level involves more internalising of the value or attitude. The behaviour associated with a particular value or attitude gradually becomes automatic. For example, in the laboratory situation, pupils will at first simply be told about safety and why particular rules apply. Gradually, safety concerns should become internalised so that they are 'automatic' and pupils no longer need to be reminded of them. They will be safety conscious not simply because it is expected, but because they understand and accept the reasons for it.

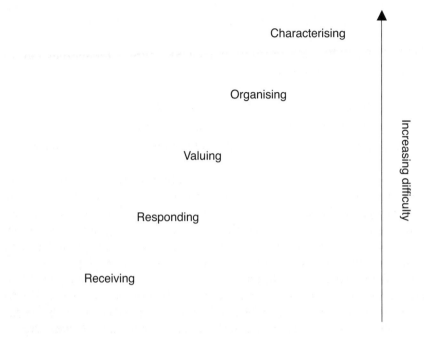

FIGURE 4.5 Major categories in the affective domain

Reflection point

Do you feel that creating an ethos in which pupils refrain from racist and sexist name-calling can be achieved in the same way that safety in a laboratory is achieved? What factors would assist or inhibit the success of this objective?

The answer is 'yes'. If something is considered important enough to be made a priority then there is a good chance that it can be achieved. The likelihood of success will be increased greatly if senior members of staff support the initiative and all colleagues in the school embrace it (in the example cited school policies would certainly support the behaviour required). Where individual teachers try and push a value that is at odds with the overall ethos of the school the chances of success are slight. If parents are also supportive of the initiative it will be more likely to succeed. Of course, it is impossible to measure what pupils think and feel and so, as with safety, there may be some pupils who conform in school, but behave differently away from school because they haven't internalised the value or attitude.

Phrasing aims and objectives clearly

Aims are broad ranging and general, often cover more than one domain of learning, are long-term intentions, often contain more than one verb, can be difficult to observe directly and give a sense of direction and 'flavour' of a course.

In contrast objectives should be specific, related to only one domain of learning, short-term and contain only one verb. Successful achievement of objectives should be able to be observed or measured.

The following are three aims taken from a GCSE course – the syllabus aims to provide students with opportunities to:

- Acquire knowledge and understanding of the human past;
- Investigate historical events, people, changes and issues;
- Provide a sound basis for further study and the pursuit of personal interest.

These are broad and general as is typical of aims. In order to achieve these broad aims, more precise objectives relating to topics and lessons would need to be written. Very tightly phrased objectives are sometimes called 'product objectives' because they state very precisely what the product or learning outcome will be. Verbs such as recall, select, organise, deploy, classify, describe, analyse and explain are related to specific events in the writing of objectives. For example, related to the syllabus above a teacher might set as a lesson objective that pupils would be able to recall the territories Hitler gained control of before the outbreak of World War 2, or explain why Chamberlain followed a policy of appeasement in the 1930s.

Product objectives have several advantages. They give students clear targets, inform assessment, inform teaching strategies, provide clear standards and are unambiguous. It is sensible practice for teachers to share objectives with pupils at the start of a lesson. However, all teachers should take care not to focus solely on product objectives and thus lose sight of legitimate aims that are less easy to measure. Product objectives used rigidly can constrain teachers and pupils, can be given status beyond their worth, and can limit the achievement of ambitious overall aims. The important thing in planning is always to keep in mind overall aims, vision and direction, while writing sensible, clearly focused objectives to be achieved in the short-term. In this way you should be able to see how each lesson contributes towards the achievement of your overall aims, but building gradually on what has gone before.

It is important to use language clearly when writing objectives. Thinking carefully about the verbs you use will help you to realise that some of your objectives will be much easier to assess than others.

Reflection point

Consider the verbs below. Which are unambiguous and which are open to many interpretations? What are the implications for the writing of lesson objectives?

- Know
- Understand
- State

- Write
- Construct
- Explain
- Think
- Solve
- Identify
- Distinguish
- Compare
- Differentiate
- Enjoy
- Believe
- Remember
- Draw
- Design
- Appreciate.

Many of the above words could be used for the writing of product objectives. Applied appropriately, words such as state, identify and compare would make unambiguous and clearly measurable objectives. This doesn't mean that words such as appreciate and enjoy should never be used. It may be that they are better used when writing programme aims, but if they are linked to objectives then thinking carefully about how you might assess pupils' achievement of the objectives will be very important. The words and phrases provided in Table 4.2 should help you to write appropriate objectives that reflect the expected cognitive development of pupils.

Action point

Consider the following objectives and decide how each one could be improved.

1. The objective of this lesson is to teach Faraday's laws of electro-magnetic induction.
2. The objective of this lesson is for the pupils to gain knowledge of Harvey's theory of blood circulation.
3. The objective of the lesson is to cover the causes of the Industrial Revolution.
4. The objective of the lesson is that the pupils should know the meaning of 'scientific method' and be able to apply it effectively.

The first objective stresses what the teacher will teach, but clear objectives should always be phrased in terms that indicate what *pupils* will know, understand or be able to do as a result of the lesson.

TABLE 4.2 Verbs and phrases for writing learning objectives

BLOOM'S TAXONOMY	VERBS AND PHRASES FOR WRITING OBJECTIVES
Knowledge	Draw Record Identify Describe Remember List Explain what
Comprehension	Sort Discuss Define Select Present Explain why
Application	Classify Demonstrate how Calculate Solve
Analysis	Analyse Conclude Interpret Use the evidence to . . .
Synthesis	Design Formulate Plan Predict Explain the differences between . . .
Evaluation	Assess Compare/contrast Make connections between Evaluate the evidence for . . .

The second objective is better in that it indicates what the pupils will learn about. However, the exact level of knowledge expected will need to be clarified within the lesson plan. It is likely, of course, that there will be other objectives associated with this lesson that go beyond the knowledge level of Bloom's taxonomy.

The third example is a poor objective because it is written as if a good lesson is simply about 'covering' or 'getting through' a chunk of a syllabus. It doesn't say what the pupils will be expected to achieve. For example, will they be expected to remember the causes of the Industrial Revolution (if so, how many causes), show some knowledge of each cause studied or understand the causes and their inter-relationship?

The final objective is actually not one but two objectives put together. Each one should be presented on a lesson plan as a separate objective. When evaluating a lesson it is important to be able to say if each learning outcome has been achieved and so it is best not to confuse matters by combining objectives. The second part of objective number 4 is also vague. What is the scientific method to be applied to? It is important that this is clear in the mind of the teacher at the planning stage.

Other elements in planning

A few years ago the government of the day used the *Key Stage 3 Strategy* to raise standards and improve pupils' rates of progress from Year 7 to Year 9. Key ideas underpinning the Strategy included establishing high expectations for all pupils, strengthening progression across key Stage 3 and motivating pupils through active engagement in the classroom. Some schools retain features of the Strategy to ensure a common approach to lesson planning. In such schools the following are looked for in all teachers' lessons:

- A variety of activities in each lesson;
- Sharing of lesson objectives with pupils;
- Being clear about standards and expectations;
- Encouraging independent learning;
- Effective use of 'starters' with good questioning of pupils;
- Effective use of the plenary part of the lesson to review learning.

You should recognise these expectations as being features of good practice already mentioned in this book. Guidance on how learning objectives can be shared with a class, how pupils can be helped to recognise standards being aimed for and how to provide effective starter and plenary sessions will be discussed in Chapter 5. The important thing to note in this chapter is the need to plan for short and well-focused starter and plenary sessions in most lessons of fifty minutes or over, with a variety of activities (usually two or three) in between.

Planning for inclusion

In Chapter 6 the issue of inclusion is discussed. At the lesson planning stage it is important to consider how well your proposed lesson will meet the needs of *all* pupils and especially those with special educational needs and those pupils classed as gifted and talented. Although children identified as having special needs require individual learning plans, it isn't realistic for secondary school teachers to write individualised learning plans for all pupils, nor is it necessary. In schools and subjects where streaming is the norm, you are unlikely to meet extremes of ability in the groups you teach, compared with subjects where mixed ability teaching is favoured. However, you will still need to adjust your delivery and support to meet the needs of some pupils. After all, all pupils are unique and although you have a lesson plan suited to the average ability of the group you will need to be aware of pupils that need further challenge and those that need support and reassurance. In mixed ability teaching situations planning will be more complex. Although the teacher-led part of the lesson will be the same for all, you will need to use a variety of resources to meet different needs. How this can be done is considered in Chapter 6. You will need to be clear about this in your planning. One way to proceed is to break down the topic of the lesson into: knowledge, concepts and skills *all* children must know or show by the end of the lesson; those *most* children should know or show by the end of the lesson; and those some children *could* know or show by the end of he lesson. This 'must-should-could' approach will force you to 'unpack' the topic you are teaching and help you to become more aware of what to expect from pupils of different levels of ability. Being able to break a topic down into parts or stages so as to make it more understandable is essential for effective differentiation. That said, a health warning about expectations applies here. While it is important to structure your lesson and learning tasks to enable all pupils to learn effectively based on your knowledge of their prior learning and capabilities, don't allow this to become a limiting factor in their learning. Never let past performance become a label that shapes and then limits what you expect of your pupils.

Action point

Think about the 'must-should-could' approach in relation to a lesson you might teach. How useful is it for thinking about intended outcomes? Could it be limiting in any way? Compare your ideas with those of other trainees.

Inclusion, of course, also involves teaching with regard to the gender, race, cultural background and socio-economic status of your pupils. An inclusive curriculum aims to acknowledge and respect the rich diversity of people that make up our nation. When you begin teaching, you have to grapple with learning new aspects of the subject you are teaching as well as trying to manage the classes you stand in front of. What is expected of you can seem overwhelming, and the prospect of having also to plan for diversity may just seem too much. You should try not to look at planning for diversity as something 'extra'. Instead, try and develop an inclusive attitude that is at the heart of the ethos of your classroom. Being inclusive has much to do with the way you relate to the students in your care, making each one feel valued and unique.

You should, of course, consider how inclusive the content of the curriculum you teach and the resources you use are. In recent years, resources have started to reflect more appropriately our multi-cultural nation and the changed position of women in society, but some older texts contain rather dated ideas and pictures. Be aware of this when planning. A checklist is provided in Chapter 6 as a stimulus to discussion on planning for inclusion.

Teachers and cross-curricular skills

Your main priority as a subject teacher is planning for pupils' progression in your subject and ensuring your lessons are both inclusive and challenging. However, if you spend a little time thinking about your subject it will soon become obvious that you will be unavoidably teaching aspects of other subjects. For example, when you use graphs and statistics in your subject you are using skills associated with mathematics. Even more obvious is the fact that – as you teach using the medium of English and mark work written in English – you may be faced with having to offer advice on, say, spelling or sentence construction in an effort to help pupils express what they know about your subject. For this reason all teachers are, to an extent, teachers of English and the Teachers' Standards (DfE 2011) makes clear that all teachers should 'demonstrate an understanding of and take responsibility for promoting high standards of literacy, articulacy and the correct use of standard English, whatever the teacher's specialist subject'. While it is not your duty to plan for developing pupils' English or Maths skills, it is your duty to understand school policies on teaching core skills across the curriculum so that the way you approach, say, correcting spellings in your subject or constructing a graph is consistent with school policy. This will ensure pupils are given clear and consistent messages and are therefore less likely to develop misunderstandings or become confused.

Saving time and effort with planning

It is not unusual to hear trainees say they 'survived' their training year and especially their time in school. Gaining QTS is extremely demanding and so it is important that you are efficient and effective in your use of time. While it is important to develop your own planning ability, it is legitimate to make use of existing resources to inform your planning. Experienced teachers absorb good ideas from other colleagues, books and training courses and build these into their planning. You can do the same when writing your lesson plans.

There are numerous sources of support on the internet. A simple Google search will reveal schemes of work and lesson plans written by teachers and offered through various on-line communities such as *The Times Educational Supplement* and *The Guardian*. Many Local Authorities offer clear guidance and schemes of work through their web-sites and, at the time of writing, Qualifications and Curriculum Authority (abolished in 2012) schemes can be located by putting 'QCA schemes of work' in Google.

A word of caution is necessary at this point. Using existing resources can save you time, but you must be sure that they are appropriate for the particular needs of *your* pupils. This usually involves modifying existing plans to some degree. This is the difference between being lazy (using someone else's planning without modification) and being effective in time management (modifying existing planning). Your school mentors and college tutors will notice the difference immediately!

There may be occasions when you are expected to plan from scratch. You may need to do this as part of a college assignment or a school based task. If so, the purpose of the exercise will be to get you to demonstrate that you can think up appropriate learning activities, unsupported. For your own development, it is useful to plan to teach a particular topic and then compare your ideas to those you find on the Internet. This will assist your self-evaluation and your planning skills.

Summary

Planning is an essential part of teaching and *those who fail to plan, plan to fail.* This is especially so in the case of trainee teachers. With none of the experience of well-established teachers to draw on you must plan in detail and on paper. You cannot carry the complicated details of every lesson in your head or on the back of an envelope! The fact that you will observe very good lessons with teachers who seem to have no written plans should not lead you to think you can do the same. All teachers had to plan as trainees and in the early stages of their careers. They gradually relied less on planning every lesson as experience and habit took over and they began to know schemes of work 'in their heads'. Eventually this will happen for you, but not for a few years yet!

Your planning will be scrutinised and assessed and unless it is of a high standard you will not be recommended for the award of QTS. With poor planning there is a greater likelihood that your lessons will be badly organised and pupils will be disruptive, thus leading to failure in other important areas of professional practice. So, the message is simple; get your planning right.

Training institutions and schools will vary slightly in the recommended lesson planning formats you are expected to use, but all will expect you to show clarity in the following, as a minimum:

- Pupils' prior knowledge and understanding;
- Your objectives for the lesson;
- What the pupils will do during the lesson;
- What you will do during the lesson;
- The timing of the various activities;
- How you will deploy other adults in the class;
- How you have catered for SEN and Gifted pupils;
- How you will assess what has been learnt.

Don't worry if your lesson plans don't always work out. At first, you will be sure to get the level of work or the timing of activities slightly wrong. The ability to be flexible and adapt your lesson in response to pupils' needs is important so don't see lesson plans as a strait jacket. Even during your training year you will find that, as time goes by, you will begin to write lesson plans more quickly and, as you get to know the classes you teach, your planning will begin to match the needs of the pupils more accurately.

References

Bloom, B.S. (1964) *Taxonomy of Educational Objectives: Handbook 1 – Cognitive Domains*, London: Longman.

DfE (2011) *Teachers' Standards*, Crown copyright.

Hay McBer (2000) *Research into Teaching Effectiveness*, London: DfEE.

Krathwohl, D.R, Bloom, B.S., and Masia, B.B. (1964) *Taxonomy of Educational Objectives, Handbook 2: Affective Domain*, New York: David McKay.

Reece, I. and Walker, S. (2000) *Teaching, Training and Learning: A Practical Guide*, Sunderland: Business Education Publishers.

5

Climate for learning and behaviour management

Introduction

Managing behaviour is often the biggest preoccupation of students during their training. It is important to make clear that behaviour management is not something that can be learnt simply through reading this chapter. Likewise, just copying approaches to behaviour management you have seen used by other teachers will not always work. In the end, your approach to behaviour management will have to reflect your personality and style of teaching.

Although this chapter is devoted to behaviour management, you must not allow yourself to think that behaviour management is something divorced from other aspects of teaching. In fact, it is more helpful to think about how to create a positive *climate for learning* than to focus on reacting to pupils' poor behaviour. In this way you think about your responsibility in creating the conditions that lead to good behaviour. Developing the approaches we discussed in Chapter 2, taking into account how children learn (Chapter 3) and planning thoroughly (Chapter 4) are all vital for achieving acceptable behaviour from pupils. Put simply, if you can enthuse the pupils, if you understand how they learn best and if your planning ensures that the work you set is pitched at the right level, the likelihood of pupils misbehaving is greatly diminished.

Having said this, there are a number of commonly accepted techniques for behaviour management which teachers use. This chapter will introduce you to these techniques as well as encouraging you to reflect more deeply on exactly what we mean by misbehaviour, what the causes of misbehaviour might be and how your own attitude and approach can have a powerful influence on behaviour. There is also some time devoted to considering how best to deal with particularly difficult individuals, as a small number of troublesome youngsters can have a negative effect on the whole class and prevent you establishing the kind of *climate for learning* you would ideally like.

While you will, of course, strive to be consistent in your approach to behaviour management, you are only human and even the most effective teacher can never be certain that their approach will work with every single child. Be prepared for pupils' behaviour showing variations from day to day. Likewise, there will be some days when you are tired and your tolerance level is lower than on other days. Don't be too hard on yourself if you don't manage to achieve with all classes the same levels of behaviour as very experienced teachers, during your training period. You will need to demonstrate that your behaviour management is effective, but 'effective' doesn't mean that you have to succeed in transforming all the pupils you teach into little angels.

What do we mean by misbehaviour?

Action point

Spend five minutes brainstorming the types of misbehaviour that might occur in classrooms. Spend a further five minutes putting the things you have come up with into rank order, with the least serious things at the top and the most serious at the bottom.

The chances are that you came up with a whole range of misbehaviours from minor irritations such as doodling to serious challenges or even physical attacks. Fortunately, physical violence against teachers is relatively rare, but some low-level misbehaviour is present in almost all schools. 'The daily effect on teachers of so-called *low level disruption*, needless chatter, equipment being dropped, and so on can be extremely draining' (Elliott 2009). However, this is nothing new and should not lead you to believe there is a crisis in behaviour in our schools. HMI reports from all decades of the second half of the last century highlight misbehaviour as an issue in many schools with teachers having to deal with 'pupils hindering others', 'lateness to lessons', 'talking out of turn', 'calculated idleness', 'work avoidance' and 'making unnecessary (non-verbal) noise' (DES 1989). These patterns of misbehaviour can, of course, be very irritating, even stressful, to teachers. They can also be a cause of underachievement. A classroom in which background noise and disruption is the norm and pupils are 'off task' is not a place that is conducive to learning.

When in school you may find teachers' perceptions vary as to what constitutes misbehaviour. What one teacher regards as healthy banter, another teacher may see as insolence. These differences are related in part to personality and also to how relaxed and secure teachers feel in their role. Some teachers are more tolerant than others, and some are stricter than others. However, it is important across a school that teachers broadly expect the same behaviour from pupils and consistently apply the agreed school behaviour policy. Research by Mortimer (1998) showed that there is usually a consensus as to what constitutes unacceptable behaviour in relation to issues such as equal opportunities, discrimination and bullying in the most effective schools. Teachers in these schools are consistent in that they all have high expectations of pupils in terms of behaviour and work hard to maintain the school behaviour policy. These findings were echoed in the report by Sir Alan Steer, *Learning Behaviour* (DCSF 2009) which makes clear the importance of consistency in a school's approach to behaviour management and stresses the need for 'consistent good quality teaching as the basis for . . . reducing low level disruption' (p.3).

Pupils need to learn what good behaviour looks like. Interestingly, when asked what good behaviour is, most pupils will still say things like 'being quiet', 'listening' and even 'working in silence'. Of course, there are times when these behaviours are entirely appropriate but much more is involved in successful *behaviour for learning*. Respecting the views and feelings of others and being able to collaborate, for example, are also essential. The following passage from the Ofsted Evaluation Schedule (2012) for 'Outstanding Behaviour' helps us to understand the need for us to develop pupils as effective learners rather than focusing only on external control of their misbehaviour. Pupils:

> 'make every effort to ensure that others learn and thrive in an atmosphere of respect and dignity. Pupils show very high levels of engagement, courtesy, collaboration and cooperation in (and out of) lessons. They have excellent, enthusiastic attitudes to learning, enabling lessons to proceed without interruption. They are highly adept at managing their own behaviour in the classroom and in social situations.

> (Ofsted 2012)

Causes of misbehaviour

Although you will come across some pupils whose misbehaviour can be explained in medical terms, the majority of mainstream children will not be misbehaving as a result of suffering from a particular syndrome or condition. There is likely to be a much more mundane explanation for their misbehaviour.

Action point

Spend a few minutes listing the possible reasons for the kinds of low-level misbehaviour we discussed above.

It is likely that you have produced a list that includes boredom, tiredness, not being listened to, failure to understand instructions, being shouted at, lack of skills to complete a task and perceptions of injustice. Some of these can clearly be laid at the door of the teacher. Let us consider these first. Many teachers say that children find it more difficult to concentrate these days than, say, twenty years ago. They get bored more easily than previous generations of children. We could spend a lot of time debating why this might be the case (assuming it is) but for the purposes of this chapter let us accept that boredom is a cause of misbehaviour in classrooms. Teachers who fail to offer activities that are interesting, varied, appropriately timed and challenging are thus more likely to face misbehaviour than those who do.

Teaching is a pressurised and demanding job. The average teacher is expected to deal with a tremendous amount each and every day. For this reason, efficient organisation is vital. If a teacher arrives late to a lesson, if s/he forgets to bring the books the class needs and if the inter-active whiteboard has not been set up in advance of the pupils arriving there is potential for disruption. It is not surprising that as a general rule, teachers who are poorly organised are more likely to face behaviour problems than those who are well organised. Of course, some eccentric and charismatic teachers are loved and respected by their pupils despite their disorganisation and some rigid but very well organised teachers will face problems because of their lack of flexibility. There are always exceptions to general rules, but as a teacher in training you would be well advised to be as organised as you possibly can if you are to succeed, whatever your personality.

We have already discussed in Chapter 4 the importance of planning. Translating planning into action requires you to be very clear in your instructions to pupils. Make sure they understand what the learning outcomes of the lesson should be and make your instructions for the work to be undertaken as simple and logical as possible. How you express these instructions will vary according to the age and ability of your class, but even the most motivated and dedicated learners need to be clear about what is expected. Always ensure that anything beyond the most simple of instructions is written down. If you have planned work that is too difficult for the ability of the pupils, or if the work offers no challenge and is just 'more of the same', then misbehaviour could result. While ensuring that your lessons have challenge, always remember that mental effort is difficult to sustain over a long period of time. This is one reason why lessons at the end of the day can often be the ones in which pupils misbehave.

So, there are several things teachers can do to reduce the likelihood of misbehaviour. However, some misbehaviour still occurs even when a teacher has acted appropriately in relation to all of the above points. Sometimes, incidents from outside the classroom spill over into lesson time. A disagreement between pupils that has occurred over a lunch break may erupt once more in your classroom, for example, or an argument with a parent before school may mean a pupil appears in your class angry and uncooperative. Good teachers try and handle such situations quietly, tactfully and without confrontation. The worst thing a teacher can do in an already tense situation is to escalate the level of aggression (see Chapter 12). Always remember, even if you cannot control pupils' behaviour you can control how you choose to respond.

Some pupils in secondary school are switched off from education for a variety of reasons. Low self-esteem resulting from years of perceived failure can leave some pupils feeling very alienated. In selective grammar schools pupils in lower sets can often exhibit anti-school behaviour due to their belief that they are failures. In non-selective schools pupils of the same ability would be seen as academic successes and their self-esteem and behaviour could be quite different as a result. Getting to know your pupils and to understand what they have to offer beyond the academic is very important if you are to help tackle their low self-esteem. Praising pupils and building up their self-belief is vital. They need to feel valued and, in the long term, this is the best way to ensure they behave well for you. Research has shown that 'if a teacher is liked and valued by a class, then generally individuals will value his or her praise and encouragement' (Fontana 1994).

Understanding why pupils misbehave will not always mean you can change their behaviour. Some pupils may have emotional difficulties resulting from neglect at home or bullying at school, which explains their misbehaviour. Some pupils come from homes where values are very different to those of the school, where little discipline exists and little respect is shown to family members. Pupils from such circumstances should not, of course, be allowed to exhibit unacceptable behaviour in your classroom. You should have high expectations of all pupils and the other pupils in your class have a right to be able to learn and to be treated with respect. However, you should not be surprised, as a trainee, if you fail to transform the attitudes and behaviours of such pupils. Do your very best, but don't feel you have failed if you need to turn to colleagues in the school for advice or support.

General advice on achieving acceptable behaviour

The Elton Report (DES 1989) contains some very down to earth advice to help teachers do all they can to ensure good behaviour in their classrooms. In brief, teachers should:

- Learn the names of all the pupils they teach;
- Get to know their pupils as individuals;
- Plan and organise both the classroom and the lesson to keep pupils interested and minimise disruption;
- Be flexible;
- Continually observe or scan the classroom;
- Be aware of and control their behaviour, especially tone of voice;
- Model the standards of courtesy they expect from pupils;
- Emphasise the positive and praise good behaviour and work;
- Make the rules of the classroom simple and clear;
- Use reprimands and punishments consistently but sparingly;
- Analyse their own classroom management performance and learn from it;
- If you have adult support in class, ensure they are empowered to assist with behaviour management.

Some of these points are worthy of expansion. For example, classroom layout is something that even many experienced teachers pay only limited attention to, yet it is very important. 'Good classroom organisation and management liberate teachers from many of the daily hassles and confrontations and enable them to establish the order without which the classroom can become a battleground'

(Watkins and Wagner 1987). Arranging the furniture appropriately can have a major impact on behaviour. If you want pupils to work in groups then it is obvious that arranging the tables for this will be necessary. However, this arrangement may not suit a more formal lesson. It offers too much potential for pupils to distract each other, for pupils to be looking at each other rather than at the teacher, and for the teacher to have their view of particular pupils obscured by others. Many teachers find a horseshoe arrangement of desks (Figure 5.1) is an excellent layout for most lessons in non-specialist rooms (providing the room is big enough to allow for this layout). It avoids the formality of rows of desks facing the front (and then the problem that most pupils can't see the face of a pupil who is making a contribution to a discussion). The horseshoe means that all pupils are visible to other pupils and to the teacher. It is easy for all pupils to look to the front. It allows the teacher to circulate easily around the room. Other teachers now use a chevron style layout, with diagonal rows of desks facing towards the teacher and other pupils across the room. If you are lucky enough to teach all your lessons in the same room try and arrange the furniture to your liking. It is more likely, however, that during training you will teach different classes in different rooms and so rearranging the furniture at the start and end of a lesson might simply not be practical.

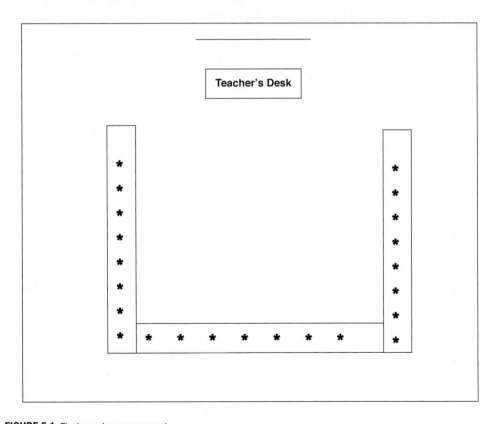

FIGURE 5.1 The horseshoe arrangement

Another point made above refers to consistent but sparing reprimands. This means being firm with pupils but not aggressive. You should try and use words in such a way that you are criticising the behaviour you are unhappy with but not the person. Private or quietly spoken reprimands are often more successful than those that cause public humiliation. Sarcasm is to be avoided, even if using it might make you temporarily feel better. Idle threats achieve nothing. Give pupils clarity about choices and consequences. If there is misbehaviour make clear what the consequences of it continuing will be. They now have a choice (and some control). Always carry through with consequences. If you don't, pupils will very quickly learn that what you are saying will happen is little more than hot air. It is the certainty of knowing the consequences will be followed through not the severity of them that is important.

Reflection point

Can you add to the above list? How do teachers with orderly classrooms behave towards their pupils? What behaviours do you see them displaying in order to keep pupils on task or when they challenge lapses in behaviour?

Bleach (2000) offers a number of additional ideas for helping to create a peaceful classroom. Some of these are included below:

- Circulate – go round the classroom asking pupils about their progress and possibly marking some pupils' work. This can help to uncover any misunderstandings at an early stage.
- Make eye contact – a well directed stare can get a pupil back on task without you having to disrupt the flow of what you are saying.
- Target questions to involve all pupils and to keep or regain particular pupils' attention.
- Use proximity – moving towards a pupil or standing by a pupil can help to keep them on task.
- Move pupils – if necessary, separate pupils whose behaviour is not acceptable, while stressing it is done in their interests.
- Correct targeting – it is important to identify correctly the pupils who are responsible for disrupting a lesson. Punishing the whole class for the misbehaviour of a few pupils can be counter-productive.
- Avoid anger – don't lose your cool, whatever the provocation. Speak assertively but not aggressively; don't let pupils wind you up.
- Avoid unfair comparisons – comparisons with other pupils or classes are unfair. It is especially unhelpful to compare a pupil to his or her brother or sister.
- Make an example – reprimanding an individual, and adding that you will not tolerate other pupils acting in this way, can be useful in the first few lessons with a new class to highlight expectations. But remember that public humiliation is rarely productive, and shouldn't be part of your long-term behaviour management strategy.

The use of effective teaching skills

There are certain aspects of almost all lessons that are similar and that you need to focus on from the outset of your training. I could have included some of these in Chapter 2 (Teaching) and others in Chapter 3 (Learning). Instead, they are included here to demonstrate that behaviour management cannot be divorced from teaching and learning. It shouldn't be considered as an afterthought. If you apply what you understand about how children learn and get your basic teaching repertoire right, most pupils will behave as you would like them to.

Arrival

Classroom management begins as soon as the first pupil arrives at your door. The whole tone of the lesson can be set at this point. Make sure you arrive at the classroom before the pupils. This can be difficult sometimes, as you may be asked to teach classes in a number of different rooms, but try your very best. If you are on school experience in a school where pupils are expected to line up outside the classroom, use this as a chance to establish order before the pupils go into the room. It is more likely that the pupils will be used to coming straight in. As they do you might offer a friendly word to one or two pupils (this becomes easier once you know names and a bit about each pupil) but try not to get involved in long discussions with individuals as your priority must be a snappy start to the lesson. A very quick calling of the register is a useful way of getting pupils settled. However, this uses up time and for this reason some teachers prefer to take the register once the children are working on a task. If there are stragglers they should be pointed to their seats. Don't make a big fuss if they are only seconds behind the other pupils, but if they are very late and this occurs regularly you will need to talk to them individually and consider sanctions for lateness. A big showdown at the start of the lesson has the potential of being very disruptive and is not a good way to begin, but any latecomers do need to know that you have noticed them, and the rest of the class need to know that this is not behaviour you will tolerate. If you are unlucky enough to be receiving pupils from all over the school, have a very short task (a challenge) ready for those arriving first to get on with. This will mean that there is an ordered, working atmosphere when the others arrive. Numerous Starter suggestions are provided in the appendix of Learning Behaviour (Steer 2009) and some of these could be used very effectively as challenges (see Table 5.1).

Lesson introduction

The class should be quiet before you begin. Use eye contact and gestures with any individuals who may still be shuffling, whispering or searching in their bags, to let them know that you want their attention. Refer to pupils by their names if any noise continues so they are in no doubt about whom you are waiting for (a seating plan can help you learn names early on). Keep your voice quiet and remain calm.

TABLE 5.1 Suggested starters (Steer 2009)

RECAP	KEY WORDS	NEW TOPIC
Summarise what you know about the topic in 5 bullet points – reduce to 5 words – reduce to one word.	Match word cards and definition cards. Can be done as card sort or snap.	60 second challenge – write down all the terms you can think of to do with a topic.
Draw a graphic summary of knowledge so far – diagram, steps, flowchart, mind/concept map (like a spidergram but shows links).	Write dictionary definitions or mnemonics for new terms learnt last lesson.	Draw a picture of current understanding of a process and redraw at end of unit e.g. Biology – digestive system or plant lifecycle.
Just a minute – pupils talk on a topic without hesitation, repetition etc.	Categorising terms – sort words into related groups, with a pile for 'not understood yet' e.g. words related to volcanoes in Geography as a 'warm-up' to activate previous knowledge.	Video clip. Class watches very short extract, then consider in pairs: What do I already know? What did I learn from the clip? What do I want to find out?
Draw a simple timeline of events covered so far.	Pictionary – draw the word without speaking or writing.	Objects – pupils are given a group of objects and asked to sort/imagine/describe/predict/explain/plan an activity, e.g. given 2 tennis balls must invent a warm-up exercise in PE.
Label or annotate a diagram or illustration – one word in each box. Can be half-complete for pupils needing some support	Bingo – as teacher reads, pupils must spot word/symbol and mark card e.g. match numbers in French with digit; match muscle with diagram of stretch in PE; match musical term and symbol.	Key question/statement snowball – pairs discuss then share ideas with another pair, 4 join another 4, and then 8 join another 8, e.g. 'What would you be prepared to die for?' to introduce unit on Martin Luther King in RS or PSHE.
Verbal tennis – divide class into 2 groups who take turns to say a word related to the current topic. No words can be repeated. Scored as tennis.	Post-it notes or stickers on foreheads – pupils work out word by asking neighbour questions which receive yes/no answers.	Concept cartoon. Choose from speech-bubble opinions of different characters, e.g. Physics – 4 different opinions about what will happen to a rocket (pictured) that has run out of fuel.

Avoid nervous gestures or defensive body language (e.g. arms folded). Don't overreact to pupils' behaviour at this stage, as a bad start could undermine everything you have planned for the rest of the lesson. If you find a class being very noisy at the start of your lesson, try counting from 1 to 5 loudly and slowly. This should result in most pupils becoming quiet before you reach number 5 (providing, of course, your voice conveys a tone of authority). Alternatively, have an agreed sound (a small bell, buzzer or horn) which everyone understands means 'be quiet'.

Try and make the introduction stimulating and interactive. You may be using the initial starter activity to find out what pupils already know and understand, to link previous learning to the next stage or to 'hook the learners'. If possible, stimulate pupils' interest with an artefact, visual source, story or piece of music. Having instructions for the first activity on the board or flipchart can be helpful. You could use pupils to read out these instructions to the whole group. By the end of the starter pupils should be clear about the purpose of the lesson and what you expect them to have learnt or accomplished before they leave. Many teachers spend too long telling pupils about the new theme or topic they are introducing. Even with the effective use of questions, most children will have 'switched off' if this goes much beyond fifteen minutes. Learning is more effective if the teacher's initial input is limited to 10–15 minutes, with the new learning points being introduced as soon as possible.

Plenaries

A plenary session should be provided at a point in the lesson (usually, but not always, the end) when learning can be assessed and reinforced. This part of the lesson can be fun, with versions of 'Mastermind' or 'The Weakest Link' used as a means of assessing learning. Sensitive selecting of questions can ensure that all abilities of children are able to take part and have learning celebrated. Some teachers use 'Phone a Friend' in Plenaries. This involves the pupils (in pairs) preparing two or three questions based on the lesson. The teacher then asks pupils in turn to 'phone a friend' in the class – the friend being the pair who must then answer the question.

Maintaining pace

By breaking up your lesson into chunks a good pace should be maintained and this will reduce the opportunities for misbehaviour through boredom. The middle bit of the lesson can be broken up by collecting in homework (if this has been done on paper rather than in exercise books). This allows some movement at the very time when children are beginning to 'wilt'.

Questioning skills

Effective starters and plenaries often depend on using questioning techniques well. Questions can be used to:

- Focus attention;
- Establish prior knowledge;
- Recapitulate previous work;
- Force comparisons;
- Seek clarification;
- Invite enquiry;
- Seek explanations;
- Force pupils to draw conclusions;
- Assess learning.

Used well, effective questioning helps behaviour management by ensuring a good pace to the lesson and keeping all pupils focused. It is important to develop your questioning skills. Many trainees use only a limited range of questions at first and tend to take answers from the first pupils with hands up. As they develop their skills they use a variety of types of questions:

- Closed questions – these have a single correct answer;
- Open questions – these have a variety of possible answers;
- Elaborate questions – these encourage development of a point already made;
- Leading questions – these focus attention on specific options or problems;
- Multiple questions – these offer a number of alternatives to the same question.

Questioning is a skill you should practice 'in your head' before teaching a lesson. You need to work on:

- Clarity of speech;
- Volume and speed of speech;
- Eye contact;
- Directing questions (especially useful for behaviour management);
- Vocabulary;
- Complexity.

Remember, one pupil answering a question correctly doesn't mean everyone else also knows the answer. Insist on hands being raised if you address a question to the whole class, so that you don't have the same few pupils shouting out the answers every time. Using 'talk partners' (pupils discussing in pairs before offering an answer) is a good way of ensuring *all* pupils are actively responding to a question. When an answer is given it is a good idea to repeat it out loud, possibly rephrasing it and emphasising key words, so that everyone can hear it. If an incomplete answer is given, encourage clarification rather than providing it yourself. Use one person's answer to pose a further question to the class, thus elaborating understanding. By directing questions appropriately, you can get pupils who are showing signs of losing concentration refocused. By offering manageable questions to the less able pupils, you can involve them and give them a sense of achievement. Always take care not to put down pupils who offer incorrect answers; you want them to feel confident enough to offer an answer next time. When you are planning lessons use Bloom's taxonomy (see Chapter 4) as a way of planning progressively more challenging questions.

Concluding lessons

Always keep an eye on the time. Allow yourself enough time to tidy up, give out homework and/or collect in books and conduct a plenary. At the very end of the lesson, when the bell goes, make sure that pupils leave in an orderly manner. Make sure that any rubbish has been put in the bin by the pupils and that the desks and chairs are left in an orderly state. As a trainee, even if your lesson has not gone according to plan, you should always aim to finish your lesson in an orderly fashion and leave the room in a good state for the next teacher and class who will be using it.

Classroom rules

Reflection point

Think back to your own school days. Can you remember any of the school rules? Do you remember thinking any of them were unfair? Which ones and why? What rules will you want in your classroom?

Most schools will have a set of rules that all teachers are required to enforce consistently. Even so, with some classes you may need to establish (or at least reinforce) some ground rules to prevent misbehaviour. This is not quite as easy for a trainee as it sounds. If you are at the early stages of your training you may have been observing a class being taught that you are now expected to teach for yourself, so you don't face a 'new' class as such and may already have established a rapport with some members of the class. Perhaps you have been teaching a small group of pupils within the class, where your approach has been able to be more 'friendly' than it will be when you face the whole class for the first time. The pupils will know the school better than you do and will be familiar with what the school rules are. They will be keen to let you know what other teachers allow. Always make sure any ground rules you agree don't go against the school rules. Some pupils are only too keen to exploit inconsistencies!

Make sure that you are clear about the school rules and the systems and procedures that are in place for dealing with misbehaviour. As a trainee, it is important that you work within the school guidelines. Even though there are likely to be rules about classroom behaviour, you should still take time with a new class to make clear what your expectations are. Getting the pupils to agree about why some ground rules are necessary (for example, why pupils should raise a hand if they want to answer a question) will help to ensure that the rules are abided by. Displaying the school rules in your classroom is a good idea. You can point to any rules pupils infringe in order to remind them of what they agreed. Use positive reinforcement with pupils by praising those who keep the rules.

It is likely that if you involve the class in making the rules they will come up with sensible ideas of what pupils must do or not do. Don't allow the list of things to be too long, or you could find you make a rod for your own back. When you have a long and rigid set of rules there are bound to be infringements that you then have to be seen to deal with. Effective teachers are often flexible in the way they apply rules. For example, if a pupil has a legitimate reason for being late to a lesson, an experienced teacher wouldn't get into a confrontation about the lateness to lesson rule being broken. Young people are capable of seeing that different responses to the infringement of rules can be fair, but they also expect overall consistency. Don't tie yourself up in too many rules or you are sure to end up appearing both unfair and inconsistent when it is impossible to enforce them all of the time and with every pupil. Often, simple phrases such as 'be considerate', 'behave well towards others', 'show respect for other people and their feelings' and 'make sure your behaviour helps you and other people to do their best' serve better than a long list of rules. They encourage pupils to reflect more carefully on their actions, though there will always, of course, be some fundamental 'dos and don'ts'. In the end, it is far better for pupils to behave well because they have thought about how their actions affect other people than because a list of rules exists.

Reprimands and punishments

This chapter has so far emphasised the need to encourage positive behaviour and reinforce this through praise. It has emphasised the need to deliver well-paced lessons and build good relationships with pupils so as to avoid the likelihood of misbehaviour occurring. This said, some pupils will misbehave and you will need to know how to respond.

Make sure you know the procedures in school relating to matters such as detention, punishments and referring pupils to other colleagues (these will be in the Staff Handbook or the materials provided for you as a trainee). Discuss with your mentor in school how these procedures apply to you. For example, if you have a very disruptive pupil in your class, you will probably be expected to send for the teacher who would normally be taking the class, rather than the head of department or year head. Most schools have strict rules about keeping pupils in detention after school and you should therefore not issue after-school detentions without discussion with an appropriate colleague. Check this out at the beginning of your time in school.

As a trainee try and avoid getting involved in confiscating pupils' property, unless you have been given very clear instructions to do so. Give children the opportunity to put things like combs and mobile phones away at the start of your lesson rather than taking them away from them. If you have to take something from a child try and give it back at the end of the lesson (this will be an incentive for good behaviour). If you decide to keep something for longer involve your mentor so that it can be locked away safely or passed to the appropriate head of year. Don't snatch things from pupils. Don't get into a battle of wills with a pupil where you are insisting something is handed over and they are refusing. This will provide entertainment of the wrong kind for the rest of the class and will be very unsettling. It is much better to deal with the matter quietly at the end of the lesson. If you do reprimand just one or two pupils at the end of a lesson, never do this behind closed doors. Ensure your classroom door is open or, better still, ask another teacher (preferably the teacher who would normally be taking the class) to be there while you speak to the pupils. Don't lay yourself open to accusations of misconduct that could be made because there were no witnesses present when you were dealing with pupils who had misbehaved.

In general, avoid punishing a whole class for the misbehaviour of a few pupils. This is very unfair, and is likely to do little towards establishing the kind of relationship you would like with a class. Try and punish only those pupils who have been misbehaving. Likewise, avoid being impulsive and punishing pupils for minor infringements of the rules. Teenagers have a strong sense of justice, and draconian punishments for small acts of misbehaviour are not seen as fair. Don't allow yourself to get into 'upping the stakes' by giving longer and longer detentions, for example. Remember, you will have to 'manage' these detentions. It could be that some pupils fail to turn up for detention and so you will then have to follow this up. If you are getting into a situation where this is happening you need to reflect very carefully on your overall management strategy and your lesson organisation. Don't be scared about asking your mentor for advice. Effective teachers use punishments very sparingly – even as a trainee you should try to do the same.

Being creative

Try and be creative in your use of rewards and punishments, taking into account the age of the pupils you are dealing with. Here are a few suggestions to get you started:

- Use quiet background music during the 'working' part of a lesson.
- Reward good behaviour by allowing the best workers to select the music for the next lesson.
- With younger pupils keep a marble jar in class. Each time a pupil earns a marble it goes in the jar. When the jar is full the whole class gets a treat.
- Instead of putting children in detention and making them write lines, get them to help you with tasks that have to be done. This will give you a chance to

get to know them, while still depriving them of their liberty during a break or lunch time.

■ If a pupil has wasted time in class and you keep them in detention to finish work stress that this is because you want them to do well and that you are helping them to achieve their full potential in your subject. You could call the time 'Learning Support' or 'Tuition Time' rather than detention to emphasise this.

Very disruptive pupils

You are likely to encounter some pupils and classes whose behaviour is particularly disruptive and who don't respond to the strategies we have discussed so far. Such students are likely to display the following behaviours:

■ Inability to sit still or be quiet;

■ Always having to answer back and have the last word;

■ Laughing loudly and shouting out;

■ Poking, kicking and generally annoying other pupils;

■ Showing no respect towards members of staff or other pupils;

■ Forgetting and losing work;

■ Coming to lessons late and with no equipment.

The following approaches should help you to manage such pupils/classes:

■ Make them sit apart from other pupils;

■ Keep all their work at school;

■ Have several short activities in every lesson;

■ Provide all equipment needed;

■ Limit class discussions;

■ Get started with the lesson even if there isn't complete silence;

■ Set measurable targets for each lesson (e.g. you must get to question 5).

Always seek advice from your mentor and other colleagues about how best to deal with really difficult pupils. Some pupils with Special Educational Needs may need to be handled in very particular ways (see Chapter 6).

Physical force

Never touch a pupil in anger. You can use physical force for purposes of restraint if a pupil is injuring themselves or others, causing damage to property, committing a criminal offence or behaving in a way that is prejudicial to maintaining good order in a school. The latter, of course, is open to a range of interpretations. If you do have to use physical force this should be 'reasonable'. That is, the minimum force necessary to achieve what is required. If you do have to physically restrain a pupil try and stay calm and say out loud as you are doing so why you are doing it, for example, to prevent X being injured.

Thinking about your own behaviour

Good teachers are reflective and honest about their own behaviours. It is important to analyse the part you might be playing in fuelling disruptive behaviour if you find yourself facing rather more hostility from pupils than other teachers seem to be receiving.

Sometimes, teachers are to blame for pupils' bad behaviour and some teachers certainly manage to escalate conflict situations rather than diffuse them. There are teachers who lack confidence in their own ability to deal with disruption and who see classes as potentially hostile. They create a negative classroom atmosphere by frequent criticism and sarcasm. They over-react to minor misdemeanours. They reprimand pupils loudly and publicly. They try and enforce petty rules rigidly. They show little interest in or respect for their pupils.

Be honest about your behaviour towards classes and pupils that you may not feel entirely comfortable with. Does your non-verbal communication (eyes and body language) give off feelings of hostility and/or fear? Do you overreact to small infringements of the rules because you are anticipating problems? It is important not to treat as a personal attack hostility you may encounter from particular classes and pupils. You need to avoid showing anger and develop the ability to show 'controlled displeasure' (Furlong and Maynard 1995).

Of course you should have high expectations of all pupils but you must avoid turning your classroom into a battleground. A pupil who is doodling as you speak may be annoying you, but there is no point having a battle over it. The rest of the class will lose out as you vent your anger on the pupil in question.

Action point

Video a lesson you teach. Use it to analyse your behaviour as a teacher. Do you display any mannerisms or habits that pupils could find amusing? Do you use any expressions or phrases that pupils are likely to laugh at? Do you seem relaxed or tense? What is the balance between praise and reprimands? Be honest about the things you need to change.

Teachers should be assertive but not aggressive with their pupils. The behaviours associated with being assertive are well documented (Table 5.2). You can work on your body language by practising how you stand, etc, and you can mentally rehearse the words you will use next time you have to deal with a difficult pupil.

TABLE 5.2 Passive, assertive and aggressive behaviour

	PASSIVE	ASSERTIVE	AGGRESSIVE
Content	Frequent justifications Rambling Excessive apologising	Clear statements Distinctions between fact and opinion Questions to find out opinions of others Ways of resolving problems	Opinions expressed as fact Threats Blame put on others Sarcasm
Voice and speech	Wobbly Soft Monotone Pauses Frequent throat clearing	Steady Warm Clear Clear Emphasises key words	Very firm Cold Strident Loud Abrupt Emphasises blaming words
Face and eyes	Evasive Looking down	Smiles when pleased Frowns when angry Firm eye contact	Scowls Eyebrows raised in amazement Tries to stare-down
Body language	Arms crossed Hand-wringing Mouth covered	Open hand movements Stands with head held up Sits upright but relaxed	Finger pointing Fist thumping Sits upright Stands tall Strides around Arms crossed

Thinking about your attitudes

It is easy for a teacher to form impressions of a pupil on which expectations are then built. The teacher's behaviour is based (consciously or unconsciously) on these expectations and the pupil then responds accordingly. Expectation theory (Rogers 1982) suggests that if teachers have low expectations of particular groups of children or individual pupils, they will find that the pupils' behaviour and achievement is poor. On the other hand, if teachers expect high standards from pupils they usually get what they expect. The important thing is to avoid stereotyping groups or 'labelling' individuals and to have high expectations of all pupils you come across.

Case study

Susan

There is one girl in a year 9 class causing you particular problems. Susan is very loud and 'in your face'. She regularly wanders into class a few minutes late, just as you are getting the class settled. When you point her to her seat or ask her why she's late, she aggressively shouts some feeble excuse for her lateness. She is physically bigger than most of the other pupils and is very intimidating. Most of the other pupils seem frightened of her. Susan shouts out during discussion sessions and even during the working part of the lesson. She constantly draws attention to herself. Ironically, the work she produces is usually of an acceptable standard and she has no difficulty in understanding your subject. Indeed, she will sometimes make very interesting comments (but doesn't wait to be asked for them). You are beginning to feel anxious about taking the class with Susan present. Although the rest of the class are fairly co-operative, you don't feel relaxed because Susan makes you feel as though you're not in control. One week she was 'on report' for bad behaviour and had to have her report card signed at the end of the lesson. She was only marginally better than usual and when you wrote 'unsatisfactory' on her card she blew her top.

REFLECTION POINT

Consider how you would manage Susan's behaviour.

Susan is not an easy pupil and it is obvious why she would make inexperienced teachers feel threatened. The fact that she has been 'on report' suggests that her bad behaviour is fairly widespread. This should at least help you to see that there is nothing personal in Susan's attitude towards you. Find out all you can about Susan from her form tutor and head of year. This should give you some insight into the reasons for her behaviour (she may have very difficult home circumstances, for example) and you are likely to feel less of a failure for hearing that she has been difficult with many other teachers. Seek their advice on what seems to work best with Susan. If there are any members of staff she relates well to try and find out how they approach Susan. If possible, arrange to observe her being taught by a more experienced teacher and note the approach that teacher takes.

Think about your own behaviour. If you feel anxious it is likely to be showing in your manner. You expect Susan to be trouble, so you probably pounce on the first little thing she does to nip the bad behaviour in the bud. This clearly hasn't worked. Try backing off a bit and not challenging the less significant things. Susan's bad behaviour is succeeding in getting your attention and this gives her power over you. If you 'notice less' this will take away some of that power. Likewise, if she can see that she succeeds in 'winding you up' this too is a form of power. Try and stay very calm and make sure your tone of voice reflects this. If she shouts out answers ignore her (even if the answers are correct) and take the answer from a pupil whose hand is up. Work on the positive by praising the good work Susan does. If there is any improvement, acknowledge it. Susan probably tried very hard to modify her behaviour while 'on report'. You were not satisfied because her behaviour still didn't match that of the rest of the class, but you could have acknowledged the improvements you saw. Positive reinforcement is very important.

With Susan you will need to work hard to resist 'manic vigilance' and 'overreaction' and to allow her choices and consequences. If she is misbehaving, calmly and quietly make clear what the consequences of continuing will be. She then has a choice. The consequences need not be draconian. The certainty of her knowing you will stick to your word is more important than the severity of the sanction or punishment, but you must always follow through. Susan is best spoken to at the end of a lesson in which there has been misbehaviour. Follow a pattern of questioning along these lines: What did you do? What were you thinking? What rule did you break? What would have been a better choice? What can I do to help you?

Sadly, Susan is likely to be a difficult pupil throughout her school career. You will only establish a better relationship with her when you can be more relaxed in her presence. Try and build a good relationship with the other pupils in the class. If the overall ethos in the classroom is positive you are doing well. Ask your mentor to observe you teaching this class and to offer advice on how you might better deal with Susan. If your mentor feels the situation is unmanageable, he may ask the usual class teacher to withdraw Susan from your lessons.

Summary

Managing behaviour will be a major challenge for you during your period of training. It is important that you don't think about behaviour management in isolation. If you plan effectively, matching work set to the ability of the pupils, and ensure your lessons are interesting, well structured and well paced, you will minimise the potential for misbehaviour. You should work on getting to know pupils as individuals and making sure that all your pupils feel valued; if you respect them they are more likely to respect you.

> Teaching has never just been about the transmission of knowledge and never will be. Establishing good relationships with pupils, encouraging them to learn to behave well have always been essential parts of a teacher's work. This cannot be achieved by talking at children, but by working with them.
>
> (DES 1989)

Don't fall into the trap of thinking that group management skills are simply a natural gift. There are tried and tested techniques which are guaranteed to assist you in making a success of classroom management. Some of these techniques have been outlined in this chapter. Consider them carefully and use them with the classes you teach. Try to avoid punishing whole classes for the misbehaviour of a few. Try not to back pupils into a corner – you have the power to offer them a way out. Use punishments sparingly and be creative. Above all else, reflect honestly on how your behaviour might be influencing the behaviour of your pupils.

Even the best teachers have difficulty in managing 'the class from hell' and particularly challenging pupils. Don't be too hard on yourself if you experience difficulties with particular classes and pupils that have a reputation for being hard to handle. Don't be embarrassed about seeking advice from your mentor or other colleagues. Listen to advice and try and learn from the strategies you see being employed by the teachers you are working with.

References

Bleach, K. (2000) *The Newly Qualified Teacher's Handbook*, London: Fulton.

DCSF (2009) *Learning Behaviour: Lessons Learned – A Review of Behaviour Standards and Practices in our Schools* (The Steer Report). Crown copyright 2009.

DES (1989) *Discipline in Schools* (The Elton Report), London: HMSO.

Elliott, A. (2009) 'Myth: Behaviour and Discipline in Schools Today are Far Worse than in the Past' in *Times Educational Supplement*, TES (11th October 2010).

Fontana, D. (1994) *Managing Classroom Behaviour*, Leicester: British Psychological Society.

Furlong, J. and Maynard, T. (1995) *Mentoring Student Teachers: The Growth of Professional Knowledge*, London: Routledge.

Mortimer, P. (1998) *The Road to Improvement: Reflections on School Effectiveness*, Lisse: Swetz & Zeitlinger.

Ofsted (2012) *The Evaluation Schedule for the Inspection of Maintained Schools and Academies*, Crown copyright.

Rogers, C. (1982) *A Social Psychology of Schooling: The Expectancy Process*, London: Routledge and Kegan Paul.

Watkins, C. and Wagner, P. (1987) *School Discipline: A Whole School Approach*, Oxford: Blackwell.

6

Inclusive practice

The challenge of meeting individual needs

Introduction

Inclusion is concerned with developing the full potential of *all* pupils so that as adults they can play an active part in society. Teachers have a duty to ensure that all pupils in their care, regardless of social background, culture, race, gender, ability and special needs and disabilities, are able to thrive and develop.

As a trainee, this responsibility can seem awesome. Nevertheless, it is a challenge you will need to rise to and having the right attitude is vital from the outset. If you see all pupils as unique individuals with a right to be educated, then you will accept that it is your duty as a teacher to do all you can to cater for their needs. If you have an inclusive frame of mind, you will welcome and celebrate diversity in your classroom and you will create an ethos in which all pupils feel valued. If you have taken on board the messages of the earlier chapters in this book, you will already appreciate that successful teaching and learning is all about creating the conditions in which individuals can thrive. You will already have a mindset that makes you determined to remove barriers to learning. Of course, you will not immediately understand how to meet the needs of all children with identified special needs, but you will have access to other professionals who do. Your commitment to ensure all pupils' needs are met and your acceptance that this will require you to differentiate your approach according to individual needs is what matters initially.

This chapter will briefly consider current interpretations of inclusion in the light of historical developments and legislation. It will provide examples of how the needs of particular groups might be met in order to illustrate the meaning of inclusion; discuss effective inclusive practice and provide a checklist in order for you to evaluate your own practice in terms of inclusion. It is not the purpose of this chapter to provide guidance on how to meet the needs of children with particular special educational needs. You will need to work on developing your understanding of how best to adjust your teaching to meet the needs of, for example, autistic pupils, pupils with dyslexia and those with attention deficit hyperactivity disorder (ADHD) during your training and early career. The Teachers Standards includes the following statement: teachers should

> have a clear understanding of the needs of all pupils, including those with special educational needs; those of high ability; those with English as an additional language; those with disabilities; and be able to use and evaluate distinctive teaching approaches to engage and support them.
>
> (DfE 2011)

Accept that developing relevant detailed knowledge will take time and you will continue learning long after your training year. Seek specialist advice from your school's inclusion manager or SEN co-ordinator and read specialist publications. Understanding your responsibilities under the SEN Code of Practice is something you must demonstrate and will thus be explained in this chapter.

Background

The drive for 'mainstreaming' or inclusion was motivated by a desire to reduce segregation in Education. The Warnock Report (DES 1978) identified that at any one time twenty per cent of the school population would have a need that would require special and additional assistance, and of these children only two per cent would have severe physical, sensory, intellectual or emotional difficulties. At the time, most of these two per cent were excluded from mainstream education. They were labelled and categorised and sent to special schools without ever being given the opportunity to experience a mainstream setting. Pressure began to grow from various quarters, including some teachers as well as many parents of these children, for mainstream education to be seen as a basic right for all. So, the push for 'mainstreaming' (integrating pupils with special needs into mainstream schools) became a driver for making educational institutions more inclusive. Alongside this, there was a growing realisation of the important role schools can play in delivering greater social equality. Across all political parties it was accepted that schools should do more to address the ways in which gender, ethnicity and social class as well as special educational needs produce differential patterns of attainment and achievement. Much legislation supported the drive for 'equality' in Education (Sex Discrimination Act 1975 and 1978, Race Relations Act 1976, Education Act 1981, 1996 and 1997, Disability Discrimination Act 1995, Special Educational Needs and Disability Act 2001, Equality Act 2010). Ofsted inspections now focus heavily on scrutinising patterns of achievement to ensure schools are meeting the needs of the diverse groups they serve.

With regard to children identified as 'disabled' the discussions and debates of the 1980s and 1990s often focused on how *disabled* and *non-disabled* children could be schooled together. Inclusion was seen as people learning together under the same roof, regardless of *weaknesses* they may have. The emphasis was on providing support within school to enable children with *disabilities* to 'cope' in the mainstream. Critics argued that this thinking was patronising (though well intentioned) defining some children as 'ordinary' and 'able' and others as 'disabled' and thus 'not able' (rather than 'differently able'). They suggested that this model of integration resulted in some mainstream teachers seeing 'differently able' pupils as lacking in some essential respect and thus a 'problem' because they didn't fit the stereotype of the ordinary child. A more appropriate model is that inclusive education values

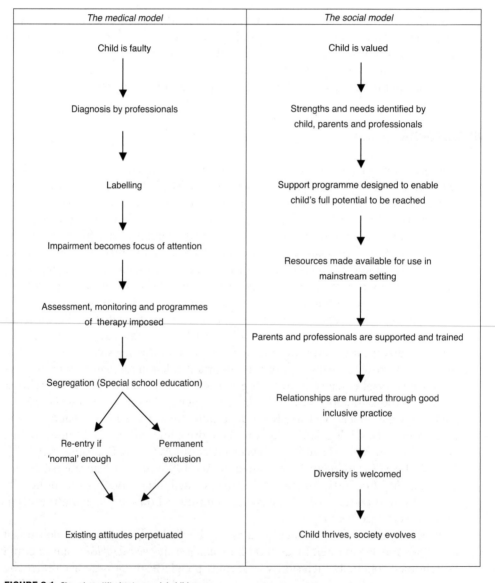

FIGURE 6.1 Changing attitudes to special children

all learners as individuals. Support services are provided for the learner in order that they might fulfil their potential. Diversity is celebrated. This approach requires school to address 'barriers to learning' and create an ethos in which all pupils are seen as unique individuals, to be valued for their differences. This should result in children growing up with less fear and prejudice than previous generations had as a result of segregated provision.

This shift from a medical model (in which the special child is seen as faulty) to a social model (in which difference is valued) has been challenging for teachers. There have been heated debates about the practicalities of mainstreaming, including the levels of support provided in mainstream schools, the cost of modifying buildings and the lack of specialist skills and training of mainstream teachers. Indeed, debates about the level of specialist support being provided for pupils in mainstream schools with clearly identified needs continue. However, few would now disagree that embracing the social model is important in a democratic and inclusive society in which all citizens are valued. As the Fish report (ILEA 1985) concluded, 'the potentially adverse effects of isolation and segregation, in whatever context, are now well-known, including the risks to social competence and to the development of a positive self-identity'.

Reflection point

How many arguments in favour of the social model of inclusion can you think of?

Here are ten very clear arguments cited by Judge (2003).

Human rights:
1. All children have the right to learn together.
2. Children should not be devalued or discriminated against by being excluded because of any differing learning needs they have whether they be based in their intellectual capabilities, their physical capabilities, their gender or their race.
3. Disabled adults, describing themselves as 'special school survivors', demand an end to segregation and exclusion.
4. There is no legitimate reason to separate children for their education.
   Children belong together – with advantages and benefits for everyone.
   They do not need to be protected from each other.

Good education:
5. Research shows that children achieve better both academically and socially in integrated settings.
6. There is no teaching or care, which can take place in a segregated school, which cannot take place in a mainstream school.

7. Given commitment and support inclusive education is a more efficient use of resources.

Social sense:

8. Segregation teaches children to be fearful, ignorant, and breeds prejudice.

9. All children need an education that will help them develop relationships and prepare them for life in the mainstream.

10. Only inclusion has the potential to reduce fear and to build friendships, respect and understanding.

Action point

When you are on school experience, ask a range of teachers for a definition of inclusion. Does everyone have the same understanding of what inclusion means? If not, why might this be so and what are the implications?

The SEN code of practice

In May 2001, legislation was passed which brought in significant amendments to the law governing the education of disabled pupils and those experiencing learning difficulties. The Special Educational Needs and Disability Act 2001 (SENDA) introduced a new Code of Practice. This emphasises that children with SEN should usually:

■ Be educated alongside other children in ordinary schools;

■ Have full access to a broad and balanced education, including the National Curriculum.

The Code recommends that schools should provide a graduated response to children with SEN by gradually increasing interventions in teaching and curriculum before embarking on statutory assessment and statementing procedures. Although most pupils with SEN will be identified in the early stages of schooling, there may be some who reach secondary school without their needs being identified. Also, there may be new arrivals to the system, such as recent immigrants, who have special needs. The stages involved in providing support are listed below:

Identification   Class teacher or form tutor identifies a child as having SEN, based on inadequate progress being made despite differentiation strategies being used.

School action   School informs parents that their child is considered to have SEN. The SEN coordinator gathers information from teachers and parents about the child. The SEN coordinator ensures that an individual education plan (IEP) is drawn up, working with the child's teachers to devise school-based interventions.

School action plus   The SEN coordinator brings in outside specialists to advise on further changes that could be made within school to meet the child's needs.

Statutory assessment   The Local Authority considers the need for statutory assessment and, if appropriate, makes a multi-disciplinary assessment.

Making a statement   The Local Authority considers the need for a statement of SEN and, if appropriate, makes a statement and arranges, monitors and reviews provision.

It is clear from this list that when you are on school experience you should:

- Know your school's SEN coordinator;
- In your classes try and meet pupils' needs through varied teaching and differentiation (sometimes called *quality first teaching* or *wave 1* provision);
- Monitor pupils' progress and behaviour carefully and discuss any pupils you feel might have SEN with their usual teacher and/or the SEN coordinator;
- Be aware of any pupils with IEPs and plan to support them in line with agreed strategies;
- Make sure you discuss your lesson plans with relevant support staff to ensure SEN pupils' learning needs are addressed;
- Keep records and evidence of progress made by pupils in your classes;
- Seek the advice of the SEN coordinator if you are unsure of how to meet SEN pupils' needs;
- Try and find time to read about how best to plan for and teach pupils with SEN.

A copy of the SEN Code of Practice and the SEN Toolkit produced to support the Code can be found on the DfE website, www.education.gov.uk. Another useful site to visit is www.nasen.org.uk

Identifying pupils with SEN

All pupils are individuals and in each classroom there will be diverse learning needs to be met. The term 'special' implies something beyond this usual diversity of needs; something out of the ordinary. Special children have a significantly greater difficulty in learning than the majority of children of the same age. They are likely to fall into one of the following categories:

- Pupils with severe learning difficulties including those with profound and multiple learning difficulties.

- Pupils with other learning difficulties including those with mild, moderate or specific learning difficulties, or those with emotional and behavioural difficulties.
- Pupils with physical or sensory impairment.
- Exceptionally able pupils.

Take care with pupils for whom English is an additional language. If they are making slow progress don't assume that this is because of their language status; they may have SEN. Pupils learning English go through clearly identified stages; they often say very little at first but are learning none the less. They benefit from stimulating learning environments but do not usually need individualised programmes. It is a good idea to seek specialist advice if you have pupils in your class who fall into this category.

Meeting the needs of pupils with SEN

All schools have a policy on SEN. This will identify the school's approach to meeting the needs of pupils with SEN. It is important that you obtain a copy of this policy for each school in which you are placed during your time as a trainee. A well-written policy will indicate how the school puts into practice their agreed philosophy on SEN. You should be able to see evidence of this in your department. All teachers are responsible for SEN pupils in their classes. Proof that this is taken seriously should be easy to find. There will be evidence of differentiated work being provided for identified pupils; schemes of work will identify possible activities and materials to support differentiation; there will be consultation between subject teachers and support staff or SEN teachers to decide on classroom approaches; there will be monitoring in place to assess the progress being made by pupils identified as having SEN and interventions in place for pupils not making expected progress.

As a trainee you should concentrate on developing good general classroom practice rather than specialist skills relating to SEN. Indeed according to NASEN (2000) 'good normal pedagogy' is the key to the inclusive classroom. Have high expectations and try and motivate all your pupils. If you single SEN youngsters out for too much of your attention this can be counterproductive and create dependency or resentment. However, you do need to be aware of some of the specific educational needs you are likely to encounter as a mainstream teacher and how you should address them.

Language impairment

Pupils in this group have limitations in understanding what is said to them (receptive impairments) or they find it difficult to convey thoughts in words (expressive impairments). This could be as a result of hearing impairment but is more likely to be linked to emotional and relationship difficulties. A speech and language therapist would usually provide specialist help for pupils with major difficulties. In class teachers can help by:

- Using visual aids and cues to the topics being discussed;
- Making sure the pupil is appropriately placed to hear and see;
- Explaining things several different ways if necessary;
- Repeating answers offered by pupils in discussions so that all pupils can hear clearly.

Cognition and learning

Dyslexia covers a wide range of needs but is most commonly associated with pupils experiencing difficulty with reading. Dyspraxia can be defined as difficulty in planning and carrying out skilled acts in the correct sequence. Difficulties with handwriting are a specific coordination issue. Autism is concerned with deficits in social interaction and communication skills (the inability to understand what another person is thinking or feeling) and repetitive behaviour. Experts believe that Asperger's syndrome and autism are on a continuum, with the former being less of an impairment.

How to teach children with these particular needs effectively will be something you need to work on well into your teaching career. You will need the support of staff with specialist knowledge and skills to begin with, and you should try and attend specialist courses during the first few years of your career, as part of your professional development. You can obtain further information from the British Dyslexia Association (www.bdadyslexia.org.uk) and the National Autistic Society (www.nas.org.uk).

Emotional and behavioural difficulties (EBD)

The definition 'emotional behavioural difficulties' is often applied to pupils whose behaviour is consistently poor or pupils who are withdrawn. These behaviours may be the result of having a special need, having a mental health need, or may be the result of an unsatisfactory school environment or an inappropriate curriculum. It is important to remember that your role in the management of such pupils is as a teacher, not a counsellor.

- Have high expectations.
- Praise successes, however small, to help build self esteem.
- Try and play to the strengths and interests of pupils with EBD.
- Be prepared to be flexible with classroom approaches.

Attention deficit disorder (ADD) and attention deficit hyperactivity disorder (ADHD) are medical diagnoses and pupils with ADHD may well be prescribed medication (Ritalin) to modify their behaviour (reduce activity). Behaviour associated with ADHD includes fidgeting, being easily distracted, being forgetful, being disrespectful of authority, interrupting others, having difficulty listening, talking incessantly and being incapable of following instructions. It is easy to see from this list that such a pupil in a class would require very careful management. Here are some general tips on how you might manage such children:

- Encourage a culture of tolerance in the group so that one child's misbehaviour doesn't disrupt the entire group.
- Work on self-esteem. Many ADHD sufferers have poor self-esteem.
- Try and establish routines, such as consistent seating. ADHD children respond well to routines.
- Seat ADHD children near to you and away from distractions such as windows.
- When talking to the pupil maintain eye contact.
- Encourage the child to use a planner to help structure his day (routines are important).
- Break the work set into timed sections with clear targets to aim for.
- Give one task at a time, not a series of tasks.
- Calmly insist on rules of politeness (such as not shouting out) and constantly reinforce these rules.
- Be aware that stress and fatigue can affect the ADHD child more severely than other children.
- As soon as bad behaviour starts employ distraction strategies.
- Give the ADHD child a job to do within a lesson, as this 'break' will help prevent disruptive behaviour.

Sensory and/or physical needs

Physical impairments may arise from physical, neurological or metabolic causes. Some children may require no more than appropriate access to buildings and equipment while others have more complex multi-sensory difficulties. You may have hearing impaired and/or visually impaired pupils in classes you teach. If so, it is likely that they will be using equipment to assist them in accessing the lesson (you may need to attach a microphone that will make you audible to a hearing impaired child, for example) and that they will have specialist support. Make sure you are aware of any such pupils and that you understand how they can get the maximum benefit from any equipment they have been supplied with. Being aware of the psychological implications for teenagers coming to terms with their self-identity as people with physical and/or sensory special needs is also important.

Remember that SEN pupils may face hostility from others and one of your duties is to break down such hostility. This is one of the aims of inclusion. Children who have physical disabilities such as cerebral palsy are sometimes treated as though their mental abilities are inferior to those of their peers, for example. Make sure that you avoid such prejudice and set the right example to your pupils. Interestingly, primary schools often find it easier to develop an inclusive ethos than do secondary schools. There are many factors that contribute to this, but without doubt the attitude of the teacher is central to successful integration.

Action point

Compile a brief report on one SEN pupil you encounter while on school experience. Write down the pupil's needs and explain how these are being met (access, differentiated work, deployment of support teacher or assistant, etc.). Also, consider the strengths shown by this pupil and note relationships s/he has with other pupils in the class. Share your case study with other trainees to identify the types of special needs you are likely to have to meet, possible strategies to employ and any particular difficulties that could arise. Remember, you may observe practice that is ineffective as well as good practice. If so, consider how the pupil concerned could be better supported.

Action point

You are responsible for deploying support staff in your lessons. Interview a support assistant. Find out what they would ideally like subject teachers to do to help them support SEN pupils effectively. Are there any practices that prevent them being effective? Be diplomatic and remember that you are trying to identify general principles and should not become involved in discussing the shortcomings of particular members of staff.

Pupils not making expected progress

Wave provision

In school, you will probably hear the terms *wave provision* and *additional and different* being used in reference to actions taken to support pupils not progressing in line with expectation, particularly in Literacy and Numeracy. There are three stages (or waves) in provision (see Figure 6.2). At Wave 1 the teacher takes into account the needs of all pupils in the class and differentiates approaches and learning materials accordingly. This *quality first teaching* will ensure most pupils' individual needs are met. At Wave 2 the school provides specific, time limited interventions for specific pupils or groups of pupils in order to help accelerate their progress so that their needs can be met through Wave 1 provision. Reading intervention programmes are typical Wave 2 provision. Wave 3 describes targeted provision for a minority of children where highly tailored and specialised interventions, often on a one to one basis, are needed.

Cultivating inclusive qualities

While the term 'inclusion' and 'SEN' often appear together, meeting the needs of SEN pupils is only part of being an inclusive teacher. As stated in the introduction, inclusion is about enabling all children to thrive while in school. In Chapter 2 we explored what makes a good teacher. It is worth now restating some particular qualities and practices that you will need as an inclusive teacher.

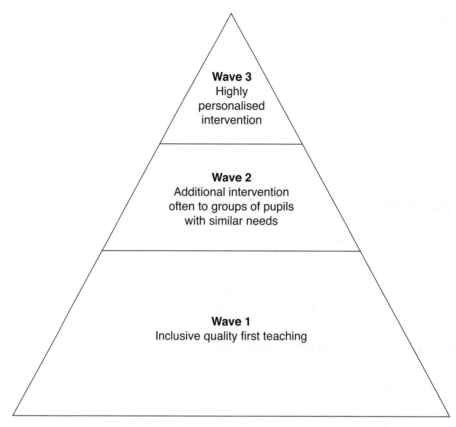

FIGURE 6.2 Waves of intervention model

- Understanding – realise that many pupils struggle to understand school work so don't respond to their efforts negatively.
- Encouragement – recognise all pupils' efforts and offer opportunities for all pupils to speak and contribute in class.
- Sensitivity – treat all pupils as individuals and help all pupils to feel successful.
- Expectation – model good behaviour, expect all pupils to concentrate, ensure there is challenge for all abilities in your class.
- Respect – believe all pupils matter and help them to respect themselves as well as others; don't allow pupils to show disrespect to each other.
- Creativity – make work relevant to pupils' lives, capture pupils' imagination.
- Flexibility – be prepared to adapt your lesson in the light of children's understanding and their changing moods.
- Critical reflection – monitor your own practice and review the progress of pupils regularly, using attainment data to inform your judgements.

These qualities and behaviours may seem obvious, but it is important not to treat them lightly. Seeing all pupils as worthy of your time and effort may not be as easy as it sounds. The first step is to engage in a thorough examination of your own values and attitudes. Why did you decide to train as a teacher? Was it by default (you couldn't think of anything else to do) or because you had a real desire to teach (you want to make a real difference in the lives of young people)? If the former, you might find it difficult to find the energy needed to engage the interest of pupils who are not very positive about education. What do you think of various groups in society (refugees, gypsies, Muslims, families on benefits, etc.)? You will teach pupils from these groups, and your attitude towards them will influence their learning. Nobody is entirely free of prejudice. You need to think about how your attitudes influence your daily behaviour and how they might influence your behaviour in the classroom. For example, Gillborn (1990) writes that white teachers sometimes regard black boys as threatening. The result has been either an unfair level of discipline imposed on black boys, or fear of reprimanding them leading to deterioration in behaviour.

It is important that you really do have high expectations of all pupils. Research has shown that underachievement is in part connected to teachers' expectations (Blair 2001). It is illogical to think that teachers are any less affected by racist and prejudicial attitudes than other members of society. The important thing is to accept this and act to overcome stereotypes you may have of particular groups. In practical terms this means getting to know pupils as individuals and not assuming that their behaviour or performance is explained by their class, gender or racial group. Effective schools monitor the achievement of pupils by gender, ethnic group and economic status. If particular groups perform less well than they should (based on prior attainment and national comparisons) teachers analyse why this is so and take action to address the situation.

Respecting pupils is straightforward, at one level. It involves not being rude and being prepared to listen to pupils' concerns. At another level, respecting pupils is more complex. It means being aware of cultural differences and taking these into account in your behaviour towards them. As a trainee, try hard to see other cultures as interesting, not inferior, and be keen to learn from your pupils about their rich and varied backgrounds. Once pupils know that you are genuinely interested they will be very keen to share their knowledge with you.

Prejudice and discrimination can affect the emotional, social and intellectual development of all pupils. Self-esteem, behaviour and ability to learn can all be adversely affected when pupils become the victims of racist behaviour. If racism goes unchallenged we are in danger of inadvertently contributing to the growth of a divided society, with all the hostilities and mistrust that follows. In terms of white youngsters, failure to challenge racism towards black people can lead them to ignore the contribution and achievements of black people and prevent them developing empathy with others (TTA 2000). It is very important to ensure you challenge all racist attitudes and behaviour as part of your approach to effective inclusive practice.

In relation to the curriculum you teach, it is important to ask yourself if the content and delivery have been made as inclusive as possible. Good, reflective teachers modify content and delivery according to the needs and backgrounds of the pupils they teach. The checklist provided in Table 6.1 should help you to reflect on the meaning of inclusive, which should in turn help you when planning. Information on helping to support pupils with English as an additional language (EAL) can be found in Chapter 10.

TABLE 6.1 Inclusion checklist

HOW INCLUSIVE ARE MY LESSONS?	*TICK*
SCHEMES OF WORK	
Allowing for the constraints of the National Curriculum do they consider pupils':	
– cultural backgrounds?	_____
– gender?	_____
– learning styles?	_____
– disability status?	_____
– English language proficiency?	_____
– values and experience?	_____
Do they take account of pupils' prior knowledge?	_____
Do they include opportunities for positive engagement with different cultures and practices?	_____
Do they include texts and/or resources that reflect a variety of perspectives?	_____
LESSON CONTENT	
Does it:	
– Acknowledge the diversity of knowledge and experience of the pupils?	_____
– Use examples and case studies free of negative stereotypes?	_____
– Encourage students to understand different ways of knowing?	_____
DELIVERY	
In my lesson do I:	
– Provide a variety of learning opportunities?	_____
– Take into account that different learners have different preferred learning styles?	_____
– Incorporate opportunities for feedback so that I can address the needs of any children who have not understood the work?	_____
– Ensure that I direct questions equally to boys and girls?	_____

Action point

Use the checklist in Table 6.1 when you are planning lessons. Make a note of any barriers to inclusion you encounter. Discuss these with fellow trainees and your college tutor.

Summary

Inclusion is currently high on the national education agenda. It is central to raising the attainment of all pupils. Inclusion is a complex concept, which includes integrating pupils with SEN into ordinary schools as well as creating approaches to teaching and learning that ensure that all pupils are able to participate and achieve, regardless of their background. Inclusion is essentially about making education accessible to all. It is fundamentally important, therefore, that you develop an inclusive mindset if you are to be effective as a teacher. You should celebrate diversity, value each child and see it as your responsibility to create a classroom ethos in which pupils respect each other and where all are expected to achieve. In order to do this, you must reflect on prejudices and assumptions you may hold about particular groups as a result of your upbringing and experience to date. You must then make a determined effort to counter these by getting to know pupils as individuals.

It is not possible during training for you to become an expert on how to address the needs of pupils diagnosed with special needs such as dyslexia and autism. Pupils with these needs will have support programmes and you should seek advice from the SEN coordinator about how best to meet their needs whilst you are in the school. Towards the end of your training you will complete a Career Entry and Development Profile in which you identify further development needs. You should consider making SEN a priority for further development during Induction. You can then expect to be given support with developing SEN strategies as part of your Induction programme. Set yourself the goal of learning as much as you can about SEN during your first few years as a teacher.

References

Blair, M. (2001) *Why Pick on Me? School Exclusion and Black Youth*, Stoke on Trent: Trentham Books.

DES (1978) *Special Educational Needs: Report of the Committee of Enquiry into the Education of Handicapped Children and Young People* (The Warnock Report). London: HMSO.

DfE (2011) *Teachers' Standards*, Crown copyright.

Gillborn, D. (1990) *'Race', Ethnicity and Education*, London: Unwin Hyman.

ILEA (1985) *Educational Opportunities for All: Report of the Committee Reviewing Provision to meet Special Educational Needs* (The Fish Report), London: Inner London Education Authority.

Judge, B. (2003) 'Inclusive Education: principles and practices' in Crawford, K. (ed.) *Contemporary Issues in Education*, Dereham: Peter Francis Publications.

National Association for Special Educational Needs (2000) 'Specialist Training for Special Educational Needs and Inclusion' Policy Paper 4 in the *SEN Fourth Policy Options* series, London: NASEN.

TTA (2000) *Raising the Attainment of Ethnic Minority Pupils*, London: TTA.

7

Assessment

Introduction

Assessment is concerned with evaluative observation or measurement of pupils and classes. It covers all the activities undertaken by teachers that measure the impact of teaching and learning. In recent years assessment has been given much greater emphasis in schools. When I was trained as a teacher in the late 1970s, this aspect of teachers' work was certainly given far less prominence than it is today. I recall discussing at great length the content of lessons and how to make my subject interesting and accessible but I can remember far fewer conversations with tutors or teachers about assessment. Marking pupils' work, testing and examining took place, of course, but it seemed to me as a trainee that there was little critical discussion of the processes or the purposes of assessment.

The situation is now very different. With much greater accountability, assessment processes have come under much closer external scrutiny. Also, teachers are now more aware of how assessment can be used to improve pupils' performance. Indeed, effective use of performance data by teachers *with pupils* is helping many schools to raise levels of attainment and achievement. Assessment, recording and reporting are, in fact, an integral part of any good teacher's repertoire of professional practice. It is therefore important that you develop a good knowledge and understanding of assessment during your time as a trainee teacher.

This chapter is intended to help you understand why and how we assess pupils' work and how schools can use assessment data to help pupils improve their performance. You will be introduced to technical terms associated with assessment and will be provided with guidance on best practice in assessment. How schools use data for target setting will be explained and the downside of the current culture of assessment and target setting will also be discussed.

The purpose of assessment

Action point

Think about why we assess pupils. Make a list and share this with a group of fellow trainees. Think about your education to date. List the various ways in which you have been assessed. Discuss with your peers which methods had a positive or negative effect on your progress or attitude and why.

There are various purposes of assessment. Here are some of the likely points from your list:

- To establish how much pupils have learnt from your teaching;
- To help teachers with future planning;
- To evaluate how well the curriculum has been delivered;
- To rank pupils in order of attainment;
- To place pupils in appropriate sets, groups and classes;
- To identify individual pupil learning needs;
- To help pupils decide which subjects to study in Key Stage 4 and Key Stage 5;
- To help pupils consider possible career options;
- To report pupils' progress to parents;
- To provide information to school managers, governors, employers and inspectors;
- To provide data for league tables;
- To prepare pupils to participate in public examinations;
- To determine the grades awarded in public examinations;
- To fulfil the statutory requirement to assess, record and report pupils' progress in National Curriculum subjects;
- To enable pupils to understand more fully how well they are progressing and how they might improve further.

You may have other points on your list; the points above do not constitute an exhaustive list nor are they in any order of importance. To help us understand the main uses of assessment for teachers let us consider the following functions:

1. *Diagnostic* assessment is used to focus on what a pupil or pupils can and cannot do. It is intended to shed light on misunderstandings and misconceptions and to reveal learning difficulties. Teachers use the information gained from diagnostic assessment to put in place appropriate provision for pupils. Formal diagnostic assessment for whole cohorts is sometimes used at transition points in schooling, for example with new cohorts of pupils joining a secondary school from various feeder primary schools.

2. *Formative* assessment is sometimes called *assessment for learning*. It is used to decide what a pupil or class needs to do next in order to make progress. Teachers use formative assessment to inform future planning. They will also adjust what they do *within a lesson* in the light of assessing learning *as they teach* (for example, by well chosen questions). Better use of formative assessment is seen as key to raising attainment and now features heavily in Ofsted inspections. Involving pupils in understanding what they need to do to improve can be a powerful tool. Meaningful targets can be set for pupils on the basis of formative assessment.

As a mainstream subject teacher you will rarely distinguish between diagnostic and formative assessment in your work. You will use formative assessment opportunities (questioning, observing, discussing, marking) to help you diagnose support needed for pupils in your classes. However, you will work with other professionals who are likely to use a variety of carefully designed diagnostic tools to assess pupils with particular educational needs. For example, pupils joining a school who do not have English as their first language will need to be assessed for very specific help, as will pupils with dyslexia.

3. *Summative* assessment is assessment of learning (as opposed to assessment *for* learning). It is used to measure *attainment* (pupil outcomes usually expressed as scores and grades) as well as *achievement* (progress made by pupils). It is typically end-point assessment, used to inform others of pupils' progress and for the awarding of grades for certificates, etc. Summative assessment is used managerially and politically for accountability purposes. For example, school effectiveness is judged in large part on pupils' performance in terminal examinations such as GCSE or Standard Assessment Tasks (SATs). While making clear where pupils (and teachers and schools) stand in the pecking order, summative assessments don't help pupils (or schools) to understand how to improve their performance in the future unless summative assessment information is used formatively (i.e. used to improve future teaching and learning). Put simply, the act of weighing a pig regularly doesn't help it get any fatter. However, using the information from weighing to inform changes to the pig's diet (or the diet of other pigs in the future) can!

Types of assessment

There are three main categories of assessment.

1. *Criterion-referenced* assessment refers to measuring a person's level of knowledge, skills and understanding against pre-agreed standards for the task. Driving tests and instrumental music exams are good examples of this kind of assessment. Also, some vocational awards use pre-specified learning outcomes against which students are assessed. Criterion-referenced exams are not designed to

establish a rank order; they are designed to determine which candidates do or do not fulfil the criteria (and therefore pass or fail).

2. *Norm-referenced* assessment refers to measuring a pupil's levels of attainment in relation to what is considered normal for a particular age group. Thus, normative assessment makes comparisons between a learner's performance and the performance of other learners. This may be within a class, a year group or even nationally, depending on the assessment in question. SATs at the end of Key Stage 2 are norm referenced, with level 4 the expected level of attainment of an eleven-year-old.

3. *Ipsative* assessment is used to help a learner consider their individual performance. Instead of measuring their performance against other learners (norm referencing) or against specified objectives (criteria referencing), a learner's performance is measured against their previous attainment. The concept of 'personal best' in athletics is an example of the use of ipsative assessment.

Whatever assessment approaches are used in schools, it is important that all involved are aware of their possible limitations. Although we live in times of league tables and what sometimes seems to be obsessive comparisons in performance between schools based on pupils' performance in national tests, it is worth noting that in recent years, there has been much nationally publicised challenging of examination results, suggesting that people in general are increasingly aware of the flaws in any system of assessment. Two concepts are important in relation to the *trustworthiness* of assessment:

■ *Validity* is the extent to which an assessment technique assesses exactly what it is intended to assess. We know that in the past some exams were badly designed and that for this reason they failed accurately to assess aptitude for and/or learning in the subject area. Take History as an example. It is acknowledged that part of being good at History involves being able to interpret and evaluate sources. An examination paper that asked pupils simply to recall information would not, therefore, provide an accurate indication of candidates' aptitude for History. It would provide an indication of their ability to learn key facts and figures, but this is not the same thing as being good at History. It is very important that in designing tests and assessments, teachers are careful to ensure that pupils are given the opportunity to show what they know, understand and can do. Some pupils never manage to show their full understanding in a subject, because their ability to write is a barrier. Don't assume that untidy, badly written responses don't contain evidence of a good level of understanding of the concepts associated with your subject. Many clever boys write very untidily! Likewise, don't phrase questions in such a way that the language used becomes a barrier for pupils. There should be no ambiguity in what you are asking of candidates.

■ *Reliability* refers to the extent to which an assessment can be trusted. Usually, assessments are seen as reliable if they produce similar results when repeated.

In other words, if a pupil sat a given test on two separate occasions s/he would perform similarly both times; likewise different teachers marking the test would award the same score. Although it is impossible to create a totally reliable assessment method, examination boards maximise reliability by using uniform mark schemes and employing moderation and standardisation procedures. In schools, effective departments use a similar approach to ensure that all teachers' judgements about pupils are trustworthy. If particular teachers are especially generous or particularly strict in their marking, this can be very confusing for pupils. Consistency between teachers within a department is very important.

Good practice in assessment

All of the above may sound very technical. It is worth simplifying matters now by considering some key points about assessment that you need to get right.

Using assessment to inform planning

Assessment is part of the 'planning loop' (Figure 7.1). You should use assessment to help you develop as a reflective practitioner. When you are evaluating how a lesson has gone, you will take into account responses from pupils given during the lesson. The plenary session should help you to get a sense overall of the learning that has taken place. However, wait until you have looked at the work done by

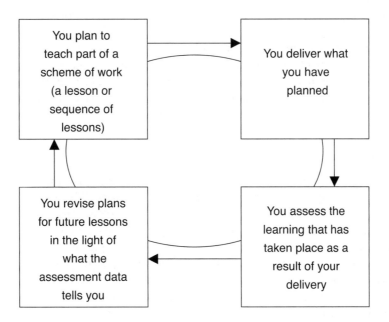

FIGURE 7.1 The planning loop

pupils before you decide on how effective the lesson has been. You may find that not all pupils have understood the concepts you covered. Use the information you gather from marking to inform the planning of your next lesson. If it is clear that particular children or groups of children have only partially understood what you have taught them, decide what you will do about this in the next lesson. You can't just plough through a scheme of work if some children in your class are being 'left behind' (though you might, of course, expect different levels of understanding – this is where differentiation is important). If you don't take learning from one lesson into account when planning the next disruptive behaviour may well be the result. You will need to modify your teaching programme if evidence of learning suggests this is necessary. Remember, learning doesn't *automatically* result from teaching and this is why monitoring through assessment is so important. The usefulness of informal, ongoing monitoring cannot be underestimated.

Using a variety of assessment techniques

Try and use a variety of assessment techniques with pupils. Remember, different people have different preferred learning styles and it follows from this that using a very limited range of assessment approaches is likely to disadvantage certain types of learner. Obviously, you have to be realistic. To some extent, the subject you teach will dictate the assessment approaches possible and the time you have available is another factor. Ultimately, you are preparing your pupils for the assessments they will face for certification, but if you concentrate on using only very formal and traditional approaches to assessment this will be very de-motivating for some of your pupils. It is sometimes possible to give pupils a sense of power by allowing them to choose how they will be assessed. For example, in RE if pupils have been researching the work of aid organizations, they could be offered the opportunity to present their findings in the form of an essay, an interview, a leaflet or a short play. All these possibilities will enable you to decide whether or not pupils have understood the role and impact of aid organisations. The critical thing will be to share with pupils in advance the criteria you will use in making your judgements about their level of understanding.

Involving pupils

Spending a lot of time marking pupils' work is of little value unless the pupils are going to be helped to improve as a result of this process. This is why *assessment for learning* is now such a high priority in schools. It is not long ago that many teachers were still assessing without the information gathered being used to help pupils move on: 'Teachers often give insufficient guidance to pupils about how to improve their work and provide few opportunities for pupils to reflect on comments' (Ofsted 2003). There is now an expectation that teachers will make clear to pupils how to improve and inspectors will look for 'how well pupils understand how to improve their learning as a result of frequent, detailed and accurate feedback from teachers following assessment of their learning' (Ofsted 2012). Never underestimate the importance of oral feedback as a means of achieving this. Try and get into the habit of marking some pupils' books each lesson as they are working. Spend a few minutes with each pupil discussing their work (you will get round the whole class over a series of lessons). This one to one feedback can be very powerful; it gives an opportunity for you to praise pupils but also help them with particular difficulties they may have. Encouraging pupils to proof-read, self-correct and redraft is made easier when you are able to discuss a particular piece of work with them.

It is important that in involving pupils you assess their approach to learning as well as their academic achievement. Pupils need to understand how to improve their knowledge, understanding and interpretation, but they also need to be able to work on their approach to learning. For example, personal and social skills, motivation and commitment all impact on achievement. According to Dweck (2006) a person's 'mindset' can have a lot to do with their chances of success in life. Those with a fixed mindset believe their intelligence is fixed whereas those with a growth mindset believe their intelligence can be expanded. Involving pupils in assessment, therefore, should include helping them to cultivate a growth mindset by giving them skills for learning. Getting them to reflect on how well they work with others, how they deal with disappointing results, how they organise their workload are all important. Of course, form tutors will play a major role in this area, but subject teachers cannot ignore the importance of pupils' approach to learning and may need to give clear guidance and set targets for pupils in this area before good academic progress can be made.

Making assessment for learning fun

A lot of assessment for learning techniques can actually add interest to your lessons as well as providing you with valuable information. Here are just a few examples of fun activities that will shed light on pupils' understanding:

- Find the Fib – display three statements about the lesson topic. Get pupils to explain which one is false and why.

- Exit ticket – near the end of a lesson ask the class a question. Give each student an index card on which to write the answer. As pupils leave they hand in the card. You use their answers when planning your next lesson.

- Be the Teacher – at the end of a lesson get the pupils to suggest what the learning objectives for the next lesson should be.

- Class Basketball – pupils stand and you pass a soft ball to one of them. This pupil gives one main idea from the lesson and then passes the ball to someone else. This pupil then has to add another idea and then pass the ball on again. Once a pupil has had the ball they sit down. The activity continues until you feel all the key ideas have been covered.

Remember, although these activities are fun, their primary purpose is to help you as a teacher assess learning and adjust your planning accordingly. Many more examples can be found on line (for example, http://twostarsandawish.co.uk).

Sharing assessment criteria with pupils

In effective departments National Curriculum level statements have been translated into 'pupil speak' and shared with pupils. These might be displayed on notice boards or given to pupils to keep in their books. Some departments provide all pupils with a simplified version of level statements and encourage pupils to assess their own level of achievement by ticking statements they felt apply to their work and level of understanding. Teachers look at pupils' self-assessments and where there is a mismatch between what pupils think about their level of achievement and what teachers think a discussion takes place to help pupils understand more clearly what is expected for each level. This empowering of pupils is very important. How can anyone know how they are doing if they are not provided with statements about what is expected?

At GCSE and 'A' level it is excellent practice to share marking criteria for various grades with the pupils. Examples of work awarded different grades can be given to pupils so that they begin to understand what is required at each level. They can be asked to mark some responses that you have prepared to see if they are able to apply the criteria successfully. Soon, they will be able to assess the quality of their own work much more objectively as they will now have the tools to do so. If the ethos of the class is good, pupils can be encouraged to mark each other's work in pairs or small groups. This is particularly useful in 'A' level classes, but care must be taken to get pairings right to avoid any pupils being adversely affected by the process. Again, this empowerment can be a very effective way of raising performance. It is really quite bizarre to think that until fairly recently pupils in many schools went in for exams never having seen the criteria that would be used to assess their answers and never having seen examples of what constituted the kind of good answers examiners would be looking for. Simplified examples for pupils of the kinds of answers needed to achieve different levels in national tests and GCSE exams are available both in printed revision aids and online (for example, www.bbc.co.uk/schools/revision).

Of course, it will not be possible to have detailed criteria for every piece of work you set. Most of the day-to-day work will be marked using the school or department's marking policy. Make sure you understand how marks and grades are used (there may be grades for effort as well as achievement, for example). Where possible, use appropriate examples of pupils' work to show the level you want pupils to aim for. Many departments hold a store of appropriate work from previous years for this purpose. Having examples of what can be achieved on display can be helpful.

Getting your judgements right

Before using mark schemes with pupils you must feel secure that you fully understand how to apply them. As with all other aspects of teaching, you need to learn from experienced teachers. It is possible that your training provider will arrange for you to undertake some trial marking away from school. If not, you need to seek guidance from your mentor in school. If possible, look at examples of GCSE course work or internal exams that have been marked and graded. If pupils sit tests and exams while you are on school experience make sure you volunteer to share the marking and to be involved in moderation meetings that take place. Scrutinise the questions set carefully and ask yourself if the language and instructions aid pupil success or act as barriers. Look carefully at the mark schemes used and reflect critically on their appropriateness. You might even be given the opportunity to attend an examination board training session with colleagues.

Providing feedback

It has already been suggested that marking criteria should be shared with pupils when significant pieces of work to be used for target setting (formative) or grading (summative) are given. This will help them to make sense of the marks they get. Your comments need to help pupils be able to improve and so you should try and make clear both what they have done well and what they need to work on. Even the weakest pupils will get something right and this will need to be praised. It is important that you then provide concrete guidance on what they can do to improve their performance. Simple and manageable targets need to be set. Your ability to break down the skills associated with your subject into steps is very important here. Don't write a long list of ways to improve; focus on a maximum of three things that can be done, otherwise most pupils will simply feel overwhelmed. Likewise, don't turn a piece of work into a sea of red ink by correcting every minor grammar and spelling error. Not only will this take you a long time, it is likely to demoralise the pupil, who will feel that there is no hope of improvement. It is better that you concentrate on a few key words, and make these targets for improvement.

As regards written feedback for parents, you will need to follow the report writing procedures used by your particular school. Some schools use computer generated reports, some use a record of achievement approach (with pupils' comments featuring alongside teachers' comments) and some use a more traditional style of report. Whatever reporting mechanism is used, you will be expected to be able to report pupils' achievement against national expectations; simply commenting on performance in relation to the rest of the class is of little use. Always make sure that you have clear evidence to back up any statements you make about pupils' achievement. Always mention pupils' attitudes to learning and study and their behaviour in class; these are of great interest to parents and are things that parents may be able to influence. Try and include simple guidance on how pupils can improve their performance. Remember to be sensitive and as positive as possible in the way you express yourself. Upsetting parents and pupils through sarcasm or negativity (however tempted you may feel) will help no one. Most parents want their children to do well and will be willing to be supportive if treated reasonably.

Keeping things manageable

Although assessment is important, you have to ensure that this aspect of your work is manageable as you have so many other equally important things to do. You will find that some teachers spend too much time on mundane aspects of assessment (such as marking pupils' books) with little evidence that their efforts improve pupils' learning and attainment. As already stated, clear feedback (based on accurate marking) relating to pieces of work to be used with pupils formatively is very important. Likewise, marking exams and course work must be done with great care. However, when it comes to marking pupils' exercise books you will find it is impossible to check these with the same attention to detail given to more significant pieces of work. You need to get a sense that what has been covered in class has been understood, but you can't be expected to correct every mistake in grammar and spelling. As discussed above, this can be counter-productive anyway. As a trainee and NQT you could so easily become overwhelmed with marking. You will need to work hard at time management and the following tips relating to marking should be helpful:

- Be flexible – some pieces of work can be treated with a light touch (monitoring) whereas others will require very detailed marking (assessment for learning).
- Try and mark some pupils' books during lessons – this will help with monitoring and will give you a chance to assess and improve pupils' understanding by talking to them.
- Think carefully about your lessons – not everything has to be written down! Learning can occur without writing taking place; equally pupils may have several pages of notes that they don't understand at all. Remember, it may be appropriate for pupils to present their ideas in the form of a diagram or poster rather than formal notes, so plan learning activities with care.
- Avoid using written work as a tool for class control. Giving pupils work to do in order to keep them quiet will simply generate mountains of marking!
- If you come across common errors as you monitor understanding, instead of giving all pupils detailed written feedback, go over the errors verbally with the class as a whole.
- As stated already, it is sometimes appropriate for pupils to mark their own work or each other's work.
- Don't forget that day-to-day assessment includes the use of questioning, observing pupils, discussing points with groups and individuals and making good use of the plenary. Doing these things effectively doesn't take any extra time but will provide valuable information which should inform your short-term planning.

Assessment and pupil progress

We have seen how *assessment for learning* can be used to help pupils improve their understanding and hence their performance in formal tests and exams (summative assessment). Formative assessment, including setting targets for pupils, can be used even more meaningfully if we have a realistic idea of what each pupil is capable of achieving. Increasingly, secondary schools have access to a wealth of data that can be used to make judgements about pupils' potential and about how effective the school and individual teachers have been in moving pupils on (adding value). RAISE on line (Reporting and Analysis for Improvement through school Self-Evaluation) data is provided by the Department for Education (DfE) and used to judge the performance of schools. Similarly, Fischer Family Trust (FFT) data on schools is used to set targets and analyse performance. In addition, some schools use cognitive ability tests (CATs) to identify pupils' potential and some use commercial packages such as Durham University's Year 11 Information System (YELLIS) and 'A' level information system (Alis) to help them review their pupils' performance. In short, a whole data industry around pupil performance has grown up in the last two decades and schools are now so data rich the challenge is how best to use all the analyses available in a meaningful way with teachers and pupils.

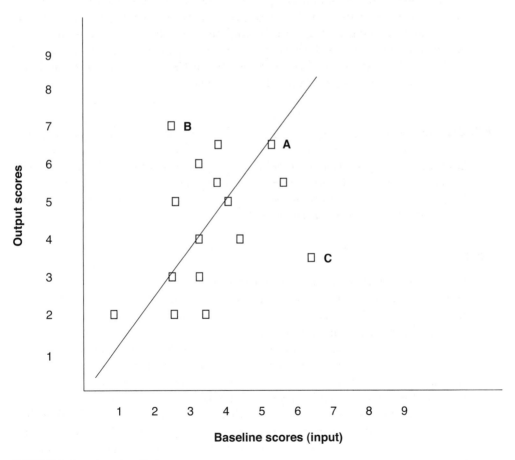

FIGURE 7.2 Measuring value added

It is not important at this stage to name and explain all of the data that schools receive (either from the DfE or through commercial packages) but it is important that you understand the basic principles involved in measuring pupil progress. At the start of a new phase of schooling a baseline assessment is used against which future progress can be measured. For example, Key Stage 2 SATs scores provide a good indication of what pupils should achieve by the end of Key Stage Three and Key Stage Four. In turn, GCSE results can be used for predicting 'A' level performance. Statistical chances graphs indicate the likelihood of pupils achieving particular results given their prior attainment (used as baseline scores). Targets can be set for pupils and progress can be tracked based on these predictions. At the end of a Key Stage summative assessment information is used to provide 'value added' information, showing how far pupils have progressed. This data is certainly more useful than league tables based on 'raw' exam results, but the information still needs to be handled carefully as there are many reasons why individual children achieve below, at, or above their predicted level. Having said this, at the level of a class, subject or school if a pattern of pupils consistently achieving below expectation is uncovered, probing questions will need to be asked. In most schools, each head of department will analyse pupils' performance as part of the yearly review and action planning process. Individual teachers and teams should be involved in discussions with their subject leader as part of this process. Individual teachers will also discuss pupils' results as part of their appraisal, as they are likely to have had targets set around pupil performance.

Action point

Look at Figure 7.2. Imagine this is value added information for your 'A' level class. The baseline represents GCSE results converted to a numerical score. The output scores represent 'A' level grades converted to a numerical score. Are you happy with the performances shown? Make particular reference to students B and C.

Reflection

Overall, your students have achieved broadly in line with expectation. This is shown by the regression line, with student A and three others performing exactly as predicted, based on prior achievement. Most other students are clustered close to the regression line. Some have performed slightly better than expected and others slightly worse. This is quite normal; predicted grades are not a guarantee of performance, they provide a statistical indication of likely performance based on what previous cohorts of students have achieved from the same starting points. Student B has done exceptionally well, performing much better than predicted. Sadly, student C has done much worse than expected. If you are able to analyse why student C did less well than expected and use this knowledge to prevent this happening to other students in future, you will have used summative data in a formative way to improve future performance.

While these results seem alright overall, a word of caution needs adding. If all the students above the line belong to a distinct category and all those below to a different category there could be an issue that needs addressing. For example, if all your boys achieved better than your girls or if a particular minority ethnic group were all below the line then you would need to think carefully about how to improve the situation. If these patterns reflected a school-wide situation, Ofsted would be very concerned.

Given that you know predicted performance at the start of a phase of schooling (in this case the start of Year Twelve) it is possible to use this to track and monitor students' progress and take action when it seems that there is underperformance. Some schools do this very systematically by asking for data on performance at regular intervals from all subject areas. Subject teachers, form tutors, Heads of Year and/or Key Stage leaders then use this information with individual pupils to discuss performance and set targets. It is a very powerful tool for motivating those who are working hard and performing above expectation as well as catching those who seem to be achieving below par. The data allows meaningful, well-focused discussions to take place, based on reliable evidence of what a student is capable of.

Assessment as a professional issue

Assessment has become a hotly debated area of educational policy over the last twenty years. Many educationalists have argued that assessment used formatively has the potential to raise standards of achievement significantly (Black and Williams 1998; Murphy 1999; Black et al 2004). By contrast, politicians have seen using summative assessment data as a means of comparing the performance of schools for accountability purposes and to assist in the creation of an educational market place in which parents make choices about where their children will be schooled based on judgements informed in part by school performance data (Gerwitz et al 1995) There now exists a complex framework of assessment structures for state school pupils and some critics argue that school improvement has become synonymous with improvements in pupils' examination scores and 'teaching to the test' is widespread. Focusing on preparing pupils for formal assessments is certainly a key priority for schools and target setting with pupils is well established. Despite significant improvements in SATs scores and GCSE and 'A' level over time, this focus on assessment is greatly criticised by many teachers and educationalists.

Reflection point

What arguments do you think are used by those who oppose the current focus on assessment and target setting in our schools?

There are many arguments offered by objectors. It is not possible in this short chapter to go into all of these arguments or to cite the supporting evidence. Nevertheless, a list of a few of the key points is provided below.

- The curriculum and teaching may become distorted in order simply to raise a school's position in the league tables. For example, pupils may be encouraged to opt for certain GCSE subjects or vocational equivalents seen as easier so that they will have more chance of gaining a higher grade. There may be a lot of 'teaching to the test' rather than exploring a subject in more detail. This 'surface learning' can enable pupils to jump through examination hoops but doesn't help them to develop a deep understanding of a subject.

- Ranking schools in league tables increases social polarisation. Middle class parents choose to send their children to schools where results are 'good', thus increasing the likelihood of some schools becoming 'sink schools'.

- Holding schools and teachers accountable for results suggests that they are in a position to make a bigger difference than they really can. This takes attention away from other factors, such as social deprivation, which are outside teachers' control. 'While schools can and do make a difference, what they can achieve is partial and limited, because schools are also part of a wider society, subject to its norms, rules and influences' (Mortimore and Whitty 1997).

- Equating school effectiveness with examination results marginalizes so many features of education that are not easily measurable. 'Most of the educational aims which parents, teachers and ordinary citizens think important – happiness, personal autonomy, moral goodness, imaginativeness, civil mindedness . . . do not appear to be measurable' (White and Barber 1997).

As you undertake your training it is important that you reflect on some of the wider educational debates such as assessment. Listen to colleagues' comments, read the educational press and observe what is happening in the schools you visit. This will enable you to develop an informed position in relation to these arguments. The provision of education cannot be divorced from politics, and as a professional you need to become acquainted with the key areas of debate.

Action point

As you near the end of your main school experience, you need to ask yourself the following questions. Your answers may identify possible areas for development in your Induction year.

- Do you use a variety of assessment approaches?
- Can you be sure that you are accurate and consistent in your assessment judgements?
- Does your assessment help pupils to improve their performance? Where is your evidence?
- Does your assessment help you to identify pupils' strengths and weaknesses?
- Does your planning show evidence that you have addressed pupils' weaknesses, identified through assessment?

- Do you share marking criteria for key pieces of work with pupils?
- Do you show pupils examples of good quality work so that they are aware of the standards they should aim for?
- Do you find time to discuss strengths and areas for development with individual pupils?
- Do you set realistic and achievable targets for individual pupils?
- Do you have records and evidence to support your judgements of pupils' achievements?
- Do you build a range of fun assessment for learning techniques into your lessons over time?

If you answered 'no' to several of these questions, make sure you identify assessment for learning as an area for development during your Induction year.

Summary

Assessment is an important aspect of a teacher's work and formative assessment is being used increasingly to help pupils improve their attainment. Improving learning through assessment depends on a number of key factors:

- Providing effective feedback to pupils so that they know what must be done to improve (small steps are important);
- Involving pupils actively in their own learning;
- Equipping pupils with the skills to assess themselves;
- Adjusting your teaching to take account of the results of assessment.

While assessment is important, you must try and limit the amount of time devoted to activities such as routine marking, so that you can devote more time to important set pieces of assessment designed to be used formatively with pupils. Use plenary sessions and in-lesson techniques to monitor a group's general understanding of the curriculum and thus to inform lesson plans. Use regular assessments (at least one each half term) with clear marking criteria to monitor pupils' achievements and set individual targets for improvement. When reporting to pupils and parents always adopt a positive tone. Try and give very precise guidance that will help pupils know how to improve.

Assessment remains a controversial issue. Results of national tests and examinations are used to produce league tables and there is still much opposition to the current testing regime. Some critics believe that the emphasis on testing distorts the kind of learning experiences provided and results in an impoverished experience for pupils. As a new teacher you will, of course, need to ensure that your pupils do well in exams. However, as a caring teacher, try not to lose sight of your duty to educate the whole child and remember that there are many worthwhile things that children will learn from you that cannot be measured.

References

Black, P J and Williams, D. (1998) *Inside the Black Box*, London: King's College.

Black, P., Harrison, C., Lee, C., Marshall, B. and William, D. (2004) *Working Inside the Black Box: Assessment for learning in the classroom*, in *Phi Delta Kappan* 86(1) 8–21 (web reference http://litd.psch.uic.edu/docs/ForSGLrngEnvAiM/BlackWrkBlBox.pdf).

Dweck, C. (2006) *Mindset – the new psychology of success*, New York: Random House.

Gerwitz, S., Ball, S.J. and Bowe, R. (1995) *Markets, Choice and Equity in Education*, Buckingham: Open University Press.

Mortimore, P. and Whitty, G. (1997) *Can School Improvement Overcome the Effects of Disadvantage?* London: Institute of Education.

Murphy, P. (ed.) (1999) *Learners, Learning and Assessment*, London: Paul Chapman.

Ofsted (2003) *Good Assessment in Secondary Schools*, London: Ofsted.

Ofsted (2012) *The Evaluation Schedule for the Inspection of Maintained Schools and Academies*, Crown copyright.

White, J. and Barber, M. (1997) *Perspectives on School Effectiveness and School Improvement*, London: Institute of Education.

8

The role of the form tutor

Introduction

It is likely that part of your school experience while in training will involve being attached to a form group (tutor group) so that you can gain experience of this aspect of a teacher's role. Although some newly qualified teachers do not serve as form tutors during the Induction, it is a responsibility that you will certainly have to take on thereafter and one that should therefore be given serious consideration during your training period.

This chapter will serve as an introduction to the work of the form tutor by considering:

- Pastoral care in schools
- The role of the form tutor
- Getting the ethos right
- Child protection
- Bullying
- Dealing with parents
- Maintaining professionalism.

From the outset it is important to accept that all teachers are teachers of *children* as well as teachers of their subject. While you may have been attracted to teaching by a desire to pass on your love of your specialist subject to pupils, you are likely also to have been motivated by a desire to contribute to pupils' development in a wider sense. This is sometimes expressed as 'wanting to make a difference' by applicants to teacher training courses. The opportunity to do just that often presents itself to teachers in their work as form tutors.

Pastoral care in schools

Form tutors operate in the context of a school's pastoral care system. The pastoral roles and responsibilities of a teacher are varied and complex and far more emphasis is given to pastoral care in British schools than in schools in most other countries. Here is a useful definition of pastoral care, provided by HMI (DES 1989).

> Pastoral care is concerned with promoting students' personal and social development and fostering positive attitudes: through the quality of teaching and learning; through the nature of relationships amongst students, teachers and adults other than teachers; through the arrangements for monitoring students' overall progress, academic, personal and social; through specific pastoral structures and support systems; and through extra-curricular activities and the school ethos. Pastoral care, accordingly, should help a school achieve success.
>
> (DES 1989)

A pastoral system operates most effectively, therefore, when academic, personal and social spheres of pupils' education are clearly and effectively linked through appropriate structures. A major change in pastoral care since the 1970s and 1980s is the emphasis now placed on how it can support students' learning and ultimately their achievement. The form tutor role is pivotal, as it involves both supporting pupils and monitoring their progress across all areas of the curriculum, including negotiating targets for improvement with individuals. In this way the form tutor provides challenge as well as support. In many schools Key Stage managers exist, with responsibility for coordinating aspects of the pastoral and academic provision within the school. These roles have been created quite deliberately to ensure the pastoral–curricular dichotomy that existed in many schools is removed.

Most schools have a written policy on pastoral care that will outline roles and responsibilities of key post holders and provide information on many areas of pastoral provision, including:

- The planning, monitoring and review of pupils' academic progress, behaviour and attendance;
- The pastoral curriculum – Personal, Social and Health and Economic Education (PSHE) and Citizenship;
- Behaviour Policy;
- Bullying Policy;
- Child Protection Procedures.

While form tutors are vital to the success of all these areas, all teachers in a school carry responsibility for pupils' pastoral care and so, even as a trainee teacher, you should be aware of the pastoral care policy operating in the schools in which you are placed for school experience. In particular, you should be aware of the school's behaviour policy, bullying policy and child protection procedures.

Form groups

In most secondary schools form groups are mixed ability and organised by age. That is to say they are typically organised so that they contain a cross-section of pupils, all from the same academic year. Normally, a pupil would remain in the form s/he joined on entry (Year 7) until the completion of GCSEs in Year 11. However, there are some secondary schools that have adopted a *vertical tutoring* model. This is where form groups contain clusters of pupils from all year groups placed together as a form. There would usually be around five pupils from each of Y7 to Y11 in a form. Schools adopting the latter model claim benefits including older pupils taking greater responsibility for nurturing younger pupils, improved behaviour as older pupils act as role models, more individualised support as the teacher has fewer pupils to deal with at critical times such as when guidance on GCSE options is required. As most schools still organise forms by year, this chapter will focus on the form tutor's role with this conventional organisation in mind.

The role of the form tutor

As a form tutor you are likely to be your pupils' first point of contact during the school day. You will see your tutor group more often than any other group you teach. In some schools form tutors see the same group of pupils through from entry in Year 7 to the end of compulsory schooling in Year 11. You are likely to get to know your pupils 'warts and all'. You will oversee their academic progress and be central to the management of their behaviour. You will be the person members of your form will be most likely to turn to if they have a problem or feel unfairly treated. Likewise, teachers and parents will come to you if they have concerns about pupils in your group. If you do your job well your form will remember you for the rest of their lives.

Action point

Most schools produce role descriptions for form tutors, with clearly defined responsibilities. Discuss with other trainees what you think are the duties and responsibilities of a form tutor. Compare your results with the list below. When you are on School Experience discuss the role of form tutor with different teachers. What do they see as the positive and negative aspects of the job?

The duties/responsibilities you came up with are likely to include:

- To take the register and monitor patterns of attendance and lateness;
- To be the first point of contact with parents of pupils in your form;

- To establish an understanding and knowledge of pupils in your form;
- To monitor the welfare of each child;
- To ensure pupil records are up to date;
- To monitor the academic and personal performance of each child;
- To set targets with each pupil;
- To establish standards of behaviour and dress;
- To deliver PSHE to your form;
- To liaise with relevant subject tutors, support staff, SEN lead and parents regarding specific pupils;
- To prepare reports and references on pupils in your form;
- To attend relevant annual parents' consultation evenings.

It should be clear from this description that good form tutors are highly skilled and flexible. They will show the attitudes discussed in Chapter 2 but will use other skills as well. Their crucial skills and attitudes include:

- Active and accurate listening;
- The ability to empathise;
- Honesty and openness;
- Approachability;
- Unconditional positive regard for each student;
- Ability to boost morale;
- Ability to solve problems;
- Nurturing skills;
- Motivational skills;
- Team building skills;
- Tact and diplomacy;
- Effective organisational skills;
- Clear thinking and good sense.

Let us consider some of these skills and attitudes a little more closely.

Listening skills

Listening is an important aspect of tutoring and knowing how to listen is essential. Pupils need to be able, at times, to 'let off steam' and kick against the system. There are times when a form tutor needs to let this happen, but without allowing it to undermine the school rules. Indeed, carefully managing pupils' anger can help to maintain good order in a school. Pupils need to feel that someone is 'on their side' and this means listening to their concerns and what they see as 'unfair'. Once steam has been let off it is possible calmly to offer alternative points of view and to try and get pupils to see other people's perspectives. Sometimes, pupils will just want to have a moan, sometimes they will be seeking support and possibly intervention from their form tutor. Of course, it takes a while to build the trust with your form that comes before the pupils start sharing their concerns with you. The mistake often made by newly qualified teachers is to try and artificially speed up this process or to be too friendly. In doing so they are in danger of losing the authority and respect needed to be a good form tutor.

Unconditional positive regard for each student

This can be very difficult to achieve. There will be some students you encounter in your career who are difficult and disruptive and who seem to reject all efforts on your part to treat them decently. Form tutors must never give up on any pupil. They must always try to find some redeeming feature that makes a child worth their effort. It is important with a difficult pupil to condemn their poor behaviour but not the person. If a child is being disruptive the chances are there will be some explanation to be found in their life outside school. The form tutor can become a point of stability in such a child's turbulent life. Consistency of approach therefore is very important. Of course, few form tutors are skilled counsellors, but they do engage in 'everyday counselling' of students, in much the same way as good parents counsel their children. It is important to be alert to the possibility that difficult children need more expert help. Never promise pupils more than you can provide. Remember that as a professional you must avoid becoming emotionally involved and you must recognise the need to involve other professionals to meet the complex needs of some pupils. Knowing when and to whom to refer a pupil is not something that will be automatic to you and different schools will have different structures of support in place anyway. For example, some schools have in-house counsellors; others have home–school liaison personnel; all have access to agencies beyond the school. This is where your Year Leader or Key Stage Coordinator comes in. It is your duty as an inexperienced teacher to discuss any concerns you have about a pupil with those in the structure who are well placed to call on additional and appropriate support, if necessary.

Boosting morale and motivating

Being at school can be hard for some pupils. They are under a great deal of pressure to perform and even the most caring secondary schools have a little of the 'education factory' about them in the way they operate. There will be times, therefore, when a form tutor has to inject a little enthusiasm into a demoralised group of pupils. Perhaps they are getting anxious about exams or have been reprimanded by teachers for the bad behaviour of a small number of pupils in the group. Your challenge is to boost morale, to create a sense that things aren't that bad, to generate some enthusiasm and to spread good cheer. Likewise, you will need to motivate your form when they are doing badly in some inter-form competition, when they feel undervalued or when they see themselves as failures compared with pupils in other forms. Being a teenager is full of angst. With individual pupils who are down in the dumps, it is often the form tutor who can make the world appear a little kinder, sometimes with a few simple words of encouragement offered at the right moment.

Team building and nurturing

Forms start as a collection of pupils put together for administrative convenience, but led by an effective form tutor they become a team. That is, they develop as a group who begin to support one another and who see the individual strengths of each pupil as valuable to the group as a whole. They become interdependent, working together and sharing in triumphs and defeats. Forms left to their own devices don't always gel as a group. There are often groups within groups, those 'in' and those 'out', winners and losers and isolated children. There can be competition and unfriendliness between groups within a form and even bullying. Boys and girls rarely mix. Forms that have been moulded into a team are a pleasure to teach; forms that become a collection of individuals and fragmented groups can be difficult to teach, as there is often falling out and infighting to deal with before teaching can begin. Here we see again how critical the form tutor is to the well-being and academic progress of their pupils.

Nurturing involves boosting the self-esteem of your pupils. If you can make every child in your form group feel better about themselves you will be doing much to make their lives happier (as well as improving their ability to learn). This is why effective form tutors try and learn what makes each child tick. They tap into their interests and in this way begin to relate to them as unique individuals. Once pupils realise that you are interested in them as people they will begin to listen to the advice you have to give. Nurturing involves encouraging pupils in different ways, depending on their level of interest and motivation. Directing, coaching, supporting and delegating all contribute to nurturing independence in pupils (see Table 8.1).

TABLE 8.1 Nurturing pupils towards independence

DIRECTING	COACHING	SUPPORTING	DELEGATING
The tutor provides very clear and specific direction to pupils and closely monitors results achieved.	The tutor directs and supervises pupils but also explains decisions, encourages suggestions and supports progress.	The tutor facilitates and supports pupils in decision making and accomplishing tasks.	The tutor delegates responsibility for decision making and task completion to pupils.

Getting the ethos right

Being a successful form tutor has a lot to do with getting the ethos right. Establishing a relationship with your form in which you are open and listening yet still uphold the school rules and enforce behaviour is very difficult and requires a great deal of skill. Building a team spirit and nurturing individuals, reprimanding and counselling, insisting on high standards for the group while continuing to show respect towards the one individual who causes the most trouble for the group, are difficult to manage. However, with a consistent approach and a generosity of spirit they can be achieved.

Your personality and behaviour will be key factors in establishing the tone of your tutor group. You can set high expectations by modelling the kind of behaviour you expect from your group. Nowhere are covert curriculum messages more important than in how you operate as a form tutor. The following are examples to think about:

- If you are punctual your pupils are more likely to be.

- If you are well organised and well prepared you can rightly expect this of your pupils.

- If you create routines you will establish appropriate behaviour more easily. For example, silence when notices are being read out, checking of homework diaries on a daily basis.

- If you encourage your form to look after their form room and take pride in keeping it tidy this will help them to feel greater 'ownership' and a sense of belonging.

- If you celebrate individual birthdays you are helping to show that each pupil is valued.

- If you celebrate cultural difference and show respect to all your pupils regardless of their social class, gender, faith or level of ability you are helping to prepare your tutees to be citizens in a pluralistic society.

- If you strive to be fair, balanced and consistent you are encouraging these behaviours in your pupils.

- If you use English well and sensitively explain to your form members why they should communicate with each other clearly and respectfully you are promoting social skills they will need in the workplace as well as 'promoting high standards of literacy, articulacy and the correct use of standard English' (DfE 2011) as required of all teachers.

Central to creating the right ethos is valuing each individual while at the same time building a sense of the form as a team. There are many opportunities for this:

- Use any spare time in tutor periods to chat to your class, trying to get to know pupils as individuals. Use circle time (see Chapter 9) as a vehicle for giving pupils an opportunity to speak. Don't allow very confident pupils to occupy all of your time or to dominate others in the group.

- Try and remember small details from your tutees' lives such as the music they are interested in, the football team they support and their favourite films. Use their birthdays as a way of boosting their self-esteem and making them feel special. Celebrate the achievements of pupils in your form as a group.

- If there are behaviour problems in the group make sure these are discussed openly with strategies for how to address the problem being proposed by group members.

- Keep a note of pupils who experience personal trauma and make sure you take the trouble to monitor their behaviour and performance. For example, there will be pupils whose parents undergo divorce or who suffer the death of a family member. They may not want to talk to you about their feelings, but you can help by keeping an eye on how such events seem to be affecting them and offering encouragement in a low-key manner.

- Prepare your tutor periods as thoroughly as you prepare your subject lessons. Your way of working may need to be very different to how you operate as a subject teacher (see Chapter 9). Try and provide opportunities for your tutees to set the agenda and include issues they feel are important to them.

If you get the ethos right, you will look forward to form periods. Sadly, some teachers don't! What is more, you will find that your tutees begin to boost your morale, notice when you're a bit under the weather and offer support when you're under pressure. When this begins to happen, you can rightly feel pride in the relationship you have achieved.

Actively engaging your form

Early on in your time as a form tutor you need to set the expectation that your form works as a team, while also showing them you value each individual. There are numerous activities you can use to get them working together. These activities work especially well with the new Y7 intake as all the pupils will be new to school and will be open to establishing new friendships. A few examples of the sort of approach you can take are provided in Table 8.2. You would use these activities over several sessions, not all at once.

Action point

When you are on School Experience see if you can talk to groups of pupils in Year 7, Year 9 and Year 11 about their expectations of a form tutor. Note how pupils' ideas change as they get older. What kinds of activities and tasks do form tutors involve their form in at these different stages?

TABLE 8.2 Examples of activities to use with a new form

Activity 1	–	Think of an adjective which starts with the same letter as your surname. (I am Fantastic Fleming.)
	–	Take turns to say your adjective and name. Everyone else must listen very carefully and repeat.
	–	Say your adjective and name and then throw the ball to another person in the class. Remember to say their adjective and name first, e.g. Fantastic Fleming – Superb Susie – Throw.
	–	Who can remember the most names?
Activity 2	–	The class stand in a line that snakes around the class according to first name alphabetical order. They turn to the person next to them and share something about their likes and interests.
	–	The line re-forms in surnames alphabetical order. The sharing takes place again.
	–	The line re-forms based on date of birth order. The sharing takes place again.
	–	The line re-forms according to number of brothers and sisters. The sharing takes place again.
	–	Etc.
Activity 3	–	The pupils write down three statements about themselves. One should be true and two should be false. Encourage the inclusion of unusual facts so that guessing the truth is difficult.
	–	Pupils work in pairs trying to guess the truthful statements.
	–	As teacher, you decide the method for moving to new partners according to the mixing you want to achieve.

Child protection

Through their daily contact with pupils, form tutors are in a critical position to identify children suffering abuse. You need to be familiar with your school's child protection procedures for this reason. You are obliged to 'act on suspicion' by referring your observations or concerns to the school's 'named person' (the Child Protection Liaison Teacher) who in turn will make referrals to appropriate agencies, if required. It is better to refer your concerns to the 'named person' (even if you think and hope you are wrong in your suspicions) than to ignore signs of abuse. Those with greater experience than you will be in a better position to consider the significance of what you have noticed. They are likely to proceed with caution. 'Although it is better to be wrong than to leave a child in an abusive situation, one should always try to find out if there is a reasonable explanation, not connected with abuse, for any signs seen' (Cole 1999). This is exactly what the 'named person' will do, and something you will become more confident about doing as your pastoral skills develop over time.

Reflection point

Consider the signs that might lead you to suspect a child is suffering abuse.

Abuse can happen to boys and girls of all ages and backgrounds. It can be physical, emotional, sexual, or simply neglect. The following are signs to be aware of:

- Changes in behaviour, for example a child becoming very withdrawn or unusually aggressive;
- Overheard remarks that trigger suspicion;
- Bruises, scratches, burns and scalds that don't look accidental;
- Symptoms of neglect, for example a child falling asleep in class or looking undernourished;
- Overworldliness and behaviour with sexual overtones that seems inappropriate to their age and development;
- A sudden drop in performance in work;
- A sudden reluctance to participate in PE;
- Signs of self-harm, e.g. weight loss, scratches or cuts on arms.

Of course, as a caring form tutor it may be that a child tries to confide in you. Disclosures of abuse are sometimes made in this way. It is important that you listen to the child but don't ask leading questions. You should under no circumstances promise to keep what is told to you 'a secret', in fact you should make it clear to the child that you might need to pass information that is disclosed on to another person in order to ensure that appropriate help and support is provided. You should immediately refer disclosures to the 'named person' in school. When you pass information on (as a result of your suspicions or disclosure) you should make careful notes of anything that you have seen or that has been said to you. Theses notes should be dated and signed and put in the pupil's record file. They might help to establish any pattern of abuse that is occurring, and they allow information from different people to be collected in one place.

Action point

As a trainee if you have not been given one already, ask your placement school for a copy of their Child Protection Policy.

As a Newly Qualified Teacher your Induction programme should include child protection. It is also important that you visit your Local Authority's website where you are likely to find training and support materials relating to child protection and your duties as a teacher.

Bullying

Sadly, bullying exists in all schools, though in some it is far worse than in others. It seems almost inevitable that some individuals will attempt to intimidate shy and less forceful people or those who are different. Bullying can take many forms, including name calling, teasing, malicious comments and gossip, intimidation, ostracising, damaging school work, damaging property, extortion, jostling, punching, kicking, and violent assault. As technology has advanced cyber-bullying has become the preferred modus operandi of many bullies. For pupils on the receiving end of any form of bullying life is not pleasant; for those who are the victims of a sustained campaign of bullying their lives can, quite literally, become hell. Indeed, there have in recent years been well-publicised cases of teenagers subjected to a sustained campaign of bullying taking their own lives.

Action point

Discuss with other trainees what the possible causes of bullying are and why particular children become victims.

There are many possible explanations for why some people bully and why others become the victims of bullying. Victimisation may occur because of things such as a child's race, colour, family background, level of intelligence (very able or having special needs), wealth (affluent or poor), or some other difference. Often, victims are children who are less assertive, anxious, loners, or those with few friends. Children may become bullies because they enjoy the feeling of power, they are copying behaviour they receive at home, they are secretly jealous of the victims, or they are unhappy and lacking in self-esteem (even though their behaviour might not suggest this). Sometimes, children get drawn into bullying by fearing what will happen to them if they don't join in with the instigator of the bullying. It takes a very brave child to stand up to a bully on behalf of the bullied; such action carries the risk of becoming ostracised or bullied in turn.

Victims of bullying often try to keep what is happening quiet. They can feel frightened and ashamed. They often believe that if teachers or parents try and do anything about what is happening the situation will only be made worse. Children who are being bullied may become withdrawn, their work may deteriorate, they may begin to miss school (sometimes with patterns of missing particular lessons where bullying is at its worst), and their personality can change. At home, they can become withdrawn or aggressive, taking out their frustration on their parents. They can begin bed-wetting and complain of feeling unwell so as to avoid going to school. Bullying can be very traumatic for parents as well as children, and it is important that schools take the issue very seriously.

Your school will have a bullying policy (or anti-bullying strategy), which will outline good practice and how to deal with incidents of bullying. It will also make clear the reporting procedures for such incidents. As a form tutor the ethos you create should go a long way towards preventing bullying. The more you can build a sense of the form being a team and each individual being valued the less chance there will be of bullying; the higher each pupil's self-esteem, the less likely they will become a victim of bullying. You can use PSHE as an opportunity to encourage mutual respect and tolerance (see Chapter 9) and there are other things you can do:

- Stress to pupils that those who stand by and witness bullying are condoning it;
- Be very strict about not allowing racist, sexist and unkind names to be used;
- Praise non-aggressive behaviour and acts of kindness that you witness;
- Ensure you set the right example by never bullying pupils (even those who are themselves bullies).

Working with parents

It is normally the form tutor who writes a summative report on a child's performance, typically once each year. The form tutor is in a good position to pull together themes from across all subject areas and to make accurate judgements about overall progress and the extent to which a child is achieving their full potential. S/he may also have insights into the child that shed light on the reasons for changes in their level of performance and motivation. Form tutors are likely to be responsible for helping their tutees agree targets for improvement, choose options for Key Stage 4 and think about possible career paths. All these activities could bring the tutor into direct contact with parents and carers, as well as the possible need to see them as a result of difficult issues such as bullying or unacceptable behaviour. Effective form tutors establish successful relationships with the parents or carers of their tutees and become their first point of contact in the event of them having any concern about their child's education.

It is unlikely that you will meet parents directly as a trainee, but you might get the opportunity to shadow a form tutor during parents' evening. Newly qualified teachers are sometimes daunted by the prospect of meeting parents and so it is worth considering during your training how to build effective relationships with them. Always remember that many parents are, in fact, reluctant to visit schools, as they feel inferior and out of their depth in the school environment. 'Those who are involved in their children's schooling tend to be those whose cultural framework echoes that of the school . . . that is, middle–class, white heterosexual families' (Ofsted 1999). It is very important, therefore, that all parents and carers are made to feel welcome and at ease if useful 'partnerships' are to be established. The vast majority of your dealings with parents will be positive but you will from time to time come across difficult parents. The points below are offered as general guidance on how to behave with parents in a number of different contexts. Guidance on dealing with difficult parents is provided in Chapter 12.

Parents' evenings

The exact format of these events will vary from school to school, but typically you will be seated in a classroom or the hall with several other teachers. Your desk will have two chairs for parents to sit at. You will only have a few minutes to spend with each parent (or parents) discussing their child's overall progress. Most parents will be pleasant people and most pupils will be making steady progress, though there may be a few who are not performing well or whose behaviour is poor. The points below should help you to get ready for dealing appropriately with parents:

- Prepare your comments in advance. Take assessment records and examples of pupils' work as evidence to support what you have to say.

- Dress formally, stand up to greet parents and shake hands. Offer a broad smile and a firm grip. You need to convey an impression of professionalism if you are to be taken seriously.

- Always start with the positive, but make sure you draw areas of concern to parents' attention. Don't hide the truth from parents; many are naturally defensive of their offspring but they do appreciate being given the full picture. Negative comments will more readily be accepted if they can see that you are genuinely interested in their child, you are caring and want them to do well.

- Don't make personal or sarcastic comments about pupils. Focus on behaviour not personality. Be analytical and constructive. Listen carefully to what parents have to say. Show empathy. Try and agree a way forward that involves parents in helping their children with punctuality, uniform, completion of homework, etc.

- Avoid a 'them' and 'us' situation by using the term 'we' to suggest collective concern and responsibility.

- If a parent tries to deflect you from what you are saying by raising issues about other teachers or the school in general, try and get them back to the topic in hand by referring them politely to relevant colleagues to discuss their other concerns.

- Don't allow argumentative situations to develop. If you feel you need more time with parents try and arrange a meeting for a later date when you may be able to call on your Head of Year for support.

- If problems have been discussed always try and close the meeting having agreed a way forward. If you have promised to do something following the meeting always follow through and keep parents informed of outcomes.

Effective schools maintain contact with parents throughout the school year, not just at parents' evenings. It is now common for letters of merit to be sent home, not just letters of concern. Likewise, in some schools half-termly progress grades are being communicated as well as the once a year report. As a form tutor you are likely to be expected to contact parents when you have a concern but many schools now want form tutors to call parents to offer praise and progress updates also. This is, of course, time consuming, but the benefits of building a strong partnership with parents cannot be underestimated. Also, think of the boost a shy but hardworking pupil will get from knowing you have noticed the effort they are making and have been sufficiently impressed to bother informing their parents.

Action point

Try and shadow a form tutor at parents' evening, while on School Experience. Note all the techniques used to establish a positive rapport with parents, while at the same time providing an accurate assessment of their child's conduct and progress.

Maintaining professionalism

Action point

Discuss with other trainees what being 'friendly' means in the context of being a form tutor. How 'friendly' should a form teacher be? Why do there need to be limits? Think of examples of 'friendly' behaviour that would be unacceptable.

Just as you will take an interest in the pupils in your form, so they will take an interest in you. Regardless of the age of the pupils, you will almost certainly face questions about your personal life. While it is not desirable to keep your life a complete secret to your tutees, you need to be professional about what you reveal. Remember, you are their teacher not their friend. Friendship is a relationship between equals, and since you hold responsibility for and power over pupils you cannot be their friend, though you can be friendly. It is better to see yourself *in loco parentis* (in place of the parent). Thus, you should act towards your tutees as a caring and responsible parent would. Maintaining this balance can be difficult, at times, but you must keep a professional distance – if you don't, a pupil could feel betrayed when you have to switch role from friend to authority figure.

So, how much information should you reveal about yourself? As with so many things, there is no precise answer to this, as much depends on the age of the children and the context in which the questions they ask arise. The following points should provide useful guidance, however:

- It can sometimes be appropriate to talk to a pupil about an aspect of your personal life to reassure him or her. Sometimes an anecdote from your own past can help a pupil to feel better about a situation they are facing.

- Never reveal something to a pupil that you don't want to become public knowledge. Be prepared for anything you tell a pupil to become exaggerated as it gets passed around the school.

- Keep certain aspects of your life back from your class. It is inappropriate for them to know all about your partner, exactly where you live and your social activities.

- Never share a private e-mail address or phone number with a pupil. Do not allow your pupils to access your Facebook pages. Be judicious with what you put on any social networking site.

Intimate relations (or even discussions) between teachers and their pupils should be strictly avoided. They represent a gross misuse of a teacher's position. If a pupil attempts to get personal, for example by declaring undying love for you, you must not keep what has been said to yourself. You must protect yourself by reporting it to the Year Head and ensuring the encounter is documented. You must then make sure you never put yourself in a situation where you are alone with the pupil; always talk to them in a public place or with another colleague present. If you 'let them down gently' from their infatuation it will probably soon pass, but you must under no circumstances do anything that could later be misinterpreted. It is important to remember that in the *Personal and Professional Conduct* section of the Teachers' Standards teachers are reminded that they should 'at all times observe proper boundaries appropriate to a teacher's professional position' (DfE 2011). If you fail to do so you risk losing your career.

Case study and reflection point

It has already been suggested that form tutors often have to decide on a course of action having considered a number of alternatives. Consider each case below and think about how you might proceed before reading the accompanying reflections.

Case 1

You are a Year 10 Form Tutor. Halfway through the year, three teachers in the same week tell you that Paul, a bright student, has failed to hand in GCSE course work by the deadline given. Paul has previously had a very positive attitude to school and you haven't noticed any change in his behaviour in form sessions. However, he has had a few one day absences in recent weeks, though these have all been accounted for with signed notes from a parent.

What would you do?

Clearly, there are a number of possible ways to proceed. You could choose to do nothing, believing on the basis of past performance that Paul will sort things out. This is not a good idea. Three missed deadlines is very worrying and Paul is risking damaging his chances of the grades he is capable of and even access to the sixth form as a result. Therefore, you must take some action. As a minimum, you should talk to Paul and try and establish what, if anything, the problem might be that has prevented him handing coursework in. You should negotiate new handing in dates with him and his subject teachers (we will assume this is an option, though pupils may not be permitted to submit work late in some circumstances) and then monitor what he is doing carefully to ensure the new deadlines are met. The pressure of three pieces of coursework all required at the same time might simply have been too great for him. Guidance on effective time management may be needed to ensure the problem doesn't arise again.

You should consider probing further into his performance if you are worried as a result of your discussions with Paul. This would mean contacting all his subject teachers for an update on his performance and also re-examining the absence notes to see if they really were genuine. You must decide whether you believe that as a result of your talk Paul will be back on track or whether there are underlying issues affecting his performance that you haven't been able to identify. Remember, you have a duty of care towards Paul and so you should let his Year Head know what has happened and what you have found out from your discussion with him. You also have to decide whether to let Paul's parents know about his failure to complete the coursework. If you do let them know, they may put Paul under severe pressure to succeed, which might have a positive or negative result depending on Paul's state of mind and his relationship with his parents. If you have learnt something about a family difficulty as a result of your discussion with Paul, such as a parent being seriously ill, then a letter or phone call could cause additional stress to the family. On the other hand, if you don't let them know and Paul's performance deteriorates further, his parents could, with justification, be very upset and angry they were not informed earlier. Teachers are increasingly accountable for their actions and so I would recommend that parents are made aware of the missed deadlines. Parents are 'partners' in education and they have a right to be kept informed of their child's performance. This can be done sensitively with a phone call. On the phone it is possible to be more 'human'. Parents' questions can be answered and anxieties eased. It is also possible to discuss how the school and Paul's parents can both help him to get back on track. If there is a serious family problem then other subject teachers should be informed so that they can deal sensitively with Paul.

You can see from these possible levels of response that form tutors have to think carefully about how to react to pastoral issues that crop up. As an inexperienced teacher, you should discuss situations like this one with your Year Head so that the decision on how to proceed is jointly agreed.

Case 2

You are a Year 9 Form Tutor. During a registration period you half-hear a furtive conversation in which the word 'drugs' is mentioned. You have had no reason to suspect these pupils of any involvement with drugs and their work and behaviour is fine.

What would you do?

Again, there are various possible courses of action open to you. You could speak to the group you heard discussing drugs, or individuals in the group, and probe further. This could have a number of possible outcomes. They might, from their perspective, feel that you are being nosy and that you have no right to be listening to their private conversation. They may point out that if you allow them some 'chat time' during registration then they should be able to chat about what they see fit. They may feel deeply offended that you are even thinking that they have anything to do with drugs; after all, their conversation could simply have been about the drugs raid on *East Enders* they witnessed the previous evening. This shouldn't worry you as it is important your pupils understand you have a duty of care towards them and as such you need to be aware of anything happening that might adversely affect their performance or health and well-being. If, though it seems unlikely from what we know, these pupils are involved in some way with drugs, they are unlikely to admit this simply as a result of your enquiry. On the other hand, if you have a good relationship with these pupils and they are whispering about something that is happening elsewhere in school, they may tell you what they know as a result of your probing and this information could be very important. Form tutors who have worked with a group since Year 7 will be at an advantage in this situation, as they will know their pupils extremely well.

Given that you have had no reason to suspect these pupils are involved in drugs, and your friendly enquiry reveals nothing to alarm you or raise suspicions, it would be reasonable to take no action beyond keeping an eye on the group and your ears open in the coming days. The fact is that as a teacher you will catch snippets of all kinds of conversations between pupils and if you attempted to probe each one of them your job would become quite impossible. Clearly, it would be ridiculous to consider contacting parents about a conversation you only half-heard between a few excitable fourteen-year-olds, when you have no evidence or reason at this stage to suspect they are involved in drugs in any way. If, however, you have the slightest concern, secure advice from your Year Head.

Action point

When you are on School Experience discuss these case studies with the Form Tutor you are placed with and see what course of action they would have taken.

Summary

Effective pastoral care integrates the management of pupils' personal, social and academic development. The work of the form tutor is vital to the well-being of pupils; effective form tutors make a real difference to the lives of pupils and to the overall success of a school. Good form tutors are caring and well organised, with high expectations linked to an ability to listen and a genuine interest in the well-being of all their tutees, including those who are difficult and un-cooperative. Pupils on the whole no longer respect teachers just because of their position. Thus, it is very important that form tutors develop good relationships with pupils in their care. The form tutor will also be an important link to the home, probably knowing pupils in their form better than any other single member of staff. A well managed form should begin to function as a team, with each pupil showing respect towards other form members. Form tutors help to achieve this by being respectful to pupils, being consistent, modelling the behaviour they expect, building pupils' self-esteem and being robust in challenging unacceptable behaviour and bullying.

References

Cole, M. (1999) *Professional Issues for Teachers and Student Teachers*, London: Fulton.

DES (1989) *Report of Her Majesty's Inspectors on Pastoral Care in Secondary Schools: An Inspection of Some Aspects of Pastoral Care in 1987–8*, London: DES 1989.

DfE (2011) *Teachers' Standards*, Crown copyright.

Ofsted (1999) *Primary Education: A Review of Primary Schools in England 1994–98*, London: Ofsted.

9

Teaching beyond your subject specialism

Introduction

The training programme you are on will prepare you to teach your specialist subject to secondary school pupils. Most courses are designed to prepare you to teach across Key Stage 3 and Key Stage 4, with some also offering a preparation for working in the sixth form. There are a few courses aimed at training teachers for teaching in the middle years of schooling, these typically involve coverage of Key Stage 2 and Key Stage 3. Once you are a fully qualified teacher, you will not be restricted to teaching only the subject or age phases for which you trained, and a number of secondary teachers, for various reasons, move into primary or Further Education during their careers. Likewise, there are lots of teachers who successfully teach subjects other than their specialism during the course of their career.

Flexibility is an asset, and having the ability and willingness to teach more than a single subject and across the whole of the secondary age range is a good thing. In most schools, teachers are less and less able to live on small academic islands, and will be likely to be involved in the delivery of programmes such as Personal, Social, Health and Economic Education (PSHE), Citizenship and/or Social & Emotional Aspects of Learning (SEAL) as part of their duties as a form tutor. Additionally, most schools offer a range of enrichment activities, often known as extra-curricular activities, provided by teachers working outside the classroom. In order to make a full contribution to the corporate life of a school, you should be willing to consider carefully what you have to offer beyond your specialist subject. Indeed, this may be something you are asked while on interview.

This chapter will consider:

- Issues involved in teaching additional subjects;
- Teaching PSHE and Citizenship;
- Contributing to curriculum enrichment activities.

If you came into teaching because you want to 'make a difference' and because you want to be involved in the education of the 'whole person', you should have no difficulty in seeing yourself as teaching beyond your specialist subject. If this prospect seems daunting, however, this chapter will hopefully give you an understanding of what is involved, and whet your appetite for becoming involved in areas of a teacher's work that can be extremely rewarding.

Issues involved in teaching additional subjects

Your training course will prepare you for teaching a specialist subject you are committed to. This is likely to be a subject you studied at degree level. You will probably seek a post teaching this subject, but in most schools an element of flexibility over what teachers deliver is required. Indeed, teachers' conditions of employment mean that head teachers can direct their staff to undertake duties deemed 'reasonable', including teaching beyond their subject specialism. It is reasonable to expect most teachers in a school to be form tutors and therefore to participate in the teaching of PSHE and Citizenship; it is reasonable also, for example, to expect a teacher trained in Religious Education, and with 'A' levels in History and Geography, to teach a certain amount of History or Geography, if required.

When you attend an interview for a job try and get a clear statement on what you are likely to be expected to teach. For example, if a job is advertised as a Chemistry post, will you be expected to teach some Combined Science or even some Physics and/or Biology also? If so, what proportion of your timetable will be devoted to your main subject? Staffing requirements do change each year, based on factors such as pupils' GCSE and 'A' level choices and staff promotions, and so no teacher can expect to have exactly the same timetable year after year. It is reasonable to expect you to teach subjects related to your main specialism, but it isn't reasonable to expect you to teach subjects for which you are ill equipped. This would result in a bad experience both for you and your pupils. In my own career, I have always been happy to teach across all Humanities subjects, even though I trained to be a History teacher. However, I was once asked to consider being timetabled to take a lower school Maths class for a year, and I resisted this very strongly. I didn't feel my own understanding of Maths was such that I was capable of teaching it well. It simply wouldn't have worked. Most head teachers are reasonable people, and wouldn't want to put teachers into situations that would be bad for all concerned. If you find you have been asked to teach something you really don't feel capable of, then discuss matters straight away with your Induction tutor. Of course, there will be lots of new things you will be teaching related to your main subject. This is to be expected and these new topics should be treated as a stimulating challenge.

Some jobs will be advertised which make it clear that a teacher who is capable of teaching more than one subject is being sought. You will need to think carefully about such jobs before applying. Find out if the teaching will allow you to have contact with the whole secondary age range, all abilities of pupils, and to offer the possibility of 'A' level work in the future in your main subject. This will help you to decide whether or not to apply for the post. Always remember, most teaching skills are generic and therefore transferable across subjects. If you are willing to do the necessary reading and research relating to the subjects concerned you will not let your pupils down. However, if teaching your specialist subject is really important to you, the idea of having a timetable that limits your involvement in this area might not appeal.

If you end up teaching subjects from different faculty areas this can pose particular difficulties, as subject team meetings are likely to be scheduled for the same time each week and you won't be able to be in two places at once! As a new teacher you are entitled to an appropriate level of support and so the head of department of your second subject should be willing to meet with you regularly if you can't attend meetings. This will allow you to get focused support, which will probably be more appropriate for you than sitting through a lot of business that isn't directly relevant. If you are teaching just one or two groups for your second subject, the chances are there will be parallel groups being taught the same area of the curriculum. Try and arrange to meet with a teacher of a parallel group to share planning; this will help you to get to grips with the topics you have to cover. Observations of parallel groups being taught will also be useful. If you are teaching a GCSE course, make sure you get the syllabus and several past papers from the relevant head of department so that you can prepare thoroughly. Your flexibility over teaching a second subject will be appreciated, but it is your right to be supported. As a new teacher you shouldn't simply be left to get on with things, so make sure through your Induction tutor that appropriate support is in place. The legislation around Induction requires schools to provide appropriate support so don't feel guilty for asking for it!

Teaching PSHE and Citizenship

In most secondary schools form tutors teach PSHE and Citizenship. In some respects this is a shame, as the teaching of these important areas of the curriculum requires a particular approach and methodology that some teachers find difficult. In other respects it is good that PSHE and Citizenship are taught to form groups by the teacher who should know them better than any other member of staff – their form tutor.

PSHE involves helping pupils to develop skills for living healthy, safe and productive lives. Useful guidance can be found in various places (e.g. www.pshe-association.org.uk) and it is likely that your Local Authority will have schemes of work and resources available to support you. Most of the themes mentioned above have always been at the core of good pastoral work undertaken by form tutors, though there has been and still is healthy debate about exactly how each area should be covered and developed. Citizenship is more contentious, as there are fierce debates about the nature of citizenship and what it means to be a 'good citizen', and many teachers are reluctant to teach about politics. There are various possible reasons for this, including 'a lack of tradition; few teachers who were professionally committed to the field; a belief that politics was solely an adult domain; and fear of indoctrination' (Davies 2003).

Citizenship has achieved a great deal of attention in recent years, however. It became part of the National Curriculum for secondary schools in England in 2002. Politicians had high hopes for citizenship at a time when there were 'worrying signs of alienation and cynicism among young people about public life and participation, leading to their possible disconnection and disengagement from it' (Kerr 1999). The model of citizenship education argued for in the Crick Report (DfEE 1998) emphasizes the development of social and moral responsibility, political literacy (knowledge and critical understanding of democratic society) and community involvement, as a preparation for pupils' active participation as adults in civic affairs. These ideas are central to the National Curriculum for citizenship.

> Citizenship gives pupils the knowledge, skills and understanding to play an effective role in society at local, national and international levels. It helps them to become informed, thoughtful and responsible citizens who are aware of their duties and rights.
>
> (QCA/DfEE 1999)

Most schools retain a PSHE programme even though it is not a statutory curriculum requirement. At the time of writing Citizenship remains part of the National Curriculum and the Teachers' Standards make clear that teachers are required 'not to undermine fundamental British values, including democracy, the rule of law, individual liberty and mutual respect, and tolerance of those with different faiths and beliefs' (DfE 2011). This suggests all teachers are, in fact, teaching Citizenship, even if this is not through a formal programme of study.

The overall school ethos and organisation should encourage respect for individuals and provide opportunities for pupil involvement in decision making through the development of 'pupil voice'. The most common evidence of this in schools is the existence of a School Council, but in some schools pupils are also involved in shaping Teaching & Learning policy, staff appointments, lesson observations and co-construction of schemes of work. The school itself is a community and therefore acts as a model of Citizenship. The importance of teachers' behaviour in the classroom should never be underestimated. 'The indirect moral influence on children is deeply embedded in the daily life of the school, either within normal teaching activities or within the contingent interactions at classroom level' (Halstead and Taylor 2000). Beyond this, Citizenship can be taught through other subjects, as a discrete subject on the timetable, and through special events and the use of outside speakers. Most schools probably opt for a combination of all these approaches, but with the major elements of citizenship being provided by form tutors as part of a PSHE/Citizenship package.

Some of the issues that are covered within PSHE/Citizenship require very sensitive handling. These 'big issues' are very important but can cause anxiety for some teachers who may not feel well equipped or relaxed when covering topics on racism, sexism, social disadvantage and sexual relationships, for example. An effective form tutor must establish a relationship with their form in which discussion and debate can take place in an atmosphere of trust. This takes time and requires form tutors to respect each individual pupil and allow them to express their views in a secure environment. It means giving pupils a sense that their views are valued. As a reflective professional you need to allow your views to be challenged and changed by feedback from pupils. Actively listening to pupils' concerns is very important. Teachers who listen and learn from their pupils are showing they value them.

Circle time is used very effectively in many primary schools and is now appearing in some secondary schools. It can certainly make a difference, especially if introduced as normal practice in form period from Year 7. Essentially, circle time provides pupils with an opportunity to be heard. They sit in a circle so that all pupils can see each other and each pupil takes it in turn to raise or pass comment on a particular issue (but they only speak if they want to). All pupils agree the ground rules, for example that only one person can speak at a time and that all contributions will be listened to with respect. The passing of an object to the pupil whose turn it is to speak can help establish appropriate behaviour. Circle time can be used to discuss something that has occurred in the form, such as reported bad behaviour, or wider issues that need disciplined discussion, such as drug abuse.

> Circle time may also help pupils to learn to talk about their feelings, to gain a sense of belonging to a group or community, to develop qualities such as trust, responsibility, empathy, co-operation, caring behaviour and respect for the feelings of others and to engage in personal reflection and clarify their own values.
>
> (Halstead and Taylor 2000)

Circle time will only work, of course, if teachers are committed to it and understand its purpose; if they believe in the idea of empowering their pupils. Added to lessons taken by an authoritarian teacher (see Chapter 2) the chances are that it simply won't work, as the teacher's underlying values will not be consistent with those needed for circle time; the teacher's relationship with their form won't be conducive to pupils revealing their thoughts and feelings in public.

There are numerous activities you can undertake with your form group in order to try and establish the kind of ethos that will be supportive of effective learning in PSHE/Citizenship. Bear in mind that these activities will need to be modified according to the age of the pupils in your form group.

- Encourage your tutees to help you settle into your new school (providing they aren't new as well). Ask them about the school, its good and bad points, but don't get drawn into discussions about particular members of staff.
- If you have a Year 7 form it will contain pupils from different primary schools. Take photographs of your tutees and get them to write a summary about themselves. After they have used these to tell the rest of the form about themselves, they can be displayed in your form room.

- Save these photos and summaries when you change the wall display; you can bring them out again some years later and use them to help pupils consider how they have developed and changed.

- Split your form group into 'care groups'. Give each group a responsibility, for example collecting the register, making the room tidy, and keeping the form notice board up to date. These tasks should be rotated, and each group must decide between them how they will accomplish the tasks.

- Give the pupils an inspirational 'thought for the week'. Display it on the form notice board. Later, pupils can take it in turn to find a thought for the week.

- When problems occur, use the circle time approach to solve them. For example, if a particular subject teacher is complaining about the form's behaviour.

- Celebrate each pupil's birthday. This can be very low key, but helps to show each pupil is valued.

- Create a list of topics for discussion that pupils can choose from; later let the pupils put their own ideas on the list. Have discussion sessions as a regular part of form period, if time allows.

- Encourage pupils to value all members of the school community, for example by getting them to organise a Christmas present for the cleaner of their form room.

- Have end of term parties during form period, during which time you can publicly celebrate the achievements of the group and individuals. Get the pupils to take responsibility for organising food, arranging furniture in the room and tidying up afterwards. Make sure you gain approval for this from your Year Head first!

- If you have a form group from the senior end of the school try and get them involved in helping younger pupils. Some schools have paired reading schemes, pupil counsellors, etc.

Action point

When you are on school experience, investigate the following:

- What arrangements exist to give pupils a voice and involve them in decision-making?

- Is there a School Council? If so, what do pupils think of it?

- Are you able to detect aspects of the 'hidden curriculum' that might reinforce or detract from what the school is trying to achieve through citizenship education?

Contributing to curriculum enrichment activities

In most schools there are activities organised for pupils that take place beyond the normal school day. Some of these, like sporting activities and homework clubs, are closely related to the curriculum and provide pupils with opportunities to build on work undertaken in class. Others, such as accelerated learning techniques and voluntary work in the community, help to build pupils' self-esteem and this, in turn, can impact on their performance in all areas. These activities are given a variety of titles in school: curriculum enrichment, extra-curricular activities, personal enhancement programme, out of school hours learning and study support.

> Study support is learning activity outside normal lessons which young people take part in voluntarily. Study support is, accordingly, an inclusive term, embracing many activities – with many different names and guises. Its purpose is to improve young people's motivation, build their self-esteem and help them become effective learners. Above all it aims to raise achievement.
>
> (DfES 2000)

Action point

List all of the things from the school you last attended or from a school you are placed for school experience that fit this definition. Can you distinguish between activities that are designed to 'enable', those designed to 'extend' and those designed to 'enrich'?

Your list probably includes such things as:

- Support classes for key skills such as literacy, numeracy and ICT;
- Study clubs linked to curriculum subjects;
- Homework clubs;
- Coursework support sessions;
- Sports, games and outdoor activities;
- Creative activities (music, drama, dance);
- Residential opportunities;
- Opportunities to do voluntary work in the community;
- Debating society and discussion groups (e.g. book clubs);
- Mentoring by adults;
- Learning about learning (thinking skills);
- Religious groups (Christian club, Islamic society);
- Gifted and Talented provision.

Enabling activities provide pupils with opportunities to develop basic and key skills needed to access the curriculum effectively, for example ICT skills. Extension activities allow pupils the chance of extending their knowledge and understanding of activities covered in class. Enrichment activities provide new opportunities for pupils. Certain activities, of course, will cover more than one type of opportunity. For example, being in a music group might extend work done in lessons, but also provide new opportunities such as performing in public. Highly successful schools find ways of ensuring their most vulnerable pupils and those at risk of under-achieving are involved in appropriate additional activities as a means of addressing very specific issues these pupils face. This is an important stage beyond simply offering enrichment activities to those who choose to opt in and is one sign of a truly inclusive school.

As a trainee and newly qualified teacher you will be very busy and may be wondering what the point of volunteering to be involved in enrichment activities is. Firstly, there is a good deal of evidence to support the belief that pupils benefit from the activities discussed above in very tangible ways. 'It is possible to state that the research evidence has established a link between young people's participation in a range of activities outside school hours and a number of desirable outcomes, including attitudes to school, attendance and academic achievement' (NFER 1999). Secondly, there are obvious benefits for you as a teacher. Your involvement in enrichment activities should result in:

- Enhanced relationships with pupils;
- Getting to know your colleagues better;
- Increased respect from pupils;
- A deeper understanding of how children learn;
- The opportunity to try out new ideas;
- Increased job satisfaction.

Let us consider these reasons for involvement a little more closely.

Reflection point

Discuss with a fellow trainee the differences between lesson time and out of lesson learning and why some pupils might be more enthusiastic about the latter.

There are many points you are likely to have uncovered. Some of these are listed in Table 9.1. It really is quite amazing how many pupils come alive once they are placed in less formal learning environments, especially situations away from school. Some pupils really shine in contexts where practical skills, common sense and the ability to 'muck in' become more valuable than a natural capacity for academic work and willingness to conform. Allowing pupils who learn in more practical ways, and those who possess forms of intelligence not always valued in school, the opportunity to excel can show them in a different light to their peers

TABLE 9.1 Contrast between in lesson learning and out of lesson learning

IN LESSON	OUT OF LESSON
Compulsory	Voluntary
Little choice	More choice
Pupils grouped by age and ability	Mixed age groupings by shared interest
Formalised pupil teacher roles and relationships	Varied range of different adult pupil roles and relationships
Testing	No testing
Competition	Cooperation
Focus on individual achievement	Focus on team achievement
Duty	Fun
Day in day out	Short bursts
Learning is routine	Learning has novelty/variety
Pupils have limited responsibility	Pupils have enhanced responsibility
Academic skills valued	A range of skills valued
Auditory learners thrive most easily	All styles of learner thrive

and do wonders for their self-confidence. Of course, effective teachers try and incorporate aspects of out of lesson learning (choice, co-operation, group work) into everyday lessons (see Chapter 3), but the opportunities for this are so much greater away from a formal classroom situation.

As far as the benefits to you as a trainee or teacher are concerned, seeing pupils in less formal contexts can be very enlightening. It allows you the opportunity to get to know them as individuals, and to appreciate them for their skills and qualities beyond the academic. Your relationship with them is likely to improve; you will be more relaxed and the pupils will see another side to you, just as you will see another side to them. It is very rare that pupils take advantage of this once back in the classroom. It is a good idea to try and become involved with Year 7 pupils in out of lesson contexts; the relationship you develop at this stage will help you in your dealings with them as they move through the school.

Clearly, then, involvement in enrichment activities is a good thing, but there are some practicalities to consider. Firstly, you need to be aware of the time involved. During training and the Induction the time you devote to school will already be considerable. Your first priority is successfully to complete Induction by developing as a capable subject teacher. However, getting involved in extra-curricular activities will help you establish yourself with pupils, work with colleagues in less formal situations and show a commitment to the school. A good way in is to support activities that are already in place, rather than starting something new. For example, if you join a department that offers homework support sessions during lunch break, then you can make sure you contribute to these with the rest of the team. If the school runs activities such as the Duke of Edinburgh scheme, you could offer to help, but making clear what the limit of your involvement will be.

Health and Safety issues need to be considered very carefully. Most enrichment activities done in classrooms will carry no greater risk than your usual teaching, but activities out of class are a different matter. This is a good reason for supporting what is already happening as a newly qualified teacher, rather than pioneering something new. This will give you a chance to learn from experienced colleagues how to handle planning and risk assessment and how to conduct yourself with children away from school. Essentially, teachers are bound by a 'duty of care'. This concept is a complex matter, especially when teachers are engaged in activities that take place off the school site. The law on negligence is particularly significant here, as a few highly publicised cases have demonstrated in recent times. The Induction programme your school provides for you should include Health & Safety and Risk Assessment so that you learn what procedures have to be followed. It is important to discuss with your Induction tutor (mentor) issues in working with children off-site before you consider any out of class learning. You can also seek advice from your professional body or union representative. The following publication will also prove useful: DfES *The Code of Practice: Study Support: A Guide for Secondary Schools* (DfES 1998). It can be found using the search engine at www.education. gov.uk.

Summary

Being willing and able to be flexible is an asset. Being able to teach your specialist subject effectively to all ages and abilities of pupils is important, but the likelihood is that at some point you will be called upon to contribute to the teaching of a second subject. This should not be viewed negatively or with dread; your teaching skills will be transferable, and providing you feel secure in your understanding of the subject you have nothing to be worried about. As a newly qualified teacher, though, you must make sure you receive appropriate support if called upon to teach beyond your subject area. You should not be asked to teach subjects that you don't feel suitably equipped to deliver.

Although you might not be given a form group in your first year of teaching, you almost certainly will in subsequent years. It is likely that you will have to teach PSHE/Citizenship to your form. This should be seen as a really important aspect of your work and should be taken every bit as seriously as the teaching of your main subject. Your delivery of PSHE/Citizenship will be effective if you have created with your form an ethos that is inclusive and which encourages pupils' autonomy. You need to develop active learning approaches, through which pupils develop the ability to evaluate, question and be critical, as well as learning basic facts about key issues you will cover.

Try and become involved in activities beyond the classroom, though be careful not to take on too much during the Induction. Working with pupils on activities they volunteer for and which are not compulsory will allow you to see different aspects of their personality, and this will strengthen your relationship with them. Use your first year as an opportunity to learn from other teachers who are running extra-curricular activities. In particular, try and gain a thorough understanding of Health & Safety issues and how to conduct risk assessments.

References

Davies, I. (2003) 'Citizenship Education: origins, challenges and possibilities' in Crawford, K. (ed.) *Contemporary Issues in Education*, Dereham: Peter Francis Publishers.

DFE (2011) *Teachers' Standards*, Crown copyright.

DfEE *(1998) Education for Citizenship and the Teaching of Democracy in Schools: Final Report of the Advisory Group on Citizenship (The Crick Report)*, London: QCA.

DfES (1998), *The Code of Practice: Study Support: A Guide for Secondary Schools*, London: DfES.

DfES (2000) *Extending Opportunity: A National Framework for Study Support*, London: DfES.

Halstead, J.M. and Taylor, M.J. (2000) 'Learning and Teaching About Values: A Review of Recent Research', *Cambridge Journal of Education*, 3(2) 169–202.

Kerr, D. (1999) 'Re-examining Citizenship in England' in Torney-Purta, J., Schwille, J. and Amadeo, J.A. (eds.) *Civic Education Across Countries: 22 Case Studies from the Civic Education Project*, Amsterdam: Eberon Publishers.

National Foundation for Educational Research (1999) *The Benefits of Study Support: A Review of Opinion and Research*, London: DfES.

Qualifications and Assessment Authority (QCA) and Department for Education and Employment (DfEE) (1999) *Citizenship*, London: QCA/DfEE.

10

Teaching in schools in challenging circumstances

Introduction

All schools are different and all schools present challenges of one sort or another. However, schools serving severely disadvantaged communities pose challenges that might seem especially daunting to those new to the profession. Social disadvantage and educational underachievement are closely linked and teachers in schools in challenging circumstances find themselves on the front line in the battle to improve outcomes for socially disadvantaged pupils.

This chapter includes a brief discussion of the reasons for underachievement in schools in challenging circumstances. This is followed by a consideration of the particular challenges that arise in educating pupils in such schools and what is known about best practice, learnt from schools that have rapidly improved outcomes for pupils from disadvantaged communities. Although the challenges are considerable, the work can be very rewarding and exciting. I taught for eleven years in an inner city school, and have very fond memories of this chapter of my career. There are many excellent schools doing a remarkable job in difficult circumstances, and I would encourage you to arrange to visit such a school or to undertake a school placement in one, if your programme doesn't already offer this opportunity. Many trainees come away from such an experience determined to take up a post in a school in challenging circumstances. They have seen very quickly the potential rewards of being able to make a difference in the lives of pupils from disadvantaged communities.

Features of schools in challenging circumstances

Schools in challenging circumstances usually serve significant numbers of pupils from poorer backgrounds (often identified as pupils eligible for free school meals) and typically share most of the following features:

- In the main they have a history of low levels of academic achievement when judged by 'raw' examination results (though value-added data suggests that some of these schools are very effective).

- They are often located in areas of significant socio-economic deprivation. These may be inner urban areas, areas of local authority housing characterised by high unemployment, or former industrial communities blighted by unemployment. It should be remembered that some rural communities face poverty and deprivation also, and that challenging circumstances are therefore not confined to urban schools.

- They often contain a significant number of pupils for whom English is an additional language.

- There is a high level of pupil mobility and transience.

- Pupils often display poor social skills.

Explaining lower levels of attainment and achievement in schools in challenging circumstances

Statistics on educational achievement indicate that particular groups of pupils consistently achieve more highly than others. For example, the children of professional parents do better than children from non-professional families. Likewise, Gillborn and Mirza (2000) have demonstrated the persistence of underachievement of some ethnic minority groups (for example, Pakistani, Bangladeshi and African-Caribbean) over the years. This is not to say that all children from working class families and all Pakistani, Bangladeshi and African-Caribbean minority ethnic pupils underachieve. Some individuals from these groups do well, but *overall* these groups underperform.

There are several interlinked factors that help to explain why particular groups consistently underachieve. Some factors lie outside the school, others operate through institutional processes. While some factors apply to specific ethnic groups, others affect all groups identified as underachieving.

Poverty

Politicians insist that poverty is 'no excuse' for low achievement. Social background, they argue, should not determine a child's chances of success. Yet the evidence of a link between poverty and achievement is overwhelming. for example, in 2008, only 35% of pupils eligible for free school meals obtained five or more A★ to C GCSE grades, compared with 63% of pupils from wealthier backgrounds and between the early 80s and the late 90s, the proportion of poorer children graduating from university had risen by only 3%, compared to 26% from wealthier families (Narey 2009). Research undertaken for the Joseph Rowntree Foundation showed only 21 per cent of the poorest fifth (measured by parental socio-economic position or SEP managed to gain five good GCSEs (grades A★ to C, including English and Maths), compared with 75 per cent of the top quintile (Goodman 2010).

Unemployment is the biggest cause of poverty, though not the only cause. People from minority ethnic groups are more likely to live in poverty than the white population, though poverty is not restricted to ethnic minorities. Many largely white communities where the traditional industry has declined, such as some mining areas, suffer from serious social and economic disadvantage. Features of communities suffering from poverty that can impact on pupils' performance in school include:

- Low incomes
- Poor quality housing
- Poor diets
- Poor health
- High levels of stress
- High levels of crime
- High levels of drug use.

'Underclass' is the term used to describe people on the margins of society who live in a state of permanent poverty. In these circumstances, there can be tremendous instability within families.

> Poverty breeds stress and stress breeds unstable relationships, giving rise to complicated family structures; many women have a number of different children, each by different fathers. There may be frequent changes of arrangement for childcare, with friends or extended family involved. Even in families with stability, relationships are difficult. The cause is poverty. When life is dominated by the fact that there is no way the ends can meet, it is not surprising that tempers get frayed, people get emotionally exhausted and people look for ways out or for ways to forget.
>
> (Johnson 1999)

Reflection point

How might each of the features listed above impact on pupils' ability to perform well in school?

Background and impact on aspiration

The parents of children living in poverty are unlikely to have the levels of skill and education needed to gain employment beyond unskilled work. For some families unemployment has been the norm for many years or even generations. Such parents probably had little success at school and may be unaware of what they can do to help their children succeed. Thus, a cycle of deprivation operates in which the children of our nation's poorest families do badly at school and as a result live in poverty when they become adults. Children from poor backgrounds typically begin schooling with lower levels of language and social skills than children from more economically successful families. This holds back their initial progress in school. As teenagers, they have few academically successful role models in their own community to emulate and can often see little incentive for working hard at school. Background has a very strong influence on pupils' attitudes towards teachers, behaviour in school and homework. Education is seen by politicians as a means of breaking this cycle of learnt failure and low aspiration.

For older children, peer expectations also become very important. There is much evidence to suggest that peer pressure prevents teenage boys applying themselves to study, as it isn't seen as 'cool' to work hard. According to Epstein (1998) 'one of the dominant notions of masculinity in many schools is the avoidance of academic work'. While this may be true for the majority of boys in all schools, it is at its most extreme in the subcultures associated with poor, working class communities, both black and white.

Flecknoe (2001) argues that the use of target setting with pupils is especially problematic in schools serving poor communities:

> For academic targets to be perceived as valid they must be seen to have currency in terms of lifestyle. This is an economic problem; perceptions in some areas are such that, whatever a child achieves at school, there is little to look forward to. Schools in such areas and with such pupils face a different and more difficult task than do schools where there is an accepted link between achievement in school and future success.

The acceptance of the fact that a large number of pupils become disaffected as they move through secondary school because the academic curriculum is not perceived as relevant to their needs is one of the factors fuelling the on-going debate about the content of the school curriculum and which prompted the Labour administration pre-2010 to introduce alternative vocational pathways at Key Stage 4.

Action point

When you are on school experience, get permission to interview a number of pupils about their attitudes to school and their hopes and aspirations. Do any of the factors in Figure 10.1 emerge as significant influences on their thinking and achievement?

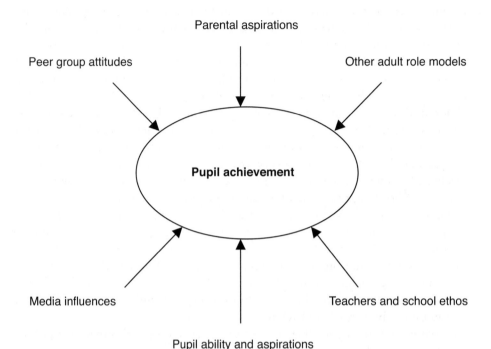

Parental aspirations

Peer group attitudes

Other adult role models

Pupil achievement

Media influences

Teachers and school ethos

Pupil ability and aspirations

FIGURE 10.1 Influences on pupil achievement

National policy towards schools in challenging circumstances

Politicians of all mainstream political persuasions state they want to close the attainment gap between pupils from more affluent backgrounds and those from socially disadvantaged families as a means of securing greater social mobility. It is not the purpose of this book to offer comments for or against the policies of any particular government. However, it is important to explain briefly what trainees considering working in schools in challenging circumstances might need to be aware of. All schools nationally are expected to reach minimum *floor targets*. At the time of writing (2012) the target for secondary schools is a minimum of 35% of pupils attaining 5 or more GCSE passes at grades A★ to C, including English and Maths. This will rise to 50% by 2015. Teachers in schools in challenging circumstances with historical low levels of attainment will clearly face a great deal of pressure to achieve these targets. Schools with data showing low levels of attainment will also be vulnerable when it comes to Ofsted inspection. It was announced in 2012 that an inspection judgement of 'satisfactory' will be renamed 'requires improvement' and schools judged by Ofsted to be in this category for three consecutive inspections will be served a notice to improve. While it is clear that coasting schools in more affluent areas will be under close scrutiny as a result of these changes, the clear link between poverty and attainment makes the challenges facing schools in deprived areas particularly daunting.

Over the years various changes in organisation designed to bring about improvements for our most disadvantaged pupils have been tried. Under the Labour administration pre-2010 many inner city areas saw the creation of sponsored academies. State-of-the-art buildings were created, with private sector sponsors helping with funding. There were also many new schools built through private finance initiatives (PFIs) in an attempt to improve the physical environment in which pupils learn. The coalition government since 2010 has focused on removing the influence of local authorities on education and allowing outstanding schools to become academies which are then able to operate with greater independence. Academies are encouraged to become partners of underachieving schools or even create a chain of academy schools in a bid to spread a culture of success with weaker schools learning best practice from stronger schools.

What all this means is that if you choose to work in a school in challenging circumstances you might well find yourself in a purpose-built school with very good facilities. The image of dilapidated inner city schools is now outdated (though there are still some). While the challenges you face will be enormous and a lot will be demanded of you, the work can be very rewarding. The chances are you will be working with experienced colleagues from inside your school and beyond and in these circumstances you could develop your skills as a teacher very rapidly indeed, getting your career off to a good start. However, you need to be sure that the school you start your career in has a culture that will enable you to thrive and not simply survive. You need to join a school with a positive culture. Be realistic about the risks and challenges. More schools serving poor communities have been placed in 'special measures' or found to have 'serious weaknesses' than schools serving more prosperous communities. (These two terms, used by Ofsted inspectors, indicate that a school is not providing an acceptable level of education. Immediate action to redress weaknesses is required if a school is placed in 'special measures'. Schools that fail to improve can be closed down). Without good leadership and highly skilled and focused teaching across all subjects, schools serving pupils from disadvantaged communities can quickly spiral downwards into a situation in which poor discipline and poor attendance sap the energies of teachers and the culture of the school becomes one of 'survival'. If this happens, teaching in these circumstances can rapidly become a source of stress rather than an exhilarating experience.

Positive school cultures and teachers' behaviour

Schools in challenging circumstances identified as doing an excellent job have managed, against the odds, to create a culture in which order prevails, students respect each other and their teachers and there is a relentless drive for improvement and achievement. The aggregate effects of home background are very clear, but time after time individual children have proved themselves capable of defying their home circumstances and, with the right support, achieving well. While GCSE results have a high correlation with home background for pupils in general, for individual pupils the correlation is much weaker. It is for this reason that teachers working in schools in challenging circumstances must have high expectations of all the pupils they teach. Although poverty and cultural backgrounds are explanations for underachievement, they must not be used as excuses. Applying labels to children because of their backgrounds can result in a self-fulfilling prophecy, in which teachers' attitudes to pupils brings about the very behaviour they were expecting. The power of high expectations is now widely understood, and is one reason why many effective schools in challenging circumstances focus on creating a high achievement culture among teachers, pupils and the local community as a fundamental ingredient of school improvement. This was done successfully some years ago at Hanson School in Bradford, for example: 'the aim high and achievement culture entered our whole school jargon, repeated constantly to get the message across' (Chaplain 1999). Similarly, Christ the King College, located in an inner city area of London, has established over time an ethos and culture of high attainment resulting in outstanding outcomes for students (Ofsted 2011).

Schools that do very well with pupils from disadvantaged communities display particular characteristics:

- Strong and shared leadership;
- Clear vision translated into clear expectations of staff and pupils;
- Well-focused curriculum, with attention paid to basic skills;
- Collective planning and sharing of successful pedagogy;
- Good teaching, with direct and sustained interaction with pupils;
- Effective and focused staff development;
- Systematic monitoring, evaluation (including monitoring of attainment by ethnic group) and assessment for learning (AfL);
- Well focused SEN arrangements;
- Effective use of support staff;
- Effective personal support for pupils;
- Clear communication with parents;
- United approach to improving attitudes, behaviour and attendance;
- Clear procedures for responding to bullying and racial harassment.

Many of these characteristics, of course, will be present in successful schools not classed as challenging. Ofsted 2000 identified the following features of lessons in challenging circumstances schools in which teaching was very successful:

- Clear and uncomplicated classroom routines, for example on the use of equipment and materials and the way work is presented;

- Good use of time and learning resources;
- An insistence that pupils do their best, coupled with support to help them meet the challenges set;
- Sustained interaction between teachers and pupils, including the skilled use of questions and the call for pupils to articulate their thinking.

You will again notice that these features would be present in many lessons in schools other than those in challenging circumstances. High expectations backed up by practical support are at the heart of successful teaching in challenging circumstances schools. Support can be provided by:

- Structured support for homework and coursework outside normal school hours, for example through homework clubs;
- Providing very clear instructions (based on formative assessments) on exactly what pupils need to do to improve their work;
- Careful joint planning between teachers and support staff so that SEN pupils' needs are met effectively.

The need for consistency and clarity in classroom procedures as a means of improving behaviour is spelled out in more detail in another HMI report published in 2001:

> Good teaching is clear in routines, expectations, objectives, instructions, explanations, examples, structure, discipline and language. Teachers manage classrooms effectively by controlling entry and seating, giving definite instructions and explanations, using interesting material and activities, challenging and supporting pupils, keeping them on task and responding fully to their work.
>
> (Ofsted 2001)

Boys, in particular, are likely to respond to teachers who:

- Set clear limits on behaviour;
- Give strong direction over work;
- Show enthusiasm;
- Use humour;
- Reward good work;
- Praise quietly rather than in public;
- Include practical activities in lessons;
- Use short-term targets;
- Use ICT in the classroom.

Very successful teachers in schools in challenging circumstances possess a high level of commitment and highly developed skill in relating to their pupils. They operate with a genuine moral purpose and this leads them to display an honest respect and interest in their pupils while accepting no nonsense in the classroom. In many ways these teachers provide pupils with the guidance and setting of aspirations that can be lacking in their homes.

> The personal and professional qualities that teachers exhibited towards students, the calibre and honesty of relationships between them, their images of teaching, their motives, passion, and 'moral purposes', were all crucial to 'success'. These qualities were manifested in valuing pupils and getting to know them for who they were in and out of school and by creating climates in the classroom based upon trust, mutual respect and rapport.
>
> (Lancashire LEA 2004)

The iceberg model (Fig 10.2) helps us to understand this success when we observe a highly successful teacher (the skills above the water line) but we aren't always conscious of the deep and emotional commitment that drives them in their work (what lies below the water), making them such very special teachers.

Much was made in Chapter 6 of the need to respect and embrace all pupils in order to create an inclusive ethos. Racial equality should be a priority for all schools, including those with an all or mainly white population, not just those inner urban schools where you are likely to find classes that contain pupils from a wide variety of cultural and ethnic backgrounds. You need to avoid the danger of holding stereotypes about any groups you encounter. Cultures are dynamic and multi-

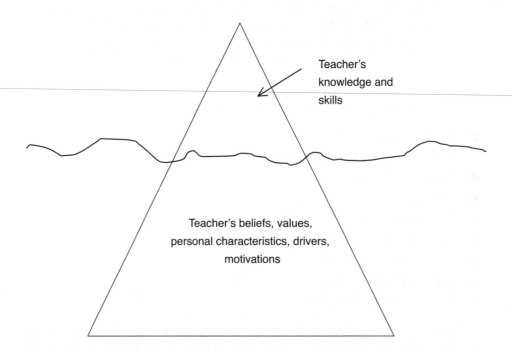

Teacher's knowledge and skills

Teacher's beliefs, values, personal characteristics, drivers, motivations

FIGURE 10.2 The iceberg model

TABLE 10.1 Culture clash: tensions between street norms and school norms

WITH REGARD TO	STREET NORMS	SCHOOL NORMS
Demeanour, posture, gait and gesture	Body language shows you mean to be respected – not messed with, not hassled, or bothered or provoked.	Through body language and your general attitude show you 'accept the role of pupil' – you respect and defer to authority, tradition and the rules.
Provocation	Get your retaliation in first . . . shoot from the hip . . . swear and use verbal abuse . . . signal you are ready to use force . . . use force (fists, weapons) if necessary.	If provoked by a teacher, back down. Never swear at a teacher or threaten or use force. If provoked by another student, keep cool and don't fight.
View of outsiders	Anyone who doesn't conform is not allowed in.	Official view is that schools should be as inclusive as possible and should respect diversity and pluralism.

layered, and many teenagers are coming to a sense of personal identity through combining elements of different cultures into an identity that makes sense to them (for example being Black and British and a Muslim).

You must also guard against the likelihood of tensions between street culture and school culture, and think carefully about how you handle situations in the light of this. Table 10.1, modified from Richardson and Wood (1999) shows clearly how misunderstandings can arise.

Getting the tone right can be very challenging for trainee teachers, especially when you come across cultural norms that are different to your own. It can be especially difficult to set clear expectations of behaviour, while taking account of cultural differences, for example. An important point to remember is that pupils are more likely to conform if they feel respected. It is not *what* you ask of pupils that will offend, but *how* you ask.

> We need to consider when to accommodate students' cultural backgrounds, and when to expect students to accommodate. In mutual accommodation, teachers accept and build on students' language and culture but also equip students and their families to function within the culture of the school.
>
> (Weinstein et al 2004)

Language support

Throughout England over two hundred different languages are used with varying degrees of fluency. Many pupils in English schools speak a language other than English in their homes. According to the DfE (2010) 11.6 per cent (378,200) of all state funded secondary school children have a first language known to or believed to be a language other than English. Most teachers will teach pupils learning English as an additional language (EAL) at some stage in their careers. You could encounter such pupils in any school, but in inner urban schools, children with EAL will be greater in number. As a trainee you should understand the needs of such pupils and know how best to support them. Their social and academic progress will depend greatly on their progress in the use of English.

It is important to remember that pupils learning English as an additional language will not all be the same: some will be fluent speakers, readers and writers of another language (or languages); others may be fluent speakers of another language but may have limited literacy skills in that language. Pupils can be at very different stages of learning English. The range can be from pupils who have been learning English all their lives (but where English is not the first language spoken in the home) to pupils new to English, entering the education system at a late stage, for example some refugees and asylum seekers. Clearly the needs of these pupils will be very different, but broadly the approach taken to children with EAL is to integrate them into mainstream schools as quickly as possible.

> The language of the mainstream classroom offers the best context for learning language, because bilingual students are learning English for the purpose of learning the subject being taught and not in the abstract. They learn language in context, which is how language is most effectively learnt. They are offered a motivating experience to learn English in wanting to join in the activities of their peers, both inside and outside lessons.
>
> (Heilbronn and Jones 1997)

As a trainee, you will be provided with specialist support in school to help you plan to meet the needs of EAL pupils in your classes. The following points should help you to begin to think about how you might manage such pupils.

- Language, culture and identity are closely linked. While you want pupils to improve their English skills as rapidly as possible, it is important not to undervalue their first language. Acknowledging and valuing the pupils' linguistic heritage can be achieved by creating opportunities for pupils to use their first language. Providing peer support using pupils you know speak the same language as your new arrival can be helpful.

- Provide learning opportunities with the level of English development matched to curriculum content. Differentiated activities and close liaison with support staff will be needed. If a pupil can write in his home language but not English, having some dual language texts and/or key word cards can be helpful. Simplified English texts can be used with some pupils until their reading and writing of English improves. Provide activities such as labelling diagrams (specialist vocabulary provided), matching notes to pictures and writing up work with picture prompts. Use planning grids to help pupils to structure their writing.

- Ensure EAL pupils are involved in listening to your input to a lesson and whole class discussions. Try and have visual and/or auditory resources to illustrate points during whole class teaching. For example, artefacts, maps, diagrams, graphs, time lines, video-clips, web pages, etc. Share learning objectives with the whole class and try and keep the discussion focused on these.
- Display key words linked to tasks around your classroom as you introduce them.
- Provide plenty of opportunities for EAL pupils to work collaboratively.
- Remember to support pupils with English skills as well as with the content and vocabulary relating to your subject. In using formative assessment, focus on language development as well as subject targets.
- Many EAL pupils remain silent until they feel confident enough to begin to use English. Don't assume silence means a child doesn't follow what is being said.
- Remember that although learners may acquire fluency in conversational English quite quickly, it takes much longer to acquire a level of proficiency that is required for learning within the school curriculum. Support in class could still be needed for EAL pupils who are fluent orally but produce poor written work.

Bear in mind that the EAL learners new to this country are likely to be under tremendous pressure. In addition to the obvious challenges being faced by their families, they must:

- Begin their learning at a different starting point to the other children;
- Learn a new language;
- Learn a new curriculum in a new language;
- Acquire new social skills;
- Accommodate the new language, values, culture and expectations alongside the existing ones learnt at home.

Under these circumstances it is important that they are made to feel welcome and given encouragement and practical support (see Chapter 6 for ideas on inclusive practice). Take every opportunity to praise oral contributions from pupils who are new to English as this will help build their self-esteem.

Action point

Visit a successful inner urban school and learn as much as you can about how the school operates and how the particular challenges it faces are met. Use the guidance below to make the most of your visit.

Visit guidance

It is quite possible that your training provider will arrange for all trainees to visit a multi-ethnic school. Indeed, some providers located in or close to urban areas will use such schools for school placements. If this is so, then you will be offered guidance on how to get the most out of your visit or placement. If no such visit is arranged or a visit is only for one day, you should consider taking the initiative to spend at least a week in a 'good' inner urban school. This could be done at any time during your training or immediately following the completion of your programme. You could seek advice on the best schools to approach from your college tutors or by contacting the adviser for Newly Qualified Teachers (NQTs) or the teacher recruitment officer in the Local Authority in which you are considering your visit. No school is obliged to offer you the chance to visit and some may simply be too stretched to do so. Having said this, successful schools are usually keen to accommodate visitors.

Undertaking a visit is really the only way to find out about what interesting and exciting places some schools in challenging circumstances can be. If you aren't keen to work in such a school as a result of your visit, you should still come away having seen some good teaching ideas that can be used in other contexts. The suggested intended outcomes list below is for people who initiate their own visit to an inner urban school.

Intended outcomes

Be clear about the purpose of your visit. By the end of your time there you should:

- Be aware of the particular challenges facing inner urban schools;
- Understand whole-school strategies being used to raise achievement;
- Understand the school's approach to inclusion and equal opportunities;
- Be aware of effective classroom management strategies being employed;
- Know more about differentiation and strategies for meeting individual needs;
- Understand how EAL pupils' language needs are assessed and how teachers can support language development within mainstream/subject classes;
- Understand the roles of a range of professionals who work with teachers, for example, learning mentor, SEN support assistant, school liaison officer;
- Have some knowledge of how pupil data is used to track progress and set targets;
- Understand how pastoral support mechanisms operate.

Tasks in school

Bear in mind that schools are busy places and that it might not be possible for teachers to devote large amounts of time to you. You cannot expect a school to accommodate all your requests. However, if you show enthusiasm and interest it is more likely that schools will do their best to help you. See if you can be placed with a form group during your stay, as well as being given the opportunity to observe teachers in your own and other subjects. Accomplish as many of the tasks below as you can. You won't be able to achieve them all, so rearrange the list in order of interest.

- Drive or walk around the local area to get a feel of the housing conditions in which pupils attending the school live.
- Gather statistical data on the school: ethnic groups, attainment and achievement, attendance, etc.
- Read through key documents and policies, for example prospectus, Behaviour Policy, Equal Opportunities Policy.
- Find out about the curriculum and about learning opportunities beyond the curriculum (clubs, trips, study support, etc). How does curriculum planning take account of ethnicity, background and language needs of pupils?
- Summarise from the documents and your meetings with key staff the approaches being used to raise achievement in school.
- Look at documents relating to your subject specialism: department handbook, schemes of work, teacher-produced booklets, etc.
- Gather information on how the language needs of EAL pupils are assessed and how support is provided. Get copies of any diagnostic tools being used with EAL pupils.
- Note the causes and nature of any disruptive behaviour you observe.
- Record the strategies you see being employed to manage the behaviour of classes and individuals.
- Make notes on effective teaching and behaviour management strategies you see being employed.
- Note how teachers set targets with students (verbal, written comments on work, formalised whole-school systems).
- Find out how data is used to track achievement. Are results analysed by gender (if mixed school) and ethnic group? What action is taken following analysis?
- Discuss with teachers how they take account of the needs of pupils from different ethnic groups in their lessons.
- Note examples of techniques used by staff for challenging racism and stereotyping.
- Note approaches being used to encourage positive attitudes to ethnic difference and cultural diversity.
- Find out how 'racist incidents' are dealt with.
- Note similarities and differences in approach between teachers in this school and other schools you have been in as a trainee.

In addition to being attached to a tutor group and observing teachers at work, you should try and negotiate to undertake some of the following:

- Meet the SEN coordinator to learn more about inclusion and how support for pupils is managed.

- Meet the co-coordinator of Language Support to learn more about assessing EAL pupils' needs and providing support.

- Meet the teacher with responsibility for data and target setting to learn more about how the school monitors pupils' progress.

- Meet the head of department of your subject to discuss approaches to teaching the subject in an inner urban school.

- Interview a learning mentor about their role.

- Interview the school liaison officer about their role.

- Interview a pupil support assistant about their role.

- Interview a sixth former (or a successful Year 11 pupil if the school has no sixth form) about their aspirations and about their attitude to school. Find out what approaches to teaching helped them to succeed.

- Interview a range of ages and abilities of pupils about their aspirations and their attitude to school. Find out how they define a 'good lesson' and a 'good teacher'.

- Shadow a pupil for a day and observe their responses in different lessons.

- Attend assemblies.

- Accompany a teacher on break duty.

- Plan for and teach a 'group within a group'.

- Plan for and teach one or more lessons.

- Go round the school and identify good practice in displaying pupils' work.

Summary

Schools in challenging circumstances serve communities that suffer from serious social disadvantage, with many families living in poverty. The majority of pupils are likely to be from families in which parents are unemployed or engaged in unskilled work. Many will be from single-parent families. A number of minority ethnic groups may be represented in the same school. Teachers working in these schools face the massive challenge of raising the achievement of pupils from families where educational success has been limited.

While this poses particular challenges for teachers, tremendous rewards are also on offer. Successful schools in challenging circumstances are dynamic and vibrant institutions, where highly skilled and committed professionals make a real difference to the life chances of those they serve. As a trainee, you should try and spend time in such a school, to experience the challenges and opportunities presented. It must be remembered, however, that not all schools facing challenging circumstances are successful. Indeed, some can be very stressful places in which to commence your career. If you apply for a post in a school in challenging circumstances, try and visit the school before the day of the interview to make sure that you feel positive about the prospect of working there. It is vital that the school and its ethos suit your skills and personality and will allow you to thrive and develop.

References

Chaplain, I. (1999) 'Improving Achievement by Raising the Community's Expectations' in *Sustaining School Improvement*, Bromley: Funding Agency for Schools.

DfE (2010) *Annual Schools Census*, http://www.education.gov.uk/rsgateway/DB/SFR/s000925/index.shtml.

Epstein, D. (1998) 'Real Boys Don't Work: underachievement, masculinity and the harassment of 'sissies'' in D. Epstein, J. Elwood, V. Hey, and J. Maw (eds.) *Failing Boys*, Buckingham: Open University Press.

Flecknoe, M. (2001) Target Setting: Will it Help to Raise Achievement, *Educational Management and Administration* 29(2) 217–228.

Gillborn, D. and Mirza, H. (2000) *Educational Inequality: Mapping Race, Class and Gender*, London: Ofsted.

Goodman, A. (2010) *The Importance of Attitudes and Behaviour for Poorer Children's Educational Attainment*, Joseph Rowntree Foundation.

Heilbronn, R. and Jones, C. (1997) 'Supporting Bilingual Learners' in Heilbronn, R. and Jones, C. (eds.) *New Teachers in an Urban Comprehensive: Learning in Partnership*, Stoke on Trent: Trentham Books.

Johnson, M. (1999) *Failing School, Failing City*, Charlbury: Jon Carpenter.

Lancashire LEA and St Martin's College (2004) *Successful Teachers in Schools in Challenging Circumstances*, Lancaster: Lancashire LEA.

Narey, M. (2009) *Report from the Independent Commission on Social Mobility*, http://www.tuc.org.uk/extras/Social_Mobility_Report_Final.pdf.

Ofsted (2000) *Improving City Schools*, HMI 222, London: Ofsted.

Ofsted (2001) *Improving Attendance and Behaviour in Secondary Schools*, HMI 242, Windsor Print: Crown copyright (London).

Ofsted (2011) *Good Practice Example: The personal, social and spiritual development of young people in an inner city area – Christ the King College*, http://www.ofsted.gov.uk/resources/good-practice-resource-%E2%80%93-personal-social-and-spiritual-development-of-young-people-inner-city-area.

Richardson, R. and Wood, A. (1999) *Inclusive Schools, Inclusive Society*, London: Trentham Books.

Weinstein, C., Tomlinson-Clarke S. and Curran, M. (2004) Towards a Conception of Culturally Responsive Classroom Management, *Journal of Teacher Education* 55(1) 25–38.

11

Getting your first post

Introduction

Successfully completing your initial teacher training is a great achievement. It will give you much to celebrate. However, ensuring your first year of teaching is successful is equally important. Induction is a statutory requirement and failure to complete Induction successfully will make you ineligible to teach in maintained schools (see Chapter 12). Your choice of first teaching post may be one of the most important decisions you ever make and so you need to think very carefully about the type of post you want. You also need to know how to maximise your chances of getting the type of job you want. You are likely to be applying for your first post during the final stages of your training, when you will be under great pressure and probably undertaking a school placement, and so the challenge of securing a suitable post is a considerable one. This chapter is intended to help.

There are various stages you will need to go through:

- Deciding where you want to teach and the type of school you want to teach in;

- Looking for vacancies and accessing information;

- Completing an application;

- Preparing for and attending an interview;

- Accepting a post and preparing to join the school.

By reading this chapter carefully and reflecting on the points raised, you should become much clearer about how to apply for your first teaching post, how to make a good impression through your application, and how to prepare for the interview day in order to cope confidently with likely selection procedures. This greater clarity should help you to feel more confident and relaxed, and this in turn should increase your chances of success in the application process.

Thinking about where you want to teach

Over the years the Training & Development Agency for Schools (now the Teaching Agency) ran many successful campaigns to recruit trainee teachers, ensuring a good supply of new qualified teachers nationally. However, employment prospects for NQTs vary considerably according to area. In some places there are newly qualified teachers and recently qualified teachers claiming they are unable to obtain work when in other areas schools continue to report serious challenges in recruiting the teachers they need. The truth is there are shortages of teachers in particular subjects and particular geographical locations. Thus, as a teacher of Physics or Maths you are likely to be able to find work in most areas, whereas if you are a teacher of History wanting to teach within a very limited radius of your small home town you could have problems in securing a post. Job vacancies in London are usually plentiful across all subjects, with many posts having to be filled by teachers from abroad on exchange visits or sabbaticals.

If you are restricted to living in a particular place, perhaps because of family commitments, you need to think carefully about how far you are prepared to commute each day. Your first year of teaching will be very demanding and you will have evening commitments to honour. You will be tired at the end of the school day yet will have marking and preparation to do most evenings. Therefore, you must be realistic about how long you can spend travelling each day. An hour morning and evening spent travelling by train can feel far less tiring than an hour spent in a car, stuck in crawling traffic. A reliable train service might enable you to work forty or fifty miles away from your home, whereas a school fifteen or twenty miles away but only accessible by car, might be difficult to get to in under an hour at peak travelling times. Remember, it is possible to do some work on a train but not when you are driving. On the other hand, if you travel by train you are at the mercy of train timetables and so there is less flexibility in the times you have to travel, and getting from train stations to your school can involve walking or the use of additional public transport.

Many newly qualified teachers try to gain employment in the area in which they trained. While there are some obvious advantages to this, you must remember that if you trained in a part of the country that is very popular or desirable you could find it difficult to secure a post there. In popular areas turnover of teachers is often low and, when jobs do appear, the number and quality of applicants is usually high. If you are determined to live in a particular location, then consider looking for work in areas that may be less desirable to live in but which you could travel to fairly easily each day. Many inner city schools can be very rewarding places to work and good schools in which to start your career. It may be possible to secure a post in such a school while still living in the area in which you trained and would like to locate.

Obviously, one consideration on where you locate will be the cost of living. This is the very reason there is such a shortage of teachers in London and the South East, where renting property can be very expensive and property prices make the chance of getting on the property ladder small. However, because of this, some

London boroughs and southern Local Authorities (LAs) offer teachers subsidised housing and other incentives. If you are genuinely flexible in where you can begin your career it is certainly a good idea to look at the various packages on offer in areas that you might have dismissed because of preconceived ideas about them.

There are, of course, job opportunities abroad. While these opportunities might seem exciting, it is important to remember that if your intention is eventually to teach in maintained schools in England, you will at some stage need successfully to complete Induction. More details about this are provided in Chapter 13.

Action point

Think about where you would like to teach and about how flexible you can be in where you locate. Your ITT provider probably has publicity materials sent by various Local Authorities – look at what each one has to offer. Visit LA websites. Most have publicity packs aimed at NQTs that you can download.

Thinking about the type of school you want to teach in

There are many different types of school you might decide to work in. Most secondary schools cater for pupils aged 11–18 but there are many local and regional variations. In some areas there are schools for 11–16-year-olds, with sixth-form colleges providing education for 16–18-year-olds. In other areas middle schools exist, catering typically for 9–13-year-olds, with senior schools then educating pupils to the age of 18. Some middle schools operate like secondary schools with subject specialists; some operate more like primary schools with class teachers teaching most subjects.

Transfer to secondary school usually occurs at the age of 11. Most secondary schools are non-selective, though there can be major differences in intake depending on the particular communities a school serves. Secondary schools in small towns with just one senior school are often more genuinely comprehensive, in that they cater for all sections of the community, whereas comprehensive schools located in the more affluent areas of large towns and cities often have a very middle class intake, just as schools located in inner city areas or within local authority housing estates tend to have intakes skewed towards less affluent members of the community. In some areas grammar schools and secondary schools operate, with pupils selected by ability at the age of 11. Confusingly, some schools retain the title 'grammar school' but are actually non-selective institutions. Most schools educate boys and girls but some schools are single-sex establishments.

Most teachers are employed in mainstream schools, including state and independent schools, voluntary schools and colleges, academies and free schools. Most maintained schools are funded through the Local Authorities and supported by services from the LA. Voluntary Aided schools are part funded by LAs and part funded by another body, typically a church or diocese. Voluntary Controlled schools are state schools funded by a body such as a church or diocese and aided by the LA. Recent changes in legislation mean there are an increasing number of schools choosing to become academies. These are state schools funded directly by the government (rather than through a Local Authority) and therefore have more direct control of their budgets and operate with certain freedoms that locally maintained schools don't have. There are also city academies originally backed by a sponsor and opened in areas of high challenge. These schools were seen as vital to the regeneration of urban areas where educational attainment was low.

The existence of these varied arrangements reflects a growing belief in excellence through diversity and 'consumer choice' favoured by successive governments. There is much debate in education circles about the desirability of such a diverse range of schools and whether or not they assist or hamper efforts to achieve equality of opportunity. The purpose of this chapter will not be served by entering into these complex arguments, but there are some basic things you should think about when considering some of the types of school you could apply for beyond the 'bog standard comprehensive'. You need to be sure that your value system and world-view is not at odds with the ethos of the type of establishment you are considering applying for. You want to be happy in your first school and so make sure that what the school stands for is in harmony with the views and beliefs you hold. What all schools have in common is a desire to do the best they can for their pupils and thus they will all be seeking to appoint what they see as excellent and committed teachers who can help them achieve this. However, they will differ in how they believe schools should be organised in order to do the best for all their pupils and for this reason their view of an 'excellent teacher' will be nuanced. Excellence can show itself in different ways in different contexts. Be mindful of this when you are applying for jobs. How, for example, will you convince the head teacher of a rural selective grammar school that you will be as effective there as you have been during your training in an inner city comprehensive school?

Here are a few thoughts about some of the types of school you might consider applying to work in.

Faith schools

Most faith schools favour appointing teachers who are at least sympathetic to the doctrines the school represents. Bear in mind that many parents choosing to send their children to faith schools do so because they want their children to be educated in a school with a distinctly religious ethos. Others associate church schools with high standards and so make church schools their first choice with this in mind. It is worth remembering, however, that there are many teachers working in church schools who are not overtly religious or who hold no faith, and many inner city church schools that cater for multi-cultural communities. Church schools vary considerably so do your homework before applying for a job in one!

Academies

Most schools that have opted to become academies since 2010 were able to do so because they were classed as 'outstanding' by Ofsted or agreed to be in partnership with a school classed as 'outstanding'. This means that if you gain a post in such a school you are likely to be joining an establishment in which there is a clear vision, effective leadership and high expectations. Such a school should be able to ensure you are both challenged and supported as a newly qualified teacher. Please be aware, however, that academies are exempt from following the National Curriculum, can easily vary the length of the school day and school term times and have freedom to set their own pay and conditions.

Specialist teaching schools

At the time of writing, teaching schools are seen as central to government thinking on education. It is intended that a network of teaching schools will be established across the country and that these schools will have a major role to play in ITT and in the professional development of teachers and leaders. Only 'outstanding' schools can consider becoming teaching schools. There is no doubt that joining a teaching school should ensure expert support during Induction and is likely to afford subsequent opportunities for development and career progression. Teaching schools should be vibrant places to work, at the cutting edge of classroom practice and with enhanced opportunities to work beyond your own school.

Special schools

If you have a calling to work with pupils with special educational needs, perhaps those with severe learning difficulties, then you could consider applying for a post in a special school. However, most newly qualified teachers complete Induction in a mainstream school before beginning to specialise in pupils with SEN. Unless you have followed a specialist SEN training course, it is unlikely that your initial training will have prepared you in any depth for working with pupils with special needs and so you will need to undertake extensive professional development in order to gain the specialist knowledge and understanding required. There are now many MA programmes with specialist SEN modules, which are ideal for those moving to teach in special schools, and most courses can be followed part-time. These courses will enhance your chances of gaining employment in special education.

Single-sex schools

There is considerable discussion and research regarding the merits (or otherwise) of single-sex education. In some local authorities single-sex schools are common, whereas in others they are a rarity. If you work in a single-sex school catering for the opposite sex to your own you are likely to be in a minority, as most staff will be the same sex as the pupils. You need to think very carefully about whether or not you would suit the culture of a single-sex school. It would be wrong to generalise about the differences between boys' schools and girls' schools, but their ethos is usually very different. If you have any doubts, try and arrange to visit the school before submitting an application. Most head teachers are willing to make arrangements for prospective candidates to visit their school.

Sixth-form colleges

Some LAs operate 11–16 schools, with sixth-form colleges providing the next stage of education. If you are excited by teaching your subject at a more advanced level and wouldn't mind not having contact with the younger secondary pupils, then a sixth-form college may suit you. Most sixth-form colleges now have a fairly broad intake of students and class sizes are often just as large as those in secondary schools. You will still face the challenge of motivating some students who are struggling to keep up or who are disillusioned! Your conditions of service will be different to those of school teachers, as will your rates of pay. Pay in colleges is often lower than that of school teachers, and Further Education (FE) contracts often carry an expectation of teaching evening classes. It is important to compare these things before applying for a post in a sixth-form college. The law allows you to undertake Induction in a sixth-form college (subject to certain conditions being met) but do remember that if your early teaching experience is exclusively in a sixth-form college this will make it more difficult to gain a promoted post in a school catering for the full secondary age range.

Independent schools

In addition to all of the above, there are also independent schools to consider. These vary in size and ethos but all have the common feature that fees are paid for the education provided. In some schools bursaries, sponsorships and scholarships may be available, but these will only apply to a small proportion of the school's intake. Independent schools are not obliged to follow the National Curriculum, though in reality most do, as the pupils ultimately sit the same national examinations as their state school peers. Often, independent schools value the sporting side of the curriculum and many would boast that they do an excellent job of educating 'the whole child'. Some independent schools offer boarding facilities. If you work in a boarding school you will certainly become fully immersed in the life of the school. The experience will be very intense during term time, but you are likely to get longer holidays than your state school counterparts.

If you are considering working in the independent sector, bear in mind that pay and conditions will vary from school to school. Some prestigious schools pay more than state schools, but you will be expected to play a full and active part in the life of the school, including extra-curricular activities. Always make sure you are clear about pension arrangements. If you consider beginning your career in an independent school, check that you can complete Induction there. In order to do this there must be an agreement between the school and 'appropriate body' (usually the LA) that will be responsible for your supervision during Induction and the final decision regarding successful meeting of the Induction Standards. Also bear in mind that it might be difficult moving from the independent sector to work in the state sector, should you wish to do so.

Induction

Always check the very latest regulations regarding suitable schools for Induction by visiting the Department for Education (DfE) website or the Teaching Agency website. At the time of writing this book Induction can be completed in:

- Maintained schools
- Non-maintained special schools
- Sixth-form colleges (if certain conditions are met)
- Independent schools (if certain conditions are met)
- Pupil Referral Units (if certain conditions are met).

Further information about Induction can be found in Chapter 12.

Reflection point

Reflect on the various types of school listed. Would you be willing to work in any type of school? Do you hold any views that would put you off applying for certain types of school? Are your career plans such that you feel you need a specific type of school in which to serve Induction?

It is worth remembering the advantages of being flexible. The ideal job in the perfect location might not materialise. That being the case, do you value working in a particular area more highly than a particular type of school? Are you so opposed to working in certain types of school that you would rather take a temporary contract in a school of the type you desire than a permanent contract in a school that you see as less desirable? Only you can decide, but you need to consider these things now. My advice is not to dismiss any type of school out of hand. There are many misconceptions about all types of schools. I can think of several people who reluctantly applied for jobs in inner city schools, only to find working there incredibly rewarding. In my own case, I moved from a school in a leafy suburb to take up a head of department post in a school in the inner city. I found both the pupils and staff wonderful to work with and never regretted the move.

Looking for vacancies

The majority of advertisements for teaching posts are for specific posts in specific schools. They begin to appear around January and February for posts to commence in September, though the peak time for adverts is usually May. Independent schools often advertise earlier, from December onwards.

Teaching posts are advertised online and in the national press, sometimes in the local press (especially part-time and maternity cover jobs) and sometimes job details will be sent directly to your training institution. Some schools put current vacancies on their own school website as well as advertising through their Local Authority and/or (if they are independent of their LA) through a recruitment agency. The main paper carrying job advertisements is the *Times Educational Supplement* (TES). This is published every Friday. Jobs are also advertised in the *Guardian* (Tuesdays), the *Independent* (Thursdays), and the *Daily Telegraph* (Thursdays, mainly independent schools). Adverts can also be found in religious newspapers and those aimed at minority ethnic readers such as the *Asian Times*, *Church Times* and *Jewish Chronicle*. Most of the above newspapers have online versions where jobs are listed and you can also arrange to receive text messages when new jobs appear (for example, http://jobs.tes.co.uk/home.aspx). LAs usually have jobs listed online and there are also sites now devoted to job opportunities in education, for example www.eteach.com and www.jobsineducation.co.uk.

If you spot a job you are interested in the advert will tell you how to get further details, usually by visiting a given website.

Completing an application

You will probably be applying for your first teaching post at a time of year when you are very busy and working hard to successfully complete a long school-based experience. You will be under pressure and time will be at a premium. However, this must not become an excuse for putting in a poor application for a job. Your application letter is where you market yourself; you will not be invited for interview if you cannot write a positive and well-presented application letter. Likewise, if you are asked to complete an application form but don't bother, then don't be surprised when you are not invited for interview. First impressions are critical. Many head teachers reject applications because of:

- Poor writing or word processing errors;
- Poor spelling, grammar and punctuation;
- Cluttered presentation;
- Incorrect spelling of names of head teacher or school;
- Lack of focused response to areas asked for in instructions sent to candidates.

All of the above can be avoided and are really quite inexcusable in teachers who are supposed to be interested in encouraging high standards in their pupils. If you haven't got the time to do a polished application, it is better not to bother at all.

Once you receive details of a post you are considering applying for, read the information carefully to confirm that you are definitely interested in the post and the school. Then make sure you really are a suitable candidate before completing an application. Read through the job description and selection criteria (usually supplied as lists of essential and desirable qualities/experience) and highlight key words and phrases that you know match your knowledge, skills, expertise, experience and outlook. If there is a good match between what you have to offer and what is being looked for and your immediate reaction to what you read is that you feel confident about your ability to meet the requirements of the post, then proceed with an application. If there is a poor match, then you really have to think carefully about whether or not to apply. Have you got time to spend applying for a post that you know there is a good chance you won't be invited to interview for? If, against the odds, you managed to get the job, would you be likely to succeed if you start off with a deficit in required knowledge and skills? Induction will be demanding wherever you teach; don't make it even harder by applying for posts which will present you with even bigger challenges, if at all possible. On the other hand, do be positive about your strengths. If, for example, you see that a candidate is being sought who can teach a second subject (perhaps something you studied for 'A' level), don't be put off from applying because you didn't study the subject at degree level. The chances are that you will be able to teach it successfully as a second subject, as most teaching skills are transferable from subject to subject and you already have a good level of knowledge from your 'A' level studies.

Application forms

Completing application forms can be a time consuming process and, unfortunately, each Local Authority or school uses a slightly different form. Though the information required will be very similar for each LA and school it will need to be presented slightly differently, according to the form. Some LAs have electronic versions of application forms, which at least means you can save a copy on computer and thus save some time when applying for several jobs with the same LA. Don't try and submit your curriculum vitae instead of the proper application form. However tempting this may be, you will not be considered unless you submit your application as instructed.

Complete all sections of the form and make sure there are no mistakes on the final draft. If the form is hand written, make sure your writing is neat. It is always sensible to use black ink on application forms. Your supporting statement is, in effect, your letter of application and it is acceptable to submit this as a letter. If you do so, write 'see letter of application' in the supporting statement box on the form. Always save a copy of your application form and letter to refer to if invited to attend for interview.

Letters of application

As with forms, letters of application must be polished and free from mistakes. They can usually be hand written or word-processed. The advantages of the latter are obvious in terms of saving time and making redrafting easy. Application letters for first appointments should be between one and two sides of A4 in length (font size 12).

A letter of application should state clearly your reasons for applying for the post, matching your qualifications, experience, skills and qualities to the post details and person specification supplied to candidates. It is very important that you don't have a standard letter of application on your computer that you simply alter the school name on each time you apply for a post. A standard letter is an acceptable starting point, but you must modify it carefully so that you are demonstrating in each letter of application exactly how you meet the criteria being looked for. This process is a bit like learning information for an exam, then selecting from it carefully in order

accomplished	achieved	addressed
arranged	assessed	averted
collaborated	compiled	completed
concluded	consolidated	created
cultivated	defined	delivered
demonstrated	designed	developed
devised	documented	engaged
enacted	established	evaluated
expanded	formulated	generated
implemented	improved	improvised
incorporated	initiated	inspired
instigated	integrated	intervened
introduced	launched	led
maintained	managed	monitored
observed	organised	performed
pioneered	predicted	prevented
produced	promoted	provided
redesigned	reduced	reorganised
resolved	reviewed	revised
shaped	simplified	standardised
strengthened	structured	supported
supervised	taught	trained
unified	utilised	volunteered

FIGURE 11.1 Action words for application letters

to answer the specific question set. Sometimes, you are asked to write about particular things in your letter of application. If you ignore this instruction, you are unlikely to be invited for interview.

Remember, your letter is designed to convince the reader of why you want the *particular* job you are applying for. This is why it is so important to show that your skills match their requirements closely. Avoid being arrogant and over-confident. All newly qualified teachers have a lot to learn and most head teachers are looking for new members of staff who are good team players, willing to learn from more experienced colleagues and not reluctant to admit mistakes and seek advice when necessary. Try and use a positive and enthusiastic tone in your letter. Use 'action words' to describe the things you have done. Examples of suitable words are given in Figure 11.1. If possible, include the impact of your actions (e.g. 'interest from pupils increased as a result of . . .' or 'I found pupils' skills in X improved following . . .'). Finally, don't forget to let your personality shine through; prospective employers will read many letters that are all similar so make sure yours stand out by including something about yourself that is unique.

Your curriculum vitae

Some job adverts ask you to submit a letter and CV rather than an application form (some independent schools, for example). A CV presents the type of information usually asked for in an application form. Your CV should be no more than two sides of A4 and should be word-processed and run off on a good quality printer if being posted. You should avoid fussy and cluttered layouts and stick to print styles such as *Times Roman* or *Arial*.

Typical CVs include:

- Personal details – name, date of birth, nationality, national insurance number, DfE number, address, telephone and e-mail contact details.

- Education and qualifications – list your qualifications stating level, subject and grade for GCSE and 'A' levels/GNVQs, and degree with main subjects covered and class awarded.

- Other qualifications – music, sport, first aid, Duke of Edinburgh, etc.

- Teaching experience – give details of school experience provided during teacher training and any additional school attachments undertaken.

- Work experience – give details of previous full-time and part-time/vacation employment. Include any voluntary work you have undertaken.

- Interests and activities – hobbies, interests, membership of clubs and societies should be included.

- Referees – include the name address and telephone and e-mail contact details for two referees. Usually, the referees chosen by those applying for first posts are the programme leader from their PGCE or teaching degree course and the head teacher or head of department from their final school experience school. The programme leader will, of course, consult your personal tutor and subject tutors before writing your reference. Likewise, the head teacher will consult the relevant head of department and school mentor before writing a reference.

Preparing for and attending an interview

Before the day

Once you receive an invitation for interview, read the details carefully and quickly confirm the arrangements. This can be done by phone or with a short letter. If, for any reason, you decide you no longer want to attend for interview, let the school know as soon as possible. If the interview date clashes with something like an exam in college, let the school know straight away; they may be willing to interview you at a different time.

If the school is fairly near to where you are living, you might consider asking if you can make a visit before the day of the interview (or before you submit an application at all). If this can be arranged, it will give you an opportunity to get a feel of the school and its pupils (movement on corridors, quality of displays, pupils' behaviour around school, the local area). Try and get an opportunity to speak to a recently qualified teacher so that you can get a really good idea of what life at the chalk-face is like in the school. If the school is a long way away, check travel arrangements very carefully. It may be better to travel the day before the interview so that you are fresh on the day. This will also give you the chance of looking round the area before you arrive for interview. Most schools pay for overnight accommodation if you are travelling a long distance, but if this is not made clear in the information you are sent you can ring up and check. No one will be offended by your enquiry.

It is important that you understand current educational issues and developments. There is likely to be some discussion of educational themes on the day of the interview and you don't want to be caught out. Hopefully, you will regularly discuss important educational topics with your peers. It is a good idea to look through the *Times Educational Supplement* each week so that you are aware of anything really important that is in the news.

Many candidates now bring a portfolio of their work to interviews. In the case of practical subjects examples of your work may be asked for, but it can be helpful for any candidate to have available examples of lesson plans, reflections on lessons, learning resources they have designed, photos of classes involved in practical learning, etc. All this material should be easily available in the professional file you keep during school experience.

You should try and prepare yourself for interview by thinking carefully about typical questions you are likely to be asked (see below) and rehearsing your responses. You may find 'visualisation' helpful. This involves picturing yourself in the interview and seeing and hearing your performance. By picturing yourself being calm, positive and successful you are getting yourself ready psychologically for the big day. You may also find it useful to record your voice answering questions or to watch yourself in the mirror. By analysing your behaviour you can correct common problems such as speaking too quickly or not knowing what to do with your hands (see below).

The interview day

Although in teaching there is a more tolerant attitude to dress than in many other professions, it is sensible to dress conventionally for interviews. Whether we like it or not, the way we look (at least initially) will have an influence on what people think about us. You want to make a good impression and so you should make the effort to be smart and well groomed.

The format for interview days varies, but most involve a tour of the school, an informal talk with the head of department, meeting colleagues over lunch and a formal panel interview (possibly with a short presentation as part of the interview). It is becoming more and more common for candidates to be asked to teach a lesson as part of the interview process. The aim is obvious: the observers want to get a sense of your classroom style and how you relate to pupils. As with all lessons you teach you should know the size of the class, what you are expected to teach, what the pupils' level of ability and prior knowledge is and what resources and equipment is available. This information should be provided well in advance of the interview day. If there is anything you are unsure about, you should phone for clarification. It is a good idea not to try and make your model lesson 'all singing and all dancing'. There is great potential for things going wrong if you try and be too sophisticated. Instead, write a good lesson plan, with clear objectives and make sure each observer is given a copy. Follow the typical format of a successful lesson with a clear introduction, well-structured activities and an effective plenary. Concentrate on showing that you can make your subject interesting to the age group, that you are skilled in your use of questioning, that you have high expectations and that you use the plenary to evaluate and consolidate learning. If possible, base the lesson you teach on one that has already worked well for you on school experience. Try and use pupils' names (you could give each one a sticky label to help you) and be certain to be inclusive by ensuring that all pupils and groups are able to engage in the lesson. Remember to assess with the pupils what they have learnt by the close of your lesson.

The formal interview usually involves a panel made up of such people as the head teacher, the head of department of your subject area and a member of the governing body. Larger panels could also include another senior member of staff, an LA subject adviser and possibly even a senior pupil in the school. Interviews usually last about half an hour. The questions you are likely to be asked will vary from school to school, but most schools will want to find out:

- What you have learnt during training and especially what you have achieved while on school placement;

- Your commitment to teaching in general and why you are attracted to the specific post in question;

- Your level of subject knowledge and especially how to translate this into effective lessons;

- Your views on education and educational issues;

- Your approach to classroom management and how you create a positive climate for learning;

- What you will be like as a form teacher and any extra-curricular interests you might offer;

- How you will fit into the subject team in particular and the school in general;

- Your ability to learn from your mistakes and the level of common sense you possess;

- How effective you are with time management;

- What support you will need as a newly qualified teacher and what your career ambitions are;

- What you are like as a person beyond school – how you relax from the stresses of teaching, for example.

In order to gain this information you will be asked a variety of questions in the interview. The first question is usually intended to put you at your ease and is therefore likely to be straightforward, whereas some of the later questions will be more demanding and require more careful thought. Some of the most challenging questions will begin with 'What would you do if . . .'? Should you be unsure about the meaning of a question don't be worried about asking for clarification. The panel will not be trying to catch you out, but they will be probing to ensure that they select the right candidate for the job. They will be trying to establish what you are really like as a teacher and a colleague and how you would deal with the kinds of situations that will confront you.

Here are a few typical questions you could be confronted with:

- Why did you choose teaching as a career? Why secondary school teaching?

- Why should all pupils study your subject? Is it really accessible to all abilities of pupils?

- What has been your greatest success while on school experience? Good, now tell us about a mistake you made on school experience and how you will avoid making a similar mistake as a newly qualified teacher.

- How do you create a purposeful working environment in your classroom? That's good, but what would you do about a pupil who . . .?

- How do you feel about becoming a form tutor? Excellent . . . now tell us how you would deal with the following situation in your form group. . . .

- What targets will you set yourself for development during your first year of teaching?

- What do you do to relax after a demanding and sometimes stressful day or week at school?

At the end of the interview you will probably be asked if you would like to ask any questions and if you are still a firm candidate for the post. If you have decided, for whatever reason, that you would not accept the post if offered you should now make this clear.

Most state schools interview all candidates on the same day. This means you meet the competition and have to interact with them until the formal interviews. You must not allow yourself to be undermined by things the other candidates tell you about themselves. Remember, you would not have been invited for interview if you weren't a strong candidate. If there is someone there for interview boasting about their achievements and experience the chances are they will come across as arrogant to the interviewers, so don't let them knock your confidence. Conduct yourself politely and quietly, asking appropriate questions. Don't say too much or too little. You can talk yourself out of a job as well as into one.

The most important part of the day is the formal interview and so you need to think very carefully about how to conduct yourself. Non-verbally we all communicate a great deal. It is important that your body language doesn't give different messages to the words you are speaking. You will, of course, feel nervous, but in order to come across as being as relaxed as possible try and remember the following: rest your hands on the arms of the chair in which you are sitting or in your lap; look at the interviewer with an interested expression, and as you answer each question make eye contact with each of the panel members; keep your head raised when listening. Try and avoid fidgeting, crossing your arms, looking away from the interviewer, tapping and, of course, yawning.

Your voice should convey interest and sincerity. The panel members will want to be able to imagine you in the classroom so you should make your responses clear and well focused. Show that you are knowledgeable and caring, but try and avoid answering questions as if you were in an academic tutorial in college. If you speak with a high pitch this could convey tension. If you speak too quickly your answers may be difficult to follow (100–120 words per minute is average). Pauses in the right place can be very effective but don't fill gaps with 'ums' and 'ers'. Under no circumstances use lazy or sloppy speech (regional accents should not be a problem so long as what you say is clear and accurate).

After the interview

Where all candidates are invited for interview on the same day, you are likely to be informed of the outcome of the interview on that day. You are expected to accept or reject the offer verbally at this point. Some schools will allow you twenty four hours to consider, but others won't, so you need to be really sure that you want the job by the time the offer is made. If you accept, you normally confirm in writing within a few days. This is usually done when you receive written confirmation of your appointment from the school or LA. It is courteous to let your referees know of your success. It is unprofessional to apply for other jobs once you have accepted a post, even if you see a job that looks more appealing than the one you have accepted.

Expenses forms can usually be left at the school on the day of the interview or returned within a few days of attending for interview. You will be expected to undergo a Criminal Records Bureau check. This is standard practice, even though you will have had such a check made at the outset of your training. You will be provided with a form for this purpose. You must declare all convictions, cautions or bind-overs that you have incurred, including any that would normally be regarded as 'spent'. Failure to do so could be grounds for dismissal.

If you are unsuccessful you are sure to feel disappointed. However, there could be many reasons why you haven't been successful, and success in first interviews is quite unusual. In most cases, the successful candidate will have a more precise match of experience and skills for the job than you did. Most interview panels offer feedback to unsuccessful candidates and it is a good idea to accept, as there is much that can be learnt from their comments on your performance. This is the best way you can turn the experience into a positive learning opportunity.

Once you have succeeded in securing a post and the formalities have been concluded it is a good idea to make a couple of visits to the school before your contract commences. This should allow you to get a copy of your timetable, familiarise yourself with resources and get a better feel for the geography of the site and buildings. You should take copies of the school and department handbooks, relevant schemes of work and key textbooks away with you. This will allow you to do some preparation before September. This preparation should be fairly general, as it is quite difficult to plan lessons effectively for pupils you haven't met, even though you may have an idea of their level of ability and previous experience. You will also need a break to recharge your batteries between completing training and taking up your first post.

Supply teaching

Naturally, you will want to gain the security of a permanent contract. However, not everyone is able to locate where there is a good supply of teaching posts to apply for. If there is a shortage of jobs in your area, remember you are legally entitled to work for up to five years after gaining QTS as a supply teacher. While this is not ideal, it will enable you to gain experience in a range of different schools and may ultimately enable you to perform better when you eventually secure your first teaching post. Also, supply work might provide a 'foot in the door' as you become known to local schools. Supply work which lasts for longer than a term can count towards Induction, but only if the school registers you with the appropriate body for Induction at the outset of the contract. Supply work can usually be secured through supply agencies but some teachers prefer to make direct contact with schools they want to do supply work in. When undertaking supply work always show commitment and behave professionally. Schools want more than a 'child minder' if they are paying you as a teacher.

Summary

Securing a teaching post requires commitment, determination and organisation. You cannot leave things to chance or assume that your natural charm will enable you to perform well in the interview. If you are going to succeed you must think carefully about where you want to teach and the type of school you would like to teach in. You must then make sure in your application letter that your skills and attributes match those outlined on the person specification and/or job description. In the interview you should try and be quietly confident, revealing your enthusiasm for teaching and your interest in both your subject and young people. You must come across as someone who is a good team player and will be keen to continue to learn and hone your skills. If you don't succeed in your first few interviews, use them as learning experiences and remain positive. If you are getting feedback from each debriefing that leads you to think you have a problem in interview technique, discuss this with a college tutor who should be able to point you in the direction of the support you need, as most institutions have individuals employed to offer you more personalised advice and guidance.

12 Induction

How to succeed and flourish

Introduction

Successfully completing your training (including passing the compulsory online tests in Maths, English and ICT) and being awarded Qualified Teacher Status (QTS) will be a major achievement. However, you must remember that it is only after the successful completion of Induction (one year for those employed full time) that you will be officially recognised as a teacher with the legal status to teach in maintained schools (if you fail to complete Induction successfully you will not be eligible to teach in state schools).

In order to be successful during Induction and beyond, first and foremost you need to be a good teacher. However, you need also to use your 'people skills' (emotional intelligence) to get the best out of the adults with whom you work. New teachers have responsibility for the deployment of other adults working in their classroom (usually teaching assistants) and so understanding the importance of motivating others and of teamwork cannot be underestimated. If you are successful in the classroom and can also manage other adults effectively, you should be able to gain rapid promotion. It is never too early to consider the various career paths that exist in teaching. If you are ambitious you need to plan ahead!

This chapter will consider transition from training, statutory Induction, managing people, being an effective team player, developing reflective practice and career routes in education. It also offers guidance on how to deal with difficult parents and colleagues.

Induction

Transition from teaching

At the end of your training period you are likely to complete a career entry profile with your training provider. This is intended to allow you to reflect on your achievements, strengths and ambitions as well as to consider areas you need to prioritise for development during Induction. Before your first term in employment begins you should discuss the contents of this profile with your Induction tutor (mentor) in school to help make your transition as smooth as possible. Your likely development needs should be established so that the school can consider how best to support your further development in these areas. Don't be embarrassed about admitting any areas you need to work on as allowing you time to further develop is a key reason for having an Induction. It is very important that you take this process seriously and use it as an opportunity to be supported in the further development of your professional knowledge, understanding and skills. Common areas identified for further development by Newly Qualified Teachers (NQTs) include behaviour management, Special Educational Needs and differentiation, as these issues are particularly complex and challenging. It is not at all sensible to 'hide' or minimise any areas you have found difficult during training; as a reflective professional it is far better to take advantage of your entitlement to support and work hard to improve in these areas during Induction.

Induction

Induction is designed to ensure that newly qualified teachers are supported and continue to develop professionally. It provides a bridge between training and a career in teaching. For those in a full-time post, the Induction is normally one year. During Induction you will be provided with a programme of professional development and monitored and evaluated against the Teachers' Standards (DfE 2011).

Entitlements

In order to help you get off to a good start you are entitled to the following during Induction:

- Ten per cent NQT development time off timetable (in addition to planning, preparation and assessment or PPA time given to all teachers);
- An Induction tutor (mentor) and regular mentor meetings;
- An Induction programme designed to meet development needs you have identified;
- No unreasonable demands being placed on you (e.g. teaching outside the age range and subjects you specialised in for training, discipline challenges that are untypical for the school you are in).

During Induction you will be observed teaching and should have the opportunity to observe experienced teachers in their classrooms.

Monitoring and assessment

Lesson observations will be the main way in which you are assessed. Expect to have targets set following lesson observations. These may be expressed simply as areas to work on or they may be more precisely worded with clear success criteria stated. You can be certain that the areas you have been asked to focus on will be assessed when you are next observed so ensure that you have acted on all advice given. If you are unsure what is expected of you or what success will look like it is important to seek clarification.

At the end of each term of Induction your progress against the Teachers' Standards will be reviewed. In addition to lesson observations your planning documentation, pupils' work, pupil tracking data, your day to day behaviour, informal monitoring and informal feedback from parents and pupils will also be used to inform assessment. While most NQTs complete Induction successfully, it is important to realise a small number each year do not. If you are not successful it is possible to appeal, but if this fails then you will no longer be able to teach in maintained schools. It is very important, therefore, that you are proactive in ensuring you get your entitlements as an NQT. Most schools handle NQTs and Induction very well, but if you feel you are not being supported or unreasonable demands are being placed upon you, speak to your Induction tutor (mentor) sooner rather than later. If this doesn't help, see your head teacher. If you still feel your entitlements are not being met, contact the appropriate body responsible for quality assuring your Induction. In most cases this will be the Local Authority and they will have a named adviser who co-ordinates NQT induction across the local area. If you belong to a trade union, you could also speak to your union representative.

If you are not making the progress expected and seem unlikely to be able to meet the Standards this will be stated on your end of term review form. In these circumstances you are entitled to additional support and a support plan should be drawn up. You must make sure you are clear about what success in each area identified will look like and then work as hard as you can to do what is being asked of you. Don't waste energy challenging what is being asked for unless you feel you are being treated unfairly; most Induction tutors are very experienced and know what needs to be done to ensure success.

Personalised Induction

To get the most out of Induction don't use the 10% NQT development time simply for routine tasks. This time is for you to work on your *personalised* development needs. It is likely that your school will have a common Induction programme for all NQTs but the 10% time is for differentiated elements of Induction to be provided. Depending on what your needs are this time might be used for observing other teachers, visiting other schools, joint planning, meeting with an Advanced Skills Teacher (AST), observing pupils you teach being taught by others, etc. You need to be proactive in making suggestions to your Induction tutor (mentor) rather than expecting them to initiate this plan.

Managing adults

It is highly likely that you will work closely with a range of adults in school other than fellow teachers and school leaders. Some of the adults now working in schools include special needs support assistants, classroom assistants, advanced classroom assistants, higher level teaching assistants, pupil mentors, cover supervisors, technicians, administrative staff, lunch time supervisors, cleaners and caretakers (or site managers as they may be called in secondary schools). All of these people have a valuable contribution to make to the school, even if it is not directly related to teaching and learning, and deserve to be treated with respect. This is why the Teachers' Standards (DfE 2011) expect you to 'develop effective professional relationships with colleagues, knowing how and when to draw on advice and specialist support' and 'deploy support staff effectively'.

As a trainee those who tutor you should be trying hard to support you and develop your skills and confidence. Very good mentors will make you feel capable of success while also being clear about particular areas you need to improve in. There is much you can learn from this about how you will be able to support others once you commence your teaching career.

Action point

Discuss your experience of being mentored with a fellow trainee. What things made you feel valued and capable? Did anything undermine your confidence and make you feel less capable? What can you learn from this regarding the skills you will need to support other adults working in your classroom?

There are a few important behaviours that good managers display when trying to get the best out of others.

1. *Spend time getting to know the people you work closely with*

    When you start a new job, even though you will be very busy, it is worth spending time getting to know the people with whom you will work closely. Your knowledge of these people will help you to manage situations more easily, for example by being able to anticipate their likely reactions to new ideas. As you get to know people you will become concerned for their welfare and as this begins to show it is likely to bring you a greater degree of loyalty than teachers who stand aloof. Showing that you are interested in colleagues as people and as professionals will encourage them to offer you the support you will need to do your job effectively.

2. *Communicate clearly*

    It is important that support staff with whom you work do not feel they are being kept in the dark about what you expect of them. Talk to them about your lesson plans and make clear what they are expected to do. If time pressures make talking impossible, always make sure they have a copy of your planning with what is expected of them included. Ask for their ideas; experienced support staff may well be able to offer you useful guidance initially and will certainly know the pupils better than you do when you first arrive at a school. Always take the time to explain things clearly. People are more likely to co-operate if they know what they are supposed to be doing. If teaching assistants don't perform well it is sometimes because teachers have failed to communicate with them effectively. Giving assistants a sense of ownership is really important. Try hard to allow them to contribute their ideas when you discuss your lesson plans. Remember, you are responsible for all the children in your lesson. The learning needs of SEN pupils can only be met through effective communication with the staff employed to support them.

3. *Display self-control*

Good managers calmly find ways to solve problems and they do not make mountains out of molehills. Respect is more likely to be gained by being calm when things go wrong than by creating anxiety in others by exaggerating the importance of small mistakes they have made. You will soon lose the respect of support staff if you constantly challenge them over minor matters.

4. *Lead by example*

As a teacher you should set a high standard in the quality of the work you do and in your general attitude to your pupils you should model what you expect of your support staff. Be professional at all times; you have to lead from the front. This is especially important for creating an inclusive ethos in your classroom. Value all pupils and show you care about them; this will set the tone of what you expect of support staff working with you. Try and remain positive about all pupils. Some pupils can be very challenging (they are often frustrated themselves as a result of their learning difficulties). If other members of staff offer negative comments about pupils, try and understand the cause of their comments but don't enter into an attack on a pupil's character or begin listing their failings. This can be very difficult, as sometimes teachers and support staff need to 'let off steam' if they have had a particularly bad lesson. However, verbal attacks on pupils are demeaning and ultimately show the teachers who make them in a bad light.

5. *Be considerate*

The maxim 'treat other people as you would wish to be treated yourself' is an important one for teachers. This means more than simply being pleasant and friendly towards others, it means thinking about the impact your actions will have on their self-esteem and motivation. If you show consideration towards support staff, technicians and dinner supervisors your efforts will be repaid. When you have a problem that requires them to change their plans at short notice, they are more likely to try and help you out. For example, if you treat the technician or administrator responsible for photocopying with politeness and respect, on the rare occasion when you need a 'rush job' your request is much more likely to be accommodated.

6. *Offer support*

Good teachers share relevant skills in the hope that support staff can become more effective. As a trainee and an NQT you should receive plenty of coaching and support, but as a teacher you will need also to begin coaching and supporting those working in your classroom in a support capacity. You will need to use a balance between directive behaviour and supportive behaviour. Directive behaviour involves telling people what to do, how to do it, when to do it, and then monitoring performance. Supportive behaviour involves listening to people and providing support and encouragement. Different circumstances and different individuals will require different combinations of directive and supportive behaviour and you will need to use careful judgements when considering the best approach to adopt. Typically, a directing style would be used when inducting support staff into certain classroom procedures. A coaching style might be used in order to develop their capability and encourage initiative. This would involve working closely with your teaching assistant, explaining, listening and encouraging their suggestions. A supporting style is the style that is likely to be used most often with experienced support staff. Delegation can be used with higher level teaching assistants or lesson supervisors, who have been appropriately trained for taking on a high degree of responsibility in the classroom. Such people may be ambitious to ultimately gain QTS and become teachers.

7. *Spread good cheer!*

The ability to spread good cheer should be an essential quality listed on selection criteria sheets sent to prospective candidates for any post in a school! The importance of this should never be underestimated. In far too many staff rooms you will find disgruntled teachers being negative and cynical. No doubt individual cynics will have their personal reasons for their lack of enthusiasm, but their behaviour does little to keep up morale or encourage new recruits to the profession! You can help to contribute to keeping up staff morale in a number of small but very significant ways. Praise and thanks provide what are called *positive strokes* and these help to build up morale and confidence. We all want to be appreciated and valued but, sadly, it often feels like the media and government have little that is positive to say about teachers. This can undermine morale and self-confidence and make it difficult to feel motivated. It is true that success breeds success and it is also true that negative talk can create failure or at least sap enthusiasm. By spreading good cheer you help to keep up morale. If you observe a really good lesson make sure the teacher knows how good you thought it was; if your mentor spends a great deal of time with you make sure you show that you are grateful; when your teaching assistant has an excellent idea respond enthusiastically.

Effective teams

In school you will belong to several teams, and the ability to work as part of a team is therefore very important. Some teams are permanent, for example Subject Teams, Year Teams and the Senior Management Team (SMT), although membership changes as a result of staff being promoted, staff retiring or internal restructuring. Other teams are temporary, for example working groups established to write a particular policy document or plan a school production. Some teams operate very formally, for example governing bodies, whereas other teams can be quite informal, a group of colleagues who have taken on responsibility for organising staff social events, for instance. Some teams have limited membership, for example the Senior Leadership Team (SLT), whereas other teams offer open access, for instance a working party on behaviour. Membership of some teams is voluntary but membership of other teams is contractual.

Some teams are much more effective than others. In teams that don't work well the activities of individuals frequently limit, rather than enhance the effectiveness of the whole. There may be jealousies between members, information suppressed and co-operation withheld because members see themselves as being in competition with each other. Alternatively, there may be apathy and indifference resulting from a lack of team vision or sense of direction.

Reflection point

Consider teams you have belonged to at different points in your life. What made them effective or ineffective? Share your thoughts with a fellow trainee and discuss the implications for your work in school.

It is likely that you recognised the following features in effective teams:

1. *Vision and sense of direction*

    Having shared goals is the first thing that distinguishes groups from teams. This is why it is so important that the team leader has a clear sense of direction. This should be provided partly by the vision or mission of the school, with the team leader's job being to translate the vision into something meaningful at team level. A clear sense of direction will also come from the team leader being certain about what their team is uniquely contributing to the education of young people.

2. *The behaviour of the team leader*

    Good team leaders are able to listen to the views of others and encourage participation. They adopt an inclusive style of leadership. They are self critical and committed to the idea that their authority comes more from their behaviour and the example they set than from their title. Team leaders should want individuals in their team to progress and develop and will be skillful at directing, coaching, supporting and delegating, as appropriate. The team leader will be visible and accessible and will strive to build the self-esteem of all team members.

3. *The extent to which people pull together*

A team exists if members embrace the team vision and work together to achieve it. The result is team members becoming interdependent, with particular strengths of individuals recognised and used to the benefit of the whole team and the pupils. Team members also support each other. This does not mean that there are never any disagreements. Open debate is encouraged and is one of the things that helps to clarify team values and the direction the team is going in. Team successes are celebrated publicly as are the achievements of individual team members. It is not unusual to hear laughter coming from meetings of successful teams. This indicates a relaxed rapport has been achieved and is in no way at odds with a team's serious purpose.

4. *Open lines of communication*

Team members talk to each other about issues and there is an atmosphere in which positive and negative feedback can be given. People are open-minded to the views of others and new ideas are encouraged and debated. Individual team members are assertive but not aggressive and conflicting viewpoints are seen as normal. Indeed, lively debate is seen as a constructive feature of decision making. While lines of communication are open there are also clear procedures for holding meetings and making decisions.

5. *Regular reviews of progress*

Good teams are not frightened of reviewing progress. Successes are celebrated and failures analysed so as to build on good practice and avoid repeating mistakes. All team members are involved in development planning and target setting.

An effective team combines creativity and energy to produce an output greater than the sum of its parts – this is known as *synergy*. You may have experienced synergy as part of a team putting on a public performance such as a show, or maybe in school you will experience it during an Ofsted inspection. What you will remember is the real sense of working together for a common goal. Synergy is what good team leaders try and create in the everyday work of their teams.

You may be lucky in you first post and find that you belong to a team or teams with most of the above features. On the other hand, you may join a team that doesn't function quite so well and where relationships are poor. Whatever the state of the team you are in, the important thing is for you to be professional and consistent in your behaviour, so that your actions add value to the team and help it to function well.

■ Listen to other team members respectfully (even when you disagree with what they say).

- Contribute your ideas but remember to be tactful (your colleagues will have a great deal of experience which you should respect and you must avoid appearing to 'know it all', however strongly you feel about things).

- Take on your fair share of tasks. Even though you are in your first year of teaching there are certain routine matters that you should help with. You will have a timetable that is ten per cent lighter than your colleagues (rightly so) and being seen to be willing to 'muck in' and 'roll your sleeves up' will earn you acceptance. Be careful not to take on anything that is too time-consuming, however. Being asked to take on major responsibilities in your first year is unreasonable, and if you feel this is happening you should talk to your Induction tutor (mentor) about it.

- Always be willing to accept assistance from other members of the team and seek advice and support when you feel you need it. If help is offered that you don't need make sure it is declined with good grace, so that your colleague feels their offer was appreciated.

- Showing concern for others and offering assistance in small ways will go down very well. If you have non-contact time before a team meeting have coffee ready for when your colleagues arrive, for example.

- Hopefully, the teachers you work with will plan together and share resources. Make sure you offer your ideas and teaching aids; new teachers are often very creative and take a lot of pleasure in designing work tasks. Likewise, use resources created by other teachers, but make sure they are returned to their proper home after use as 'hogging resources' will cause inconvenience to others.

- Try and avoid listening to gossip and don't allow yourself to be drawn into criticising other members of your team. Avoid becoming part of any clique; you need to be able to work effectively with all your colleagues.

Professional development and career progression

It is important that from the outset of your career you see the importance of life long learning. Education must evolve to meet the needs of our changing society and there will always be ways in which we can better meet learners' needs. Continuing Professional Development (CPD) is essential in a rapidly changing world. Successful schools realise the importance of the school being a 'learning community' where teachers continue to improve their skills and understanding through continuous development.

Showing a commitment to CPD will help you to improve your classroom performance, cope with change, increase your own capacity for learning and enhance your career prospects. You should from the start of your career see professional development as something that you are in control of and not something that is done to you! Your Induction should help you to get into the habit of setting yourself targets for development and seeking support with achieving these targets. Appraisal (performance management) procedures should continue this process following Induction.

In the past many teachers equated professional development with attending a course. This is certainly one form of professional development but there are many other ways in which teachers can develop their knowledge, understanding and practice.

Action point

List all the ways in which teachers might develop professionally.

There are many, many ways, but here are a few of the things you might have listed:

- Observing other colleagues teaching;
- Team teaching;
- Watching and reflecting on a lesson they have had recorded;
- Joint planning;
- Working with an Advanced Skills Teacher (AST);
- Shadowing a colleague doing a specific task (for example a pastoral head);
- Reading professional journals and books;
- Contributing to internet discussion groups on education;
- Undertaking marking duties for an Examination Board;
- Attending local and/or national subject meetings;
- Mentoring NQTs;
- Meeting with Local Authority advisers;
- Attending short courses;
- Attending award bearing courses (e.g. M.Ed or specialist SEN qualifications);
- Inviting outside experts to contribute to lessons;
- Joining working parties.

This is not an exhaustive list, but it gives you a clear idea that there are many opportunities for professional development and that most of them will entail no or very little cost to the school.

From the start of your career it is a good idea to keep a portfolio of your professional development. This is a collection of material and records that reflects your work. It is a way of using past experience and present activities to demonstrate and reflect on skills learnt and to identify future development needs. A well kept portfolio will show areas in which you (and your pupils) have excelled and will demonstrate how you have continued to develop professionally. A portfolio will help you with:

- Critical self reflection;
- Planning for further development;
- Producing evidence for appraisal interviews, job interviews and threshold pay progression.

In compiling your portfolio it would be sensible to be aware of all Standards relating to teachers. For now, your main concern is meeting the Teachers' Standards but at the time of writing there are plans for the introduction of Master Teacher Standards for progression to the upper pay scale. Keep aware of these changes by visiting the Department for Education or Teaching Agency websites.

Don't be shy about being ambitious. New teachers are the heads and deputy heads of tomorrow and it is never too early to consider leadership development opportunities. You can learn a lot from middle and senior leaders in school you admire and once you have completed Induction you can begin to volunteer for informal leadership experience. The National College (www.nationalcollege. org.uk) provides leadership programmes through regional contract holders and teaching schools, many universities offer leadership development programmes and many Local Authorities offer very practical leadership development sessions or even complete programmes.

In a secondary school there are numerous opportunities for promotion. Gone are the days when teachers were restricted to either a subject route (head of subject) or a pastoral route (head of year) for promotion. School leaders must now understand how the academic and pastoral elements of school life combine to impact on pupils' achievement. Posts such as Head of Key Stage, Gifted and Talented co-ordinator and Inclusion manager remove the artificial academic/pastoral divide. Likewise the language of management has changed to reflect the high expectations now placed on key post holders. Labels such as 'Year Leader' and 'Subject Leader' are not accidental. The choice of the term 'leader' implies the post holder will have a clear vision for their area of responsibility and will be capable of motivating others and being accountable for standards as well as a capable organiser. This is why it is so important that you develop effective people skills in your early years of teaching.

Of course, there are opportunities in the wider world of education for successful teachers to consider. A career in education is not the same as a career in teaching and some very successful teachers decide that their skills can be used overseas or in associated areas of work in the UK. Some teachers undertake further qualifications to work in special education or become educational psychologists, for example, while others successfully move into teaching in further education or higher education. Teachers regularly move into a career in teacher training, others into Local Authorities or private companies providing school support services. It is inappropriate in this book to explain the best routes into these various jobs, but it is important that you realise that the world of education offers enormous opportunities for those who take professional development seriously.

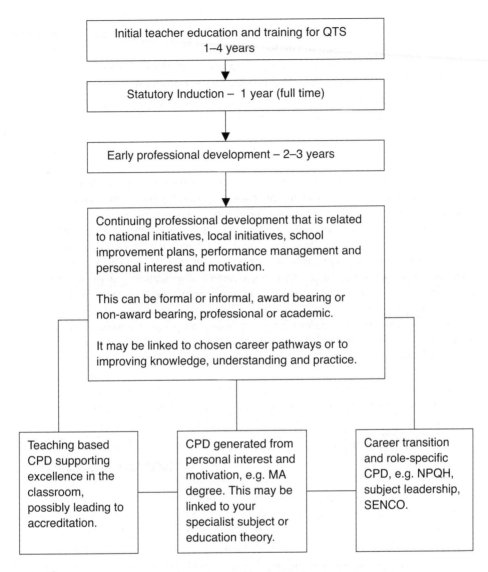

FIGURE 12.1 Career long professional development

Case study

The importance of CPD, appraisal and reflective practice

John is a teacher of RE, with three years' teaching experience, all in his present school. He made a late entry into teaching from the Church. He is a knowledgeable teacher but he leaves a lot to be desired in the areas of organisation and behaviour management. Ever since his Induction year (when he struggled with challenging classes) he has been allocated classes regarded as 'easy to handle'. He seems unaware (or chooses to ignore) his poor reputation for behaviour management and organisation he has acquired. His failings are evident in his dealings with pupils while on duty, when there are often confrontations with older pupils. On the plus side John genuinely cares about children and is always willing to help colleagues if he can. He gets his form group involved in charity events (though usually poorly organised) and he willingly contributes to extra-curricular activities.

School leaders have followed a strategy of 'working round' John rather than confronting the issues. He struggled through the school's recent Ofsted inspection, and some parents in his GCSE RE class have complained about him losing pupils' coursework. He seems unaware of the seriousness of his weaknesses and has now applied for the Head of RE post that has become available in the school due to the retirement of the current post holder.

Reflection point

- What has gone wrong with John's development since he gained QTS?
- Who is to blame for John's lack of development during his first three years in school?
- What issues will result from John's application for head of RE?

Fortunately, most schools would have dealt more effectively with John! Clearly, leaders in the school have failed John (and the pupils and parents) by working round his weaknesses and not using the Induction year and subsequent appraisal arrangements to discuss areas of weakness and set targets for improvement. Likewise, John himself has very obviously failed to develop the use of critical reflection, as he seems either unaware of his failings or unwilling to confront them. This is unprofessional, as pupils are suffering. Serious upset will be caused when John is told that he is unsuitable as an applicant for the Head of RE post. He may feel demoralised and be less willing in future to be involved in the extra-curricular activities he currently undertakes. All this could have been avoided quite easily, through target setting, monitoring and appropriate CPD opportunities (perhaps coaching in organisation and class management by experienced colleagues). The leaders in the school are largely to blame for the problem, but John must take a share also. He really should have been thinking about his career intentions and discussing these with school leaders.

The message for you as a trainee is to make sure you engage constructively with review and target setting during Induction, and thereafter with appraisal. Accept that learning is a continuous process and don't sweep areas you need to develop under the carpet. If you do, the chances are that both you and your pupils will suffer.

Some thoughts on reflective practice

The Teachers' Standards provide a valuable framework against which to 'measure' the development of essential knowledge and skills required to be an effective teacher. However, as a professional working in education you need to be able to engage critically with these Standards and think beyond a purely skills based model of teaching. Reflective practice refers to practical enquiry undertaken for the purpose of understanding and improving professional practice. It has featured in the work of many prominent educationalists, such as Dewey (1933), Schon (1983) and Zeichner (Zeichner and Liston 1987). It is possible to reflect at several levels. During training and Induction your mentors and tutors should encourage you to reflect on the technical aspects of teaching so that you develop the effective application of professional knowledge. This is likely to be done through structured reflection and review opportunities. You can help this process by keeping an ongoing log or journal of your school experience, in which you record and analyse your classroom experiences with a view to continuous improvement.

Beyond this it is legitimate that as a professional you begin to reflect on the institutional context and the wider social and political context in which you operate. Unpacking the unwritten values and assumptions within school or the underlying philosophies and assumptions that impact on education policy will help you to develop a sense of what might be possible rather than simply focusing on the world as it is. This is an important part of developing your vision for education; something you will need if you decide to climb the career ladder to a position of influence in school.

During training and Induction you should concentrate on reflecting on your subject and pedagogy (the science of teaching). The four stages of reflection involved in planning identified by Cooper and McIntyre (1996) are helpful as a means of combining subject knowledge and pedagogy in the reflective process:

- What am I teaching and why?
- How do I teach it and how else could I?
- How can I make the content relevant to the pupils in this school?
- How can I match content to the needs of pupils in this class?

As a professional you need to get into the habit of learning through experience in order continually to improve. Kolb and Fry (1975) provide a useful model for the process of experiential learning. This has four elements: concrete experience, observation and reflection, the formation of abstract concepts and testing in new situations (see Figure 12.2).

The learning process often begins with a person carrying out a particular action and then observing the effect of the action in a particular situation. The second step is to understand these observed effects in the particular situation so that if the same action were taken in the same circumstances it would be possible to anticipate what would follow from the action. The third step would be to understand the

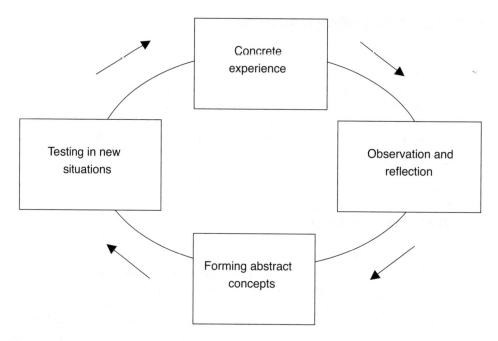

FIGURE 12.2 Kolb's experiential learning cycle

general principle under which the particular instance falls. When the general principle is understood, the last step is application through action in a new circumstance. The utility of this model for teachers is easy to appreciate.

Action research

Action research can be used to turn reflection into action. Like reflective practice action research is a generic term that embraces a variety of strategies, all of which are designed to result in improvements in some practical situation. Action research involves:

- Observing what is already happening;
- Asking a question about what you see;
- Finding evidence to shed light on your question;
- Interpreting the evidence;
- Acting on the evidence;
- Evaluating the impact of your action;
- Asking a new question.

In education, action research can be used to help evaluate the introduction of a new resource or teaching technique in the classroom by:

- Observing what is happening;
- Considering what could be done to improve matters;
- Implementing the new approach;
- Monitoring what the effects are;
- Reflecting on these effects and planning future action.

It is easy to see how action research could be used to act on a number of issues, including lesson delivery, behaviour management and assessment. It is inappropriate in this chapter to discuss research design and matters of validity and reliability in relation to action research. The important thing is that you should be willing to consider using research as a means of systematically investigating and solving particular issues you may face as a teacher. If you decide to do so during your Induction, actively involve your Induction tutor in planning and conducting the research. At a later stage in your career, undertaking a higher degree in education would help you to get to grips with and apply action research robustly. It is likely that in the future teachers will be encouraged to undertake more and more research in order to identify unique solutions to unique problems. The following websites offer further information on classroom research.

www.bera.ac.uk

www.nfer.ac.uk

Dealing with difficult people

The vast majority of teachers and parents you encounter will be pleasant and supportive. If you are behaving professionally by doing your best to teach well and showing respect towards pupils, parents and colleagues you are unlikely to encounter much hostility. However, schools are places where bullying of teachers has been known to occur and there are well-publicised examples of acts of violence being committed against teachers by parents. It is important, therefore, that you give some thought to what a new teacher can do to reduce the chances of becoming a victim of such unacceptable behaviour.

Parents

Guidance has already been provided in Chapter 8 on how best to handle parents' evenings and how to try and build fruitful relationships with parents. While on school placement during training, try and shadow a teacher at a consultation evening, so you can get an idea of how they operate. Once in your first job, try and follow the guidance below to ensure that your dealings with parents are amicable.

- If you have concerns about a child try not to save them for a consultation evening. Involve your head of department and relevant year head so that parents are informed sooner rather than later about any significant concerns.

- Keep plenty of evidence of pupils' performance and mark pupils' books regularly. Have this evidence available to support comments you make when you meet parents.

- Dress especially smartly for parents' evening; it will help you to appear professional.

- Stand up when greeting parents and shake hands with confidence.

- Speak clearly to parents. Avoid educational jargon.

- Be honest in what you say, but be sensitive to parents' feelings.

- Focus on any progress made and exactly what needs to be done to ensure further progress.

- Make a note of what you say and of anything you agree to. Always follow through.

- Make sure that you listen to what parents have to say. Show empathy. Maintain eye contact.

- Stay calm. Even if parents are raising their voice, keep your voice low.

Angry parents

Sometimes parents come into school, either by appointment or unannounced, because they have a concern about something that has happened to their child. They may misunderstand what is going on or they may be genuinely worried or angry about something. If they are not handled carefully, their anger could erupt into acts of aggression. Always try and ensure a senior colleague is with you when you meet a parent to discuss a concern they have.

The best way to take steam out of a situation is to let the parent 'offload'. Get them to sit down and then listen to their version of events, even if you know what they are saying is inaccurate. You should show concern and understanding by keeping eye contact, and nodding appropriately. Ask for points to be clarified to show that you want to understand their concerns fully. Once they have finished reassure them that you understand how they must be feeling and that you want to sort matters out. If you feel they have got only a partial version of events or that they have completely misunderstood a situation, you can calmly explain what the 'real' version of events is at this point. If you have made a mistake that has caused the anger then an explanation and apology is in order. Never patronise parents, never belittle them and never back them into a corner. You should aim to come out of a meeting with angry parents with a plan of action that both 'sides' are clear about. If you have agreed to do certain things you should make sure that these are done and reported to parents. The reporting may be by phone, letter or both, depending on the nature of the issues discussed. Alternatively, a further meeting may have been agreed to discuss progress with the issue concerned. The important thing is that you restore the trust of the parents by showing that you care and by completing anything you have agreed to do. This approach will work in the vast majority of cases, but, sadly, there are a small minority of unreasonable, truculent, even malicious parents, and this is why you should not put yourself at risk by trying to handle meetings with angry parents alone.

If you do encounter especially difficult parents *do not*:

- Retract any statements of fact you have made simply because a parent disagrees with them;
- Focus on problems rather than solutions;
- Focus on personality rather than behaviour;
- Forget that the parent may be disappointed and/or embarrassed;
- Struggle on without offering the parent a chance to speak to a senior colleague.

If parents make an appointment to see you at a time other than a parents' evening, make sure that the meeting is on the school premises (most schools have an interview room) and that senior colleagues know about it. If you are at all concerned about the reason for the meeting or the particular parents, arrange for a senior colleague to be in the meeting with you. Under no circumstances keep to yourself a conversation with a parent that has caused you concern. Share any information you have with a senior colleague and seek advice on how to respond. It is your duty to protect children and to be mindful of your own safety.

Parents as colleagues

While on School Experience and as an NQT you may find yourself involved with parents as helpers, for example they may be working as SEN support assistants in your classes. You may meet parents through Parent Teacher Association (PTA) events or parents may be used to accompany pupils on school trips. In all of these situations you should treat them professionally and with respect. If they can see that you are a caring, well-organised and committed teacher you will soon gain their respect. Under no circumstances should you gossip about pupils or colleagues with parent-helpers, even if they initiate such talk. You may also find you have the son or daughter of a colleague in your class. You should ensure you treat their child exactly as you would any other, giving them no more or no less attention than any other child and insisting on the same standards of behaviour and work as you would for other pupils. If you ever feel compromised because of how a parent who is also a teacher behaves towards you it is important to log your concerns and discuss them with a senior member of staff. Remain professional and, even if tempted, never 'bad mouth' the parent-teacher to your peers.

Colleagues

Bullying of staff does take place in some schools but this is rare. Bullying is unacceptable and should never be tolerated. Bullying includes:

- Relentless criticism;
- Threats;
- Humiliation;
- Undermining;
- Excessive work expectations;
- Inappropriate communication (shouting, ordering);
- Lack of compassion in difficult circumstances;
- Failure to recognise achievements.

Adult bullies aim to exert power negatively in order to inflict fear and cause emotional damage. Bullies are often insecure people though this wouldn't be obvious from the way they undermine others.

If you become a victim of staff room bullying it could produce:

- Anxiety
- Shattered confidence
- Reduction in performance
- Fatigue
- Digestive disorders
- Menstrual disorders
- Absenteeism.

Proving bullying can be very difficult, so make sure you keep a log of all incidents. The best people in school to speak to about it are your Induction tutor (mentor), other NQTs (for peer support), your union representative or the senior member of staff with responsibility for staff welfare. If no one in school seems to be able to make a difference, speak to the Local Authority adviser with responsibility for NQTs. Don't allow yourself to think that it is your fault that you are being bullied. You should be treated professionally and with respect even if you are not doing well during Induction.

Being assertive

Being assertive is an important skill to develop and will help you to deal with difficult people and will greatly reduce the chances of you becoming a victim of bullying. Being assertive means taking responsibility for your behaviour, having respect for yourself and others and being honest. It allows you to say what you want or feel but not at other people's expense. It means understanding the point of view of other people and being self-confident and positive. It is not about winning come what may or getting your own way all of the time. Assertiveness is about handling conflict and coming to an acceptable compromise.

Bullying involves being aggressive: getting your own way at the expense of others and making them feel worthless or incompetent. Being passive means ignoring your interests and allowing others to manipulate you by denying how you really think or feel. It is important that you are neither aggressive nor passive. You should learn to recognise passive, assertive and aggressive behaviour in order to be able to respond appropriately (see Table 5.2 in Chapter 5)

Summary

Gaining QTS represents a major achievement but is only the beginning of your career as a teacher. During Induction you will need to build on the skills you have developed. You should be supported with development needs you have identified but you need to be proactive to ensure this happens. See the 10% NQT time you get as a fantastic opportunity to develop your knowledge and skills; you won't get this opportunity again! By taking continuous professional development seriously you will be able to grow as a professional and move towards career goals you have identified. In order to be successful in teaching it is important that you are committed to making a difference to the lives of your pupils through continuously reflecting on your approach to teaching and learning. In addition, you should develop your interpersonal skills and assertiveness as in the future teachers will increasingly have to manage other adults supporting learners in their classroom. There are tremendous opportunities for rapid advancement in the profession for hardworking and skilful teachers who take their pupils' learning and their own professional development seriously.

References

Cooper, P. and McIntyre, D. (1996) *Effective Teaching and Learning: Teachers' and Students' Perspectives*, Buckingham: Open University Press.

Dewey, J. (1933) *How We Think*, New York: Heath.

DfE (2011) *Teachers' Standards*, Crown copyright.

Kolb, D.A. and Fry. R. (1975) 'Towards an Applied Theory of Experiential Learning' in Cooper, C. (ed.) *Theories of Group Process*, London: John Wiley.

Schon, D. (1983) *The Reflective Practitioner*, New York: Basic Books.

Zeichner, K. and Liston, D. (1987) Teaching Student Teachers to Reflect, *Harvard Educational Review*, 57(1), 23–48.

Bibliography

Barber, M. and Brighouse, T. (1992) *Enhancing the Teaching Profession*, London: IPPR.

Black, P. and Williams, D. (1998) *Inside the Black Box*, London: King's College.

Black, P., Harrison, C., Lee, C., Marshall, B., and William, D. (2004) *Working Inside the Black Box: Assessment for learning in the classroom*, in *Phi Delta Kappan* 86(1) 8–21, (web reference http://litd.psch.uic.edu/docs/ForSGLrngEnvAiM/BlackWrkBlBox. pdf).

Blair, M. (2001) *Why Pick on Me? School Exclusion and Black Youth*, Stoke on Trent: Trentham Books.

Bleach, K. (2000) *The Newly Qualified Teacher's Handbook*, London: Fulton.

Bloom, B.S. (1964) *Taxonomy of Educational Objectives: Handbook 1 – Cognitive Domains*, London: Longman.

Bruner, J. (1983) *Child's Talk: Learning to Use Language*, Oxford: Oxford University Press.

Capel, S. (1997) 'Changes in Students' Anxieties After Their First and Second Teaching Practices' in *Educational Research*, 39(2) 211–228.

Chaplain, I. (1999) 'Improving Achievement by Raising the Community's Expectations' in *Sustaining School Improvement*, Bromley: Funding Agency for Schools.

Cole, M. (1999) *Professional Issues for Teachers and Student Teachers*, London: Fulton.

Cooper, C. and Sutherland, V. (1997) *Thirty Minutes to Deal with Difficult People*, London: Kogan Page.

Cooper, P. and McIntyre, D. (1996) *Effective Teaching and Learning: Teachers' and Students' Perspectives*, Buckingham: Open University Press.

Covey, S. (1994) *First Things First: Coping with the Ever Increasing Demands of the Workplace*, London: Simon and Schuster.

Cowley, S. (2001) *Getting the Buggers to Behave*, London: Continuum.

Curzon, L.B. (ed.) (1990) *Teaching in Further Education*, London: Cassell.

Davies, I. (2003) 'Citizenship Education: origins, challenges and possibilities' in Crawford, K. (ed.) *Contemporary Issues in Education*, Dereham: Peter Francis Publishers.

DCSF (2009) *Learning Behaviour: Lessons Learned – A Review of Behaviour Standards and Practices in our schools* (the Steer Report), Crown copyright 2009.

DES (1978) *Special Educational Needs: Report of the Committee of Enquiry into the Education of Handicapped Children and Young People* (the Warnock Report). London: HMSO.

DES (1989) *Discipline in Schools* (The Elton Report), London: HMSO.

DES (1989) *Report of Her Majesty's Inspectors on Pastoral Care in Secondary Schools: An Inspection of Some Aspects of Pastoral Care in 1987–8*, London: HMSO.

Dewey, J. (1933) *How We Think*, New York: Heath.

DfE (2010) *Annual Schools Census*, http://www.education.gov.uk/rsgateway/DB/SFR/s000925/index.shtml.

DfE (2011) *Teachers' Standards*, Crown copyright.

DfEE (1998) *Education for Citizenship and the Teaching of Democracy in Schools: Final Report of the Advisory Group on Citizenship (The Crick Report)*, London: QCA.

DfES (1998), *The Code of Practice: Study Support: A Guide for Secondary Schools*. London: DfES.

DfES (2000) *Extending Opportunity: A National Framework for Study Support*, London: DfES.

Dryden, G. and Vos, J. (1994) *The Learning Revolution*, Stafford: Network Educational Press.

Dweck, C. (2006) *Mindset – the new psychology of success*, New York: Random House.

Education Service Advisory Committee (1992) *Managing Occupational Stress: A Guide For Managers and Teachers in the School Sector*, London: HMSO.

Elliott, A. (2009) 'Myth: Behaviour and Discipline in Schools Today are Far Worse than in the Past', in *Times Educational Supplement*, TES (6 November 2009).

Epstein, D. (1998) 'Real Boys Don't Work: underachievement, masculinity and the harassment of 'sissies'' in D. Epstein, J. Elwood, V. Hey, and J. Maw (eds.) *Failing Boys*, Buckingham: Open University Press.

Flavell J. H. (1982) 'Structures, Stages and Sequences in Cognitive Development' in W.A. Collins (ed.) *The Concept of Development: The Minnesota Symposia on Child Psychology*, Vol. 15, 1–28.

Flecknoe, M. (2001) 'Target Setting: Will it Help to Raise Achievement' in *Educational Management and Administration* 29(2) 217–228.

Fontana, D. (1989) *Managing Stress*, London: Routledge.

Fontana, D. (1994) *Managing Classroom Behaviour*, Leicester: British Psychological Society.

Furlong, J. and Maynard, T. (1995) *Mentoring Student Teachers: The Growth of Professional Knowledge*, London: Routledge.

Gardner, H. (1983) *Frames of Mind: The Theory of Multiple Intelligence*, New York: Basic Books.

Gerwitz, S., Ball, S.J. and Bowe, R. (1995) *Markets, Choice and Equity in Education*, Buckingham: Open University Press.

Gillborn, D. (1990) *'Race', Ethnicity and Education*, London: Unwin Hyman.

Gillborn, D. and Mirza, H. (2000) *Educational Inequality: Mapping Race, Class and Gender*, London: Ofsted.

Goodman, A. (2010) *The Importance of Attitudes and Behaviour for Poorer Children's Educational Attainment*, Joseph Rowntree Foundation.

Halstead, J. M. and Taylor, M. J. (2000) 'Learning and Teaching about Values: A Review of Recent Research' in *Cambridge Journal of Education*, 3(2) 169–202.

Handy, C. (1997) 'Schools for Life and Work' in P. Mortimore and Little V. M. (eds.) *Living Education: Essays in Honour of John Tomlinson*, London: Paul Chapman.

Hart, N.I. (1987) 'Student Teachers' Anxieties: Four Measured Factors and Their Relationship to Pupil Disruption in Class' in *Educational Research*, 29(1) 12–18.

Hawley, C. (1997) *Teacher Talk – What is Your Classroom Management Profile?* http://education.Indiana.edu/cas/tt/v/1i2/what.html.

Hay McBer (2000) *Research into Teacher Effectiveness*, London: DfES.

Heilbronn, R. and Jones, C. (1997) 'Supporting Bilingual Learners' in Heilbronn, R. and Jones, C. (eds.) *New Teachers in an Urban Comprehensive: Learning in Partnership*, Stoke on Trent: Trentham Books.

HMI *Annual Report of Her Majesty's Chief Inspector 1999–2000*, London: The Stationery Office.

HMI *Annual Report of Her Majesty's Chief Inspector of Education, Children's Services and Skills 2010–2011*, London: The Stationery Office.

ILEA (1985) *Educational Opportunities for All: Report of the Committee Reviewing Provision to meet Special Educational Needs* (The Fish Report), London: Inner London Education Authority.

Johnson, M. (1999) *Failing School, Failing City*, Charlbury: Jon Carpenter.

Judge, B. (2003) 'Inclusive Education: principles and practices' in Crawford, K. (ed.) *Contemporary Issues in Education*, Dereham: Peter Francis Publications.

Kerr, D. (1999) 'Re-examining Citizenship in England' in Torney-Purta, J., Schwille, J. and Amadeo, J.A. (eds.) *Civic Education Across Countries: 22 Case Studies from the Civic Education Project*, Amsterdam: Eberon Publishers.

Kolb, D.A. and Fry. R. (1975) 'Towards an Applied Theory of Experiential Learning' in Cooper, C. (ed.) *Theories of Group Process*, London: John Wiley.

Krathwohl, D.R, Bloom, B.S., and Masia, B.B. (1964) *Taxonomy of Educational Objectives, Handbook 2: Affective Domain*, New York: David McKay.

Kyriacou, C. and Stephens, P. (1999) 'Student Teachers' Concerns during Teaching Practice' in *Evaluation and Research in Education*, 13(1) 18–31.

Lancashire LEA and St Martin's College (2004) *Successful Teachers in Schools in Challenging Circumstances*, Lancaster: Lancashire LEA.

Mortimer, P. (1998) *The Road to Improvement: Reflections on School Effectiveness*, Lisse: Swetz & Zeitlinger.

Mortimore, P. and Whitty, G. (1997) *Can School Improvement Overcome the Effects of Disadvantage?* London: Institute of Education.

Murphy, P. (ed.) (1999) *Learners, Learning and Assessment*, London: Paul Chapman.

Narey, M. (2009) *Report from the Independent Commission on Social Mobility* http://www.tuc. org.uk/extras/Social_Mobility_Report_Final.pdf.

National Association for Special Educational Needs (2000) 'Specialist Training for Special Educational Needs and Inclusion' Policy Paper 4 in the *SEN Fourth Policy Options* series, London: NASEN.

National Foundation for Educational Research (NFER) (1999) *The Benefits of Study Support: A Review of Opinion and Research*, London: DfES.

Ofsted (1999) *Primary Education: A Review of Primary Schools in England 1994–98*, London: Ofsted.

Ofsted (2000) *Improving City Schools*, HMI 222, London, Ofsted.

Ofsted (2001) *Improving Attendance and Behaviour in Secondary schools*, HMI 242, London: Ofsted.

Ofsted (2003) *Good Assessment in Secondary Schools*, London: Ofsted.

Ofsted (2011) *Good Practice Example: The personal, social and spiritual development of young people in an inner city area – Christ the King College* http://www.ofsted.gov.uk/resources/ good-practice-resource-%E2%80%93-personal-social-and-spiritual-development-of-young-people-inner-city-area.

Ofsted (2012) *The Evaluation Schedule for the Inspection of Maintained Schools and Academies*, Crown copyright.

Qualifications and Assessment Authority (QCA) and Department for Education and Employment (DfEE) (1999) *Citizenship*, London: QCA/DfEE.

Reece, I. And Walker, S. (2000) *Teaching, Training and Learning: A Practical Guide*, Sunderland: Business Education Publishers.

Reynolds, D. (1999) 'Can Good Teaching Be Measured?' in *Times Educational Supplement*, TES (1st August 1999).

Richardson, R. and Wood, A. (1999) *Inclusive Schools, Inclusive Society*, London: Trentham Books.

Rogers, C. (1982) *A Social Psychology of Schooling: The Expectancy Process*, London: Routledge and Kegan Paul.

Schon, D. (1983) *The Reflective Practitioner*, New York: Basic Books.

Smith, A. (2001) *Accelerated Learning in Practice*, Stafford: Network Educational Press.

Thornton. K. (2003) 'Friendly, fun but fair – the ideal mix' in *Times Educational Supplement*, TES (25th May 2003).

TTA (2000) *Raising the Attainment of Ethnic Minority Pupils*, London: TTA.

Vygotsky, L.S. (1962) *Thought and Language*, Cambridge, Mass.: MIT Press.

Watkins, C. and Wagner, P. (1987) *School Discipline: A Whole School Approach*, Oxford: Blackwell.

Weinstein, C., Tomlinson-Clarke S. and Curran, M. (2004) 'Towards a Conception of Culturally Responsive Classroom Management' in *Journal of Teacher Education* 55(1) 25–38.

White, J. and Barber, M. (1997) *Perspectives on School Effectiveness and School Improvement*, London: Institute of Education.

Williams, E. (1999) 'Sleeplessness? Irritability? Low self-esteem? You must have Ofsteditis' in *Times Educational Supplement: Mind and Body Supplement*, TES (26th March 1999).

Wood, D. (1988) *How Children Learn and Think*, Oxford: Blackwell.

Wood, I. (1991) *Time Management in Teaching*, London: Network Educational Press.

Zeichner, K. and Liston, D. (1987) 'Teaching Student Teachers to Reflect', in *Harvard Educational Review* 57(1), 23–48.

Index